Contents

THE GOD MAKERS

ED DECKER & DAVE HUNT

HARVEST HOUSE
PUBLISHERS
EUGENE, OREGON 97402

THE GOD MAKERS
Copyright © 1984, 1994 by Ed Decker and Dave Hunt
Published by Harvest House Publishers
Eugene, Oregon 97402

Library of Congress Cataloging-in-Publication Data
Decker, Ed.
    The God makers / Ed Decker & Dave Hunt. — Rev. and updated.
        p. cm.
    Includes bibliographical references.
    ISBN 1-56507-717-2
    1. Mormon Church—Controversial literature.   2. Church of Jesus Christ of Latter-Day
    Saints—Controversial literature.   I. Hunt, Dave.   II. Title.
BX8645.D38   1997
289.3—dc21   97-2665
                                                           CIP

Printed in the United States of America.

97 98 99 00 01 02 03 / BC / 10 9 8 7 6 5 4 3 2 1

INTRODUCTION

When the original edition of *The God Makers* was released in 1984, we prayed that it would be used of the Lord to open the eyes of the world to the truth about Mormonism. We had no idea that its impact would be truly global, and that it, along with the movie *The God Makers*, would change forever the way the world would look at Mormonism.

At the same time the book became a bestseller, the film was being shown throughout the country to standing-room-only crowds in churches of every Christian denomination. In Ed's home church in Bellevue, Washington, traffic was backed up for blocks in every direction as people worked their way to the parking lots.

In one church in Colorado Springs, more than twice as many people showed up for the film as the large church building could hold. Ed had to teach on the lawn those who couldn't get in, preparing them for what they would see in the film, while the film itself was being shown inside to the first crowd. When the film was over, the crowds switched and Ed provided a question-and-answer time for the first crowd.

From city to city throughout the country, the story was the same. At one time the film was being shown at over a thousand churches per month, and entire cases of *The God Makers* book were sold at almost every showing.

Controversy and revival exploded everywhere Ed or Dave spoke. Newspaper, TV, and radio coverage converged from every perspective and viewpoint. Ministries such as Saints Alive could not keep up with the calls, counseling, letters, and necessary follow-up for those Mormons and others who trusted in the true Jesus of the Bible.

The Mormon Church was taken by surprise by all this, learning that its carefully constructed masquerade was exposed once and for all to the light of truth, and this time by people who wouldn't back down to pressure, threats, and slander.

As you read through this revised edition, you will see that several critical heresies that were pointed out in the first edition have now been revised by the LDS Church to conform to an *appearance of orthodoxy* that is so essential in its counterfeit Christianity.

But these changes have had more resemblance to the metamorphic life cycles of the insect world than to the actions of a holy-Prophet-directed "only true Church." Sadly, no matter how many heresies receive a new coat of paint, this caterpillar will never turn into a butterfly any more than the victims of Mormonism will turn into gods and goddesses.

1

THE MORMON CHALLENGE

Intent upon researching and producing an unusual feature story, *Denver Post* staff writer John Farrell, accompanied by *Post* photographer Jim Richardson, spent 13 weeks during the summer and fall of 1982 traveling throughout "The Church State"[1] of Utah. Their assignment? To penetrate what has been called "The Zion Curtain"[2] erected by the Mormon Church to protect its vast wealth and influence. The Church of Jesus Christ of Latter-day Saints so effectively controls one of the 50 American states, where it is "the largest private property owner,"[3] that "the line between worship and government has become so blurred that some civil rights have evaporated."[4] In this unusual state, "Jews are called Gentiles" and a "majority of non-Mormons" consider themselves to be "victims of discrimination."[5]

As anyone knows who has lived very long in Utah, far from encouraging freedom (as one might expect), the all-pervasive presence of the Mormon Church hangs like a heavy cloud of oppression that can't be escaped anywhere. One gradually acquires the uneasy feeling that "Big Brother" is always listening and watching. Farrell and Richardson discovered that in some ways conditions behind the Zion Curtain were uncomfortably similar to those that prevailed behind the Iron Curtain. This was particularly true concerning two of the rights that Americans have traditionally held most dear: freedom of speech and freedom of the press. In Utah these are not exercised without "widespread constraint" imposed upon everyone by the Mormon hierarchy's long arm that reaches everywhere.

These rights are further inhibited by the disturbing fact that "the state's largest evening newspaper and . . . leading TV station are owned by the church,"[6] which has been described as "America's biggest, richest and strongest home-grown faith."[7] Giving its official approval to the Church's trampling on human rights, in 1975 the Utah Supreme Court with its Mormon majority handed down a surprising decision, that, as summarized by the *Denver Post*—

> The First Amendment to the U.S. Constitution—which guarantees freedom of speech, freedom of the press, freedom of assembly and freedom of religion—did not apply in Utah but was only a limitation on the federal government.[8]

The Foundation of Mormon Authority

John Farrell's assignment was "not an exposé of the Mormon religion," but to give an honest picture of life inside Utah. Just as it was behind Marxism's Iron Curtain, however, so Farrell and Richardson discovered that in this bastion of capitalism and conservatism behind the Zion Curtain it was extremely difficult to find individuals who were willing to speak openly and freely in response to questions about the almost-omnipotent religious power that tolerates no interference in its control of the Church State. They soon learned that "the Church of Jesus Christ of Latter-day Saints does not take kindly to dissent."[9] For a resident of Utah to openly question the irresistible and self-serving influence exerted everywhere in Utah by the Mormon Church—or its activities, morals, or doctrines—could call down the wrath of a totalitarian power upon one's head. The results are sometimes frighteningly similar to those suffered by dissidents within the former Soviet Union or some other Communist country.

Dominating the skyline of downtown Salt Lake City, a huge 28-story office building, tallest in the state, houses the corporate headquarters of the Church of Jesus Christ of Latter-day Saints. Here, lawyers, accountants, and computer experts try to keep up with the day-to-day commercial activities involving the vast business interests and real-estate holdings of the multibillion-dollar worldwide financial empire of Mormonism. From his top-floor suite in the Church-owned Hotel Utah, the President of the Mormon Church (its "Prophet, Seer, and Revelator") exercises unchallenged control over the 9.7 million members[10] through a hierarchy of apostles, assistants, and advisers. Everyone entering the imposing Church headquarters is greeted by these emblazoned words:

The Course of Wisdom is the Course of Obedience.

How well Mormons know the truth of that slogan! It has been drilled into their consciousness since earliest childhood. And in Utah, the Church State, even non-Mormons feel the pressure to conform to a power that insists upon overriding both conscience and God. The authority which the Mormon hierarchy wields began with Joseph Smith's claim that every Christian on the face of the earth was following abominable creeds and was involved in a total worldwide apostasy that had completely destroyed the Church that Jesus Christ had founded. Smith claimed that he had been ordained to restore truth to the earth, and that as the modern founder of the true Church, he alone was the dispenser of God's revelation and will in this dispensation. That grandiose boast is the foundation of the absolute authority which the Mormon Presidents and Apostles claim as their divine right today. All who reject Joseph Smith's claims and do not submit obediently to his successors are "Gentiles" outside the true Church he founded and are without salvation.

Reversing the LDS Pro-Life Stand

In the 1993 Harvest House book *The God Makers II*, authors Ed Decker and Caryl Matrisciana wrote about the difficulties that faithful LDS members were having trying to balance their consciences with the dictates of The Brethren.

> When Ed was in Utah premiering the new film, one of the TV stations did a news report on church disciplinary action that was being taken against some people who were pro-lifers. In a literally *unbelievable* turn of events, the LDS church has *reversed its almost militant pro-life position* and LDS Bishops are now counseling young women to have abortions! Twenty years ago such counseling would have caused a Bishop to be immediately excommunicated from the church for such behavior. Here is the actual transcript of the report, transcribed from KTVX, Salt Lake City, on December 11, 1993:

> **ANCHOR:** The LDS Church says it has consistently opposed elective abortions, but some Mormons claim they are being disciplined for preaching the pro-life message. Paul Murphy has this exclusive report.

MURPHY: They say they are faithful Latter-day Saints, but claim they are being disciplined for their anti-abortion views.

SHARP: It is murder—the shedding of innocent blood, for which there is no forgiveness.

MURPHY: Sharp says he was excommunicated in July only over abortion. His Stake president says it was only one of four issues leading to the discipline. John Abney was a Ward clerk until he expressed his views against abortion. Now he and his wife are scheduled for a Church disciplinary court.

JOHN ABNEY: We do not want to have the blood and the sins of this generation to come upon our garments, either in or out of the Church.

MURPHY: Roxanne Abney said she couldn't believe the conversation she recently had with her Stake president.

ROXANNE ABNEY: One of the Lord's representatives, discussing abortion, me being against it, him being for it, and I'm on the wrong side of the fence.

MURPHY: The LDS General Handbook now says that abortion is not murder, and is permissible in cases of rape, incest, or when the life or health of the woman is in danger, or the fetus is not likely to survive birth. But as recently as 1975, the LDS President said abortion is wrong, even in cases of rape. And Utah's Right-to-Life Director says she has received a lot of calls from girls who say their Bishops counsel them to have abortions.

DIRECTOR: So it wasn't for rape and it wasn't for incest and it wasn't for fetal deformity...

MURPHY: And the Bishop still counseled these girls to have an abortion?

DIRECTOR: The Bishop is still advising them to have an abortion.

MURPHY:	These are confusing times for Sharp and the Abneys. They thought they were in line with Mormon doctrine. Now they find themselves on the way out. Paul Murphy, KTVX 4 News.
ANCHOR:	Tomorrow night, a group of pro-life Mormons will be meeting at the Copper View Community Center in Midvale to discuss their future in the LDS Church.

Reporter: Paul Murphy
Anchor: Randall Carlyle
1st LDS: William Sharp
LDS Couple: John and Roxanne Abney
Director of Utah Pro-Life group: Rosa Goodnight
Prophet quoted is Spencer W. Kimball, 1975

Theocracy: The Original Goal Still Intact

Aside from its vast commercial income, the Church probably receives more than four million dollars daily in tithes.[11] The billions of dollars it receives and controls are not accounted for by the Mormon hierarchy to the members who contribute so generously and sacrificially. The Mormon empire is a virtual theocracy. Its leaders claim to represent God to the people. Therefore they are accountable to no one on earth for anything. They only command, and their followers must obey without question. According to Apostle Boyd K. Packer:

> Now, about the Church money, we've never published the income figures. . . .
>
> It's been a policy. A lot of organizations are that way.[12]

The original aim of founding Prophet Joseph Smith and other early Mormon leaders was to establish a theocracy that would eventually control the entire United States. Instead, the "Saints" were successively driven from Illinois and Missouri by "Gentiles," who didn't take kindly to such a goal nor to the attempts to accomplish it by trickery and force. Under the leadership of Brigham Young, Smith's successor, the persecuted Latter-day Saints traveled westward, where they established their "nation within a nation" in the territory of Utah. Threatened with collapse of their theocratic kingdom under the onslaught of Congressional laws passed in the late 1880s that outlawed polygamy and stripped the Mormon Church of its property and power, Mormon leaders finally decided in 1890 that they couldn't win a war against the United States Army, and so capitulated. Settling into a grudging but necessary peaceful coexistence with the other states in the Union and obeying federal laws to the extent necessary in the interim, Mormon leaders were then, and still are, biding their time until that prophesied day when their original goal will at last be accomplished.

That goal of establishing a theocratic rule over the United States and planet Earth is still an integral part of the Mormon faith and the underlying motivating factor in their desire to convert the world. Speaking of the uncomfortable adjustment that has been required in the meanwhile, Mormon author Samuel Taylor has written:

> As we became accepted by the outside world, after decades of vilification and ridicule ... we went to work busily on a new public image replacing the polygamous rebel with the gentle Saint who didn't use coffee. ...
>
> They concocted a never-never land of Mormonism that presented a lovely, if unreal, façade for the outside world to admire and converts to embrace.[13]

Though he writes rather frankly, Samuel Taylor has remained a Latter-day Saint. So have the publisher and staff of *Dialogue: A Journal of Mormon Thought*, from which this quote was taken. Many other Mormons, however, have been driven by conscience to leave their Church because of what they consider to be heresies and fraud too serious to overlook any longer. Battling with just the many obvious problems of the history of their faith, such as the inconsistent versions of the First Vision, outright fraud in Smith's pretended translation of Egyptian papyri as lost Scripture, and his ridiculous attempt to foist a similar translation of the deliberately faked Kinderhook plates, many Mormons have finally come to the conclusion that they can no longer be silent. Believing they are under a moral obligation to share their knowledge about the dark side of Mormonism with the world, many former Mormons have joined forces to accomplish this goal.

The Hidden Truth

In modern pursuit of Joseph Smith's original vision, the Mormon Church circles the globe with an aggressive missionary outreach. This global force has been numbering over 50,000 full-time missionaries in the 1990s. Mormon zeal is noteworthy and their motivation must be accepted as genuine. However, their methods include a great deal of misrepresentation.

Recently the LDS church has been changing its TV and radio advertising and public service announcements to mislead all but the very wary. TV viewers watching a Billy Graham crusade were treated with an invitation to call an 800 number and receive a free copy of the Bible, with no cost or obligation. We called for one and received the Bible as promised, with a letter from the LDS Church which read in part:

> By reading this book and following the Savior's teachings found within it, your family will feel closer to each other and to Jesus Christ. You'll also better understand God's plan for each of us. Imagine the satisfaction and peace of mind that offers.
>
> If, after receiving *The Bible*, you would like to know more about how the teachings of Jesus Christ can help you and your family, please call 1-888-917-2828 and representatives of the Church of Jesus Christ of Latter-day Saints will gladly arrange a visit that is convenient for your schedule. They will also bring you a free copy of *The Book of Mormon* as mentioned below. May the message you read in *The Bible* help you find the greater love and happiness we all desire (italics in original).

A last note promises that the Book of Mormon "supports and clarifies the Savior's teachings in *The Bible*" (undated form letter from Stephen Allen, Public Programs, LDS Church).

This new public relations outreach of the LDS Church didn't just happen. Their PR experts knew that this was going to be a winner by testing it in a number of markets and then running it past select groups of their own membership first.

Ed received the following letter from an active Mormon who has worked through the problems of the LDS theology and has turned his life over to the real Jesus (He is about where I [Ed] was in my last days among The Brethren.)

Hello, brother Ed, it's _____ again. Assuming I've not already worn out my welcome, I thought you might be interested in a couple of things I found out at church today.

While the rest of the Christian world was celebrating Christ's victory over death and sin [Easter 1997], our "three-hour block" concentrated on clerical affairs and "missionary work." Our Sacrament Meeting featured a farewell talk by the First Councilor in the Bishopric and his wife, and remarks summarized from the Church News by our Bishop. Apart from a musical number by the primary children, and three Christ-centered hymns (a rarity in LDS congregational singing, I'm sure you recall), one would have been hard-pressed to know or even suspect that today was a holy day.

Our third hour was a joint Priesthood-Relief Society meeting, and it introduced something I think might interest you. Our new Second Councilor, the retiring Stake Mission President, informed us that our area—the _____ area—is part of a new missionary pilot program. Based on demographic research and (I'm not making this up) Nielsen ratings, the Church has inaugurated a new television campaign. It was introduced by an apparatchik from the Church's media department at a mission conference in Milwaukee, Wisconsin, a few weeks ago, and has been in progress and apparently is very successful.

We were shown five "homefronts"—television ads. The first two deal with the Book of Mormon and the next two with family home evening. I had seen all of them. However, the last was entitled "Truths Never Change" and it focused on three biblical principles: forgiveness, love, and peace. At the end of the spot, the announcer informed the audience that it could call a toll-free number and receive—"without obligation," of course—a King James Bible (printed in the same marbled blue mass-paperback style as the Book of Mormon).

The departing Stake Mission President excitedly announced that the fifth spot was being tested in the Milwaukee area and four other areas worldwide, and that it has generated a tremendous response—more than twice the response of all the other spots combined! Furthermore, it was pointed out that 80 percent of those contacted via the Bible ad had received the first missionary "discussion," and 60 percent had gone on to the second. The members were urged to follow up on the ad within 24 hours of a broadcast (although it wasn't made clear how this was to be done).

Nearly everyone who commented on the Bible spot said that they "felt the Spirit much more strongly" in it than they had with the Book of Mormon and Family Home Evening commercials—but nobody stopped to examine the implications of this observation. Several others pointed out that the ad was not nearly as "off-putting" to the public, as it involved something familiar. It was also noted that the ad "positions" the Church well as a denomination that reads and accepts the Bible.

I just thought you'd find all of this interesting. The Mormon missionaries who are delivering the Bibles aren't Gideons; they are using the Bible as a pretext, which is at best dishonest.

It is interesting to note that even the Mormons recognized the difference between the Bible ad and the other ads and were strongly drawn in their own hearts to the first. What a terrible manipulation of truth! Ed did not call the 888 number, but several weeks after the Bible came, two Mormon missionaries appeared to see if it had arrived and if he had any questions they could answer. The Book of Mormon wasn't even mentioned. The Bible gave them a solid ground of compatibility with which they were apparently more comfortable.

Mormon missionaries claim to be bringing true Christianity to the world. The vast majority of converts to Mormonism are proselytized from Protestant denominations. When questioned, Mormons insist that their gospel comes from the Bible and that they have the same God and the same Jesus as Christians. In actual fact, they have a completely different God from what the Bible presents, a different Jesus, and a different gospel.

These differences are denied or glossed over by the missionaries, who are often evasive and unwilling to tell the whole truth to a prospective convert for fear of losing him. Moreover, much about Mormonism cannot be revealed to sincere seekers, because those who know what is involved have taken an oath of secrecy. This means that Mormonism's most sacred and important doctrines and practices are discovered only after getting in too deeply to turn back.

Just beneath the carefully groomed façade of "true Christianity" that Mormons present to the world is another story so bizarre that non-Mormons find it difficult to believe even when the irrefutable evidence has been laid out in front of them. It is this story—the shocking and incredible truth about Mormonism—that we want to tell. Our purpose is not to harm the Latter-day Saints, but to help them by exposing what many Mormons themselves don't yet know and might otherwise learn only too late. Everything in the following pages has been thoroughly researched and fully documented.

Unfortunately, Mormons have so often been told stories of the terrible persecution suffered by the "Saints" in the early days that they react to honest criticism as though they were being persecuted once again. The *Denver Post* team of Farrell and Richardson tried unsuccessfully to get LDS leaders in Salt Lake City to tell their side of the story. "The Mormon Church's hierarchy declined repeated requests for interviews" by Farrell. "Other Utahans, fearing they might be ostracized if they spoke freely . . . would talk only if granted anonymity." Farrell, however, used nothing from anonymous sources in his article.[14]

Sincere Response to the Mormon Challenge

We have found it almost impossible to enter into a friendly and meaningful dialogue with Mormons, especially those in positions of responsibility. This attitude is strange in view of the exhortation in Mormon scripture, *Doctrine and Covenants* 71:7-8, which urges all Mormons: "Wherefore, confound your enemies; call upon them to meet you in public and in private; and inasmuch as ye are faithful their shame shall be made manifest. Wherefore, let them bring forth their strong reasons against the Lord."

Both this book and a film of the same title represent a sincere attempt to meet this challenge. We will give overwhelming evidence concerning what Mormons *really* believe and practice, and the many reasons why Mormonism is not Christian at all but a revival of primitive paganism in a modified form. We only ask for an honest hearing—the willingness to face facts and admit the truth. It is not our desire to dissuade anyone from being a Mormon who truly wants to be one. On the other hand, we want everyone who is in the Mormon Church or is considering joining it to know what this commitment really means. We sincerely accept the challenge that Mormonism presents to the world today, which early Apostle Orson Pratt explained in these words:

> The nature of the message of the Book of Mormon is such, that if true, no one can possibly be saved and reject it; if false, no one can possible be saved and receive it. . . .
>
> If, after a rigid examination, it be found an imposition, it should be extensively published to the world as such; the evidences and

arguments upon which the imposture was detected should be clearly and logically stated, that those who have been sincerely yet unfortunately deceived may perceive the nature of the deception and be reclaimed... and that those who contribute to publish the delusion may be exposed and silenced, not by physical force, neither by persecutions, bare assertions, nor ridicule, but by strong and powerful arguments—by evidences adduced from scripture and reason.[15]

This we intend to do, avoiding bare assertions and ridicule. If it continues true to form, however, the Church of Jesus Christ of Latter-day Saints may be expected, if not officially then through pressure at all levels, to discourage its members from reading this book. In good faith, we have accepted the challenge of Orson Pratt, Brigham Young, and other Mormon leaders to make the truth known—and that includes Mormonism's darkest secrets that those privy to them have sworn upon penalty of death not to reveal.

The refusal of any Mormon to consider honestly and openly the facts presented in this book can only indicate an unwillingness to face the truth in the manner urged upon LDS by their own Apostles. We challenge all who wish to know the truth to read on. It may change your life or the life of someone you love.

Tragically, the love and zeal Mormons exercise is toward a false god. Nevertheless, the true God loves them and gave His Son to die for their sins on the cross of Calvary. That truth is deliberately obscured by lying leaders and false teachers who are leading a whole people-group into eternal destruction. Christians need to face the real issue: the urgent need to speak the truth in love to set the lost free.

Let the words of Scripture awaken our concern:

> The ancient and honorable, he is the head; and the prophet that teacheth lies, he is the tail. For the leaders of this people cause them to err, and they that are led of them are destroyed.

> Therefore the Lord shall have no joy in their young men, neither shall have mercy on their fatherless and widows; for every one is a hypocrite and an evildoer, and every mouth speaketh folly. For all this his anger is not turned away, but his hand is stretched out still (Isaiah 9:15-17).

2

A Fascinating Question

Jim and Judy were typical converts to the Mormon Church. Although they had been active in a mainline Protestant denomination for years, they felt that something was still missing from their lives. Somehow they had never found that deep personal relationship with God that they sensed they needed and longed for.

In the course of his business, Jim came into contact with an active and zealous member of the Church of Jesus Christ of Latter-day Saints. Feeling themselves drawn to this man and his beautiful family, Jim and Judy gradually became more and more involved with them socially. There were so many good qualities evident in the relationships in this Mormon home that Jim and Judy began to wonder whether these people might not have found the answer to that hunger for God that still gnawed deep within their own hearts.

"These people seemed to be Christians," Judy told us. "Any people that I'd ever been around that I had felt were really Christians had the same attributes. They were fine, good, loving, family-oriented people."

Not only were the relationships of family members extremely close and loving, but they noticed something else: They took their religion very seriously. This made Jim and Judy think that perhaps these people really did have what they had been seeking.

Could Such Good People Be Wrong?

"Everything they did revolved around their Church," continued Judy. "That was appealing to us, especially since we felt pretty empty as far as our own religious experience was concerned. Something was missing from our lives that we couldn't quite explain. Looking at this family we thought, 'Boy, they really do have something!' We wanted to know what that something was, so we began to ask them questions: 'What is a Mormon? What do you really believe?'"

Jim picked up the story at this point. "At our friends' request, the missionaries came to see us and we began to take the lessons. As they would leave each night, they would encourage us to read the Book of Mormon and to pray that we might know whether it was true. At the end of the six lessons, we were encouraged to be baptized into the Mormon Church. However, these two precious young men told us that they weren't going to ask for a definite answer that last night. Instead, they would wait until the following night to see what we had decided. In the meanwhile, most of the Mormons in Mesa, Arizona, would fast and pray that our answer would be the right one."

"They were so sincere about this," added Judy. Her voice reflected both an appreciation and a sadness. "The next day Jim and I each received so many calls! Mormons we'd never met phoned me at the apartment and Jim at work. The voice on the line would say, 'This is brother and sister so-and-so. We're fasting and praying for you that your answer will be the right one.' We were sure impressed that they were a very loving people. When the missionaries came back to ask us if we wanted to be baptized, we couldn't help but say *yes!*"

It was only after several years that Jim and Judy began studying the Bible and asking God's guidance and only then realized what they were *really* involved in. The experience almost cost them their marriage. The true facts about Mormonism were entirely different from what they had been led to believe. Joining had been easy, reinforced as it had been with so much love. Getting out was something else. What they had thought was genuine love expressed over and over by Mormons who had become their closest friends suddenly turned to a severing of relationships and false accusations.

There are so many thousands of other people just like Jim and Judy. As many of them related their stories to us, it became clear that the real challenge of Mormonism involved far more than questions of religious doctrine and rituals. There are millions of lives involved—and if, as Apostle Orson Pratt declared, "no one can possibly be saved and receive" a false prophet and false gospel, then the stakes are high indeed.

Documenting the Evidence

It was in response to this side of the Mormon challenge that the documentary film titled *The God Makers* was produced. Three years in the making, it was premiered on the night of December 31, 1982, to an overflow audience of about 4000 at Grace Community Church in Sun Valley, California. After reviewing and approving the movie earlier, the internationally respected pastor of Grace Community Church, Dr. John MacArthur, had said: "This film is dynamite, the most powerful thing I've seen! Get your Mormon friends to view it!"

Those packed into the large auditorium that evening seemed to agree with Dr. MacArthur's appraisal. Long periods of stunned silence were broken intermittently with loud gasps of astonishment and utter disbelief. The documented evidence presented such a different picture of the Mormon Church from that which most people have always accepted that the audience was left in a state of shock, from which it recovered only slowly during the question-and-answer period that followed the movie and is standard at all showings.

The film centers around a dramatized reenactment of an attempt by two former members of the Mormon Melchizedek priesthood, Ed Decker and Dick Baer, to persuade a top Los Angeles law firm to file a class-action suit against the Mormon Church. The suit is proposed on behalf of numerous victims who, like Decker and Baer themselves, had seen their marriages and families destroyed, strangely enough, by the Mormon doctrine of "eternal marriage," which is a prerequisite for reaching every worthy Mormon's ultimate goal of becoming a god or goddess.

The unusual proposal is met with incredulity by the attorneys. The senior partner in the law firm demands, "Mr. Decker, Mr. Baer, just what are we dealing with here?"

Ed Decker replies, "I was involved in this group for 19 years . . . and I consider it to be one of the most dangerous and deceptive organizations in the world!" Pulling a stack of papers from his briefcase, he adds, "I've got documentation here that ties them into occultism and Satanism . . . and that's just the tip of the iceberg."

Making no attempt to hide his complete rejection of such an obviously fanatical statement, the young lawyer sitting in on the conference cuts in quickly: "Mr. Decker, I don't doubt your sincerity, but I find this very hard to

believe. These people are known for family togetherness and a very conspic-
uous form of moral rectitude."

Ed's vehement response seems only to add to the disbelief of the lawyers
and further staggers the already-stunned audience viewing the dramatization: "That's part of an incredible deception . . . and that's why we have to
expose it!"

As the director of Saints Alive (also known as Ex-Mormons for Jesus),
Ed Decker speaks from a conviction growing out of years of experience dealing both with committed Mormons and with those who are disillusioned and
want to leave the Church but don't know how.

Reactions from the "Saints"

To say that this film has aroused a strong reaction from Mormons and an
explosion of interest among non-Mormons would be a classic understate-
ment. There have been death threats against some of those who have dared to
show the film, as well as against Ed himself, who has perhaps taken the brunt
of much of the hate and anger. Mormons have demonstrated against the
movie, tried to have it banned, and pressured television stations not to air it.
Frequently they have tried to break up the showing or to disrupt the discussion afterward. All of this has only served to increase the interest of those
who want to know the truth, and it has strengthened the determination of the
film's distributors to let nothing prevent its free circulation.

In order to give the Mormon leaders an opportunity to express their
objections and point out any errors, invitations were both mailed and hand-
delivered to Church leaders for them or their representatives to attend a private afternoon showing of *The God Makers* in the downtown Salt Lake City
theater where the film's public premiere was scheduled that evening. "We are
very sincere in our desire to receive a serious response from the Mormon
Church to this film," Ed Decker told 25 to 30 Mormons, none of them top
leaders, who came to the showing. (They appeared to be attorneys and exec-
utives from Church headquarters.) Other than some whispered comments
among themselves, the only response to Ed's plea for dialogue was stony
silence and a hasty exit as soon as the film ended.

The Mormon Church has purchased several video copies of *The God
Makers* and presumably has studied the film very carefully. So far, after over
15 years of countless showings and probably close to 100,000 video copies

sold or distributed, there has been no official reaction, which we would expect if there were any factual errors. Certainly the reaction of the "Saints" so far has not been in keeping with idealistic statements from Brigham Young and Orson Pratt about welcoming investigation and confounding their "enemies" in public and private with the truth.

One time and one time only, the LDS Church agreed to have two of its official representatives meet Dave and Ed head-on. It was shortly after a showing of the film *The God Makers* on Channel 38 TV in Chicago. The LDS participants watched the film again in a private showing and spent the better part of the day in preparing for the open forum, accompanied by several men who appeared to be coaching them. Immediately after the debate, which was moderated by Channel 38 director Jerry Rose, they made a veritable rush for the door. There has never been another offer to debate the issues.

Mormons attending various showings of the film in order to publicly refute it during the open discussion time that always follows have invariably charged that it is full of lies. When asked to be specific, they have just as invariably failed to substantiate their accusations. One would think that if the Mormon Church, which has been carefully examining the film for so many years, had been able to find any inaccuracies it would have published an official refutation instead of remaining silent. No doubt the tremendous impact the film has had came as a surprise to the Church.

Neither the producer of the movie nor the authors of this book have any vendetta against the Mormon Church or against Mormons as individuals. Certainly there is no desire to deny or to lessen the right of any individual to be a Mormon if he or she freely chooses to be one. Our issue has always been with the doctrines of Mormonism, never with the people who are the victims of its deceit. *The God Makers* was intended to encourage freedom of choice on the part of those within the Mormon Church and those outside, who may be considering membership or are approached by Mormon missionaries in an attempt to persuade them to become Mormons.

No one, however, can really exercise a genuine freedom of choice without the facts upon which to base an intelligent decision. The truth alone sets free. The purpose of both the film and this book is to present the truth so that Mormons and non-Mormons alike can make a truly free choice.

Stranger Than Fiction

It has often been said that "truth is stranger than fiction." In no instance is this more apparent than when the carefully worn mask is peeled off and the truth revealed concerning the Mormon Church. That truth is so bizarre that its very "stranger-than-fiction" quality makes it difficult to believe. This is all the more so because the truth about Mormonism has been so effectively concealed by its leaders.

After months of investigation, the *Denver Post* team of Farrell and Richardson concluded that "the *Reader's Digest* image" of Mormonism most people accept "is all done with mirrors. The signs of strain inside the Mormon nation are real enough." Although Mormons pride themselves upon their abstinence from alcohol and tobacco, a government study conducted in 1973 indicated that "church members take more non-barbiturate sedatives, tranquilizers, anti-depressants, stimulants, pep pills, heroin, cocaine, and LSD" than non-Mormons. In the words of John Farrell, this fact seems to throw "some doubt on the claim that Church members only get 'high on life.'"[1] Other startling facts that the *Post* investigation uncovered include the following:

> Utah's divorce rate has always been higher than the national average . . . [and] 20 is the most common age for women in Utah to get divorced. . . .
>
> Utah's child murder rate is five times the national average.
>
> Half of all babies born in Utah have teenage mothers, and seven out of ten of these children are conceived out of wedlock. . . .
>
> But because of the fierce pressure to remain "respectable" in Utah, seven months has become the most common interval between marriage and childbirth.
>
> Mormons tend to replace vices like cigarettes and alcohol with a demanding sweet tooth. A hefty 46 percent of all adults in Utah are overweight, compared to a national average of 19 percent.[2]

The Mormon Church has worked very diligently and successfully not only to project worldwide a wholesome family image, but also to present itself as the only true representative of Christianity upon earth. Though most people reject that claim as extravagant, they are left with the impression that

Mormonism is simply an extreme form of Christian fundamentalism. Nothing could be further from the truth. On the contrary, Mormonism is a modified form of paganism which is so carefully camouflaged with a façade of Christian terminology that it even deceives most Mormons. Paganism is the universal naturalistic religion of the human race. It usually involves communication with spirits, a hierarchy of many gods, and appeasement of these powerful beings through occult rituals leading to the mastery of forces inherent in nature. Though seemingly diversified, all pagans are united in their antagonism against biblical Christianity.

How a religion that, as we shall see, is so closely linked to basic Hinduism and occultism could have managed to pose as Christian for over 150 years is a fascinating story. No less fascinating is the devout belief that the Mormon Church will rescue the United States from destruction by taking over the reins of government during a coming great crisis and that only then can Jesus Christ return to this earth—accompanied, of course, by Joseph Smith.[3]

More Than Coincidence?

Most critics of Mormonism regard Joseph Smith as a fraud who deliberately deceived his followers into joining a church of his own making whose doctrines and rituals were borrowed from Freemasonry and other pagan religions and embellished by his vivid imagination to suit his giant ego. Though partially correct, that explanation fails to account for all of the facts. Careful investigation indicates that Joseph Smith was in touch with a suprahuman source of revelation and power that has been the common inspiration behind all pagan religions down through history. Mormonism's uniqueness is in the fact that it was the first really successful attempt to pass paganism off as Christianity; *and* it thereby set the pattern for much that is happening on a broad scale today.

Joseph Smith's belief that men could turn themselves into gods was generally considered not only the rankest heresy but an absurdity in his day. Today, however, this once-radical idea permeates not only psychology, science fiction, popular films, television shows, and many other areas of secular society, but it is at the heart of an awakening religious consciousness that is sweeping the world. It is the foundation of hundreds of popular new religious movements such as Scientology, est (Erhard Seminars Training), and TM

(Transcendental Meditation). It lies at the heart of humanistic and transpersonal psychologies as well as the entire human potential movement, holistic medicine, and holistic (New Age) education and secular humanism.

How could Joseph Smith have anticipated these modern developments—or did he? Could there be something more sinister involved than even most ex-Mormons suspect? This is the most fascinating aspect of Mormonism, and a question we will seek to answer in the following pages.

Visitors from the Unseen World

One has only to look at what Joseph Smith himself claimed happened at that "sacred Grove" where Mormonism supposedly began to answer the question of demonic inspiration in the birth of Mormonism.

In the LDS scripture *The Pearl of Great Price,* Joseph Smith describes the circumstance of his seeking to know which church was true:

> 15 After I had retired to the place where I had previously designed to go, having looked around me, and finding myself alone, I kneeled down and began to offer up the desires of my heart to God. **I had scarcely done so, when immediately I was seized upon by some power which entirely overcame me, and had such an astonishing influence over me as to bind my tongue so that I could not speak. Thick darkness gathered around me, and it seemed to me for a time as if I were doomed to sudden destruction.**

> 16 But, exerting all my powers to call upon God to deliver me out of the power of this enemy which had seized upon me **and at the very moment when I was ready to sink into despair and abandon myself to destruction—not to an imaginary ruin, but to the power of some actual being from the unseen world, who had such marvelous power as I had never before felt in any being—just at this moment of great alarm, I saw a pillar of light exactly over my head, above the brightness of the sun, which descended gradually until it fell upon me.**

> 17 It no sooner appeared than I found myself delivered from the enemy which held me bound. **When the light rested upon me I saw two Personages, whose brightness and glory defy all description, standing above me in the air.** One of them spake unto me, calling me by name and said, pointing to the other—This is My beloved Son. Hear Him!

18 My object in going to inquire of the Lord was to know which of all the sects was right, that I might know which to join. No sooner, therefore, did I get possession of myself, so as to be able to speak, than I asked the Personages who stood above me in the light, which of all the sects was right (for at this time it had never entered into my heart that all were wrong)—and which I should join.

19 **I was answered that I must join none of them, for they were all wrong; and the Personage who addressed me said that all their creeds were an abomination in his sight; that those professors were all corrupt,** that: "they draw near to me with their lips, but their hearts are far from me, they teach for doctrines the commandments of men, having a form of godliness, but they deny the power thereof" *(Pearl of Great Price,* Joseph Smith History 1:15-19, emphasis added).

Please take a moment and slowly read over the bold-faced sentences again. Note that Joseph Smith is talking about some spiritual power from **the unseen world** which Smith describes as having **such marvelous power as I had never before felt in any being.** Just as he **was ready to sink into despair and abandon myself to destruction—not to an imaginary ruin, but to the power of some actual being,** two personages of light emerge from a shaft of light and tell him that he **must join none of them, for they were all wrong; and the Personage who addressed me said that all their creeds were an abomination in his sight; that those professors were all corrupt.**

Joseph Smith accepted this advice and later discovered that he would be the vessel through whom the personages would bring the real truth in the last days. Had Joseph Smith had any true biblical knowledge, he would have recognized these personages for who they really were. They certainly weren't God the Father and Jesus. And they weren't angels bringing a message from God, as an earlier version of the First Vision proclaimed. So who were they?

First, the one could not be God the Father, because the Bible tells us that Jesus is all the fullness of the godhead bodily: "For in him dwelleth all the fullness of the Godhead bodily" (Colossians 2:9). Second, this physical personage could never be God, for God is not a man. In speaking to His disciples about the nature of God, Jesus said, "God is a Spirit, and they that worship him must worship him in spirit and in truth" (John 4:24). Jesus appeared to the disciples after his death and they were frightened. He said, "Behold my hands and my feet, that it is I myself; handle me and see, for a spirit hath not flesh and bones, as ye see me have" (Luke 24:39). At another time Jesus said this about His Father: "...Blessed art thou, Simon Barjona, for flesh and blood hath not revealed it unto thee, but my Father which is in heaven" (Matthew 16:17).

Jesus not only declared that God is not a man, but spirit, but He later confirmed that a spirit does not have flesh and bones. To Peter, Jesus clearly stated that His Father does not have flesh and blood.

Shockingly, the LDS Church claims exactly the opposite: *"The Father has a body of flesh and bones as tangible as man's, the Son also; but the Holy Ghost has not a body of flesh and bones, but is a personage of Spirit. Were it not so, the Holy Ghost could not dwell in us" (Doctrine and Covenants 130:23).*

While all this should make all but the most foolish or ignorant of investigators run from the missionaries, this foundational error of Mormonism is deeply hidden from sight during the wooing process. Why so? Because Mormonism was founded on the purported visit of two personages of light who brought a different gospel, a different Christ, and a different spirit. The Bible itself identifies these two beings who appeared to Joseph as he fell under the marvelous power of that unseen being from another world: They were *beings who were the enemies of God.*

> But I fear, lest by any means, as the serpent beguiled Eve through his subtilty, so your minds should be corrupted from the simplicity that is in Christ. For if he that cometh preacheth another Jesus, whom we have not preached, or if ye receive another spirit, which ye have not received, or another gospel, which ye have not accepted, ye might well bear with him. . . . For such are false apostles, deceitful workers, transforming themselves into the apostles of Christ. And no marvel; for Satan himself is transformed into an angel of light. Therefore it is no great thing if his ministers also be transformed as the ministers of righteousness, whose end shall be according to their works (2 Corinthians 11:3,4,13-15).

According to Smith's testimony, that of Jesus, and that of the Bible itself, Joseph Smith was visited by Satan masquerading as God and pronouncing his curse upon the Christian church and the creeds of Christendom.

3

THE PAGAN CONNECTION

To the average person who only knows the mask that Mormonism wears and not the real face behind it (and this includes many Mormons), it is staggering to hear a beautiful and seemingly intelligent young woman express the incredible hopes she has as a Mormon wife. After Jolene comes on the screen in *The God Makers* and begins to tell her astonishing story, the audible gasps all through the audience voice the sudden shock felt by most viewers of this hard-hitting exposé. Then the gasps turn into embarrassed laughter. How could any intelligent person really think like that? Is it a joke? Yet Jolene is obviously sincere and deeply emotional as she says:

> Ever since I was a little girl, I was taught that my primary purpose was to become a goddess in heaven so that I could multiply an earth.
>
> I wanted that. I wanted to become a goddess with my husband . . . to be eternally pregnant and look down on an earth and say, "That's mine, and all those babies down there, I had!"

If that sounds bizarre, then Janet's testimony assures us that Jolene was not the only Mormon woman who took seriously the promise of becoming an eternally pregnant goddess. Disillusioned with Mormonism, Janet had decided to leave the Church of Jesus Christ of Latter-day Saints, when something changed her mind. It wasn't the fact that leaving the Mormon Church would cost her lifetime relationships and cause her closest friends to treat her like an enemy that made Janet decide to stay in Mormonism. Remembering very vividly, and with astonishment now, what happened when she attended that Relief Society meeting for what she had determined would be the very last time, Janet told us:

> That day they were teaching on how fortunate and privileged we were to become goddesses. I had all the qualifications, including a white skin.
>
> I thought to myself, "Wow, what I almost gave up! I can become a goddess, and I almost gave it up!"
>
> After that, I was back in the Church and I was stronger and more active than ever... [for] three more years....

It didn't seem at all unfair to Janet that people with skins darker than her own didn't have the same opportunity. She had believed the Mormon doctrine that all humans had lived in a premortal state before coming to this world. Janet had also accepted the teaching about Lucifer leading a rebellion among the spirits in that bygone era.[1] It made her proud to know, although she could remember none of it, that she had fought valiantly against the Devil on the side of Jesus. That was why she had white skin. She had earned it and the right that came with it: her worthiness to become a goddess.

There were others who had not been willing to fight in this crucial battle. Whether they had been cowards or just lazy, their failure to be valiant in the preexistence had brought the curse of a dark skin and disqualified them for the Mormon priesthood, which was a stepping-stone to godhood.[2] Since it was their own fault, they deserved that penalty. Although it became expedient for The Brethren to open the Priesthood to blacks in 1978, that alleged "revelation" did not change the Mormon explanation of the origin of a dark skin. It was also in direct contradiction to established Mormon doctrine to the effect that blacks could not have the Priesthood until after all whites had experienced "their resurrection from the dead." Brigham Young had explained it clearly in these words:

> Shall I tell you the law of God in regard to the African race? If the white man who belongs to the chosen seed mixes his blood with the seed of Cain, the penalty, under the law of God, is death on the spot.
>
> This will always be so.[3] Cain slew his brother... and the Lord put a mark upon him, which is the flat nose and black skin.

... That curse will remain upon them, and they never can hold the Priesthood or share in it until all the other descendants of Adam have received the promises and enjoyed the blessings of the Priesthood and the keys thereof.[4]

When all the other children of Adam have had the privilege of receiving the Priesthood, and of coming into the kingdom of God, and of being redeemed from the four quarters of the earth, and have received their resurrection from the dead, then it will be time enough to remove the curse from Cain and his posterity. . . .[5]

They will go down to death. And when all the rest of the children have received their blessings in the Holy Priesthood, then that curse will be removed . . . and they will then come up and possess the Priesthood. . . .[6]

John Taylor, the third Prophet and President of the Mormon Church, had this to say about the African-American in *Journal of Discourses* 22:304: "After the flood we are told that the curse that had been pronounced upon Cain was continued through Ham's wife, as he had married a wife of that seed. And why did it pass through the flood? Because it was necessary that the devil should have a representation upon the earth as well as God . . . . "

Gods-in-Embryo, Spirits-in-Waiting

As any Mormon will gladly testify, being one of the Latter-day Saints (LDS) with a "white and delightsome"[7] skin is something very special. With membership in "the only true Church" comes the added bonus of rediscovering one's own potential deity. Mormonism declares that we are all uncreated "gods-in-embryo" who have been progressing eternally upward in various forms and stages of ever-higher development in the spirit realm. Though literal sons and daughters of a "Mother and Father God,"[8] for some inexplicable reason we aren't "gods" by birth, but were required to come to this earth to take on a physical human body in order to prove ourselves worthy of godhood. Infinite numbers of our spirit ancestors have successfully earned their full godhood in this same manner and now rule as gods and goddesses over untold trillions of worlds like ours.[9]

Although the farthest reaches of the universe are now allegedly peopled with gods and goddesses with physical, resurrected bodies that were once mortal, Mormonism teaches that there are still multitudes of full-grown adult spirits out there waiting for bodies to inhabit so that they too can become gods.[10] President Joseph Fielding Smith taught that there is "possibly no greater sin" than any form of birth control.[11] This is why it is the duty of every righteous Mormon husband and wife to produce as many babies as possible. Only then can these waiting spirits come to earth to earn their full and rightful deity. The famous Osmond family has testified to their belief in this cardinal LDS doctrine in their signed, published statement of Mormon faith:

> We, as Mormons, believe that man is an eternal being, an individual of spiritual substance. We believe that we lived before coming to this earth and that in that premortal state we developed many of the attributes or qualities that our spirits now possess. . . .
>
> It also seems natural to us that our heavenly parents would want us, their offspring, to become like them. For that purpose, it was necessary for us to obtain physical bodies of flesh and bone and to become mortal as we are now.
>
> Consequently, our coming to earth at a given time or place is no accident. God does indeed control the coming to earth of the spirits born and reared in heaven. . . . He selects the most suitable locations for our birth on earth. . . .
>
> Thus, the earth was created that we might leave our heavenly parents to experience a school of challenges and to exercise our individual liberty and agency to show, through the conduct of our lives, that we fully appreciate and respect our relationship to God, our Heavenly Father, and his Son, Jesus Christ.
>
> "How do we do this?" you ask. By obedience to the laws and principles of the gospel as taught by the Savior during his period of mortality, as well as by word of his prophets.[12]

Although unable to remember anything of this fabled "preexistence" in the spirit world, every true Mormon must nevertheless believe in it because he has sworn to uphold Mormonism's founding Prophet, Joseph Smith. It was Smith who claimed he had received revelations about this premortal state from god-men who allegedly put us here and live on a distant planet near a giant star called Kolob. According to young Joseph, one of his extraterrestrial visitors, a god-man with a physical body (sometimes called "Elohim"), claimed to be the very Father of the spirits of all humans, and that we had lived with him on his home planet before being sent to earth for the purposes the Osmonds describe.

Strangely enough, the children which the gods give birth to are not gods themselves. According to Joseph Smith's "revelation," the explanation for this is stranger yet: "Gods" have bodies, but their children don't. For some peculiar reason that Joseph Smith didn't divulge, the physical womb of a mother-goddess made pregnant by her god-husband produces babies that are composed only of "spiritual substance," as the Osmonds state. So although one must have a physical body to be a god, the gods can only get their bodies from humans; for it is humans, not gods, who give birth to children with bodies. Although this may sound contradictory, this is why the Church believes that every "god-to-be" must come to an earth and take on a human body in order to become a god. For although we are all the literal children of "god-parents," we must first prove ourselves as humans before we can claim our rightful heritage as gods.

The LDS Church teaches that it was in the preexistent world that Jesus and Lucifer, two elder "brothers"[13] (sexually begotten sons of God as we all are),[14] vied before the "council of gods" for the honor of becoming the Savior of mankind. The plan that Jesus proposed was approved by the council's majority vote. In anger, Lucifer drew one-third of the brothers and sisters into rebellion against the council's decision. He then became the Devil, and his followers the demons.[15]

Mormons believe this amazing tale because of their "testimony" that Joseph Smith was a true Prophet inspired by visiting god-men. Those who have some doubts would not be very likely to admit it, for that would cost them their passport to heaven. Most Mormons rest happily in the confidence that the amazing eternal future that Joseph Smith promised is no less certain than the fabled eternal past he described (that they have completely forgotten). Why is nothing of the preexistence remembered? Early Mormon Apostle Orson Pratt explained:

> When all these spirits were sent forth from the eternal worlds, they were, no doubt, not infants; but when they entered the infant tabernacle [body], they were under the necessity, the same as our Lord and Savior, of being compressed, or diminished in size so that their spirits could be enclosed in infant tabernacles.

... When Jesus was born into our world, His previous knowledge was taken from Him. This was occasioned by His spiritual body being compressed into a smaller volume than it originally occupied.... When this spirit was compressed, so as to be wholly enclosed in an infant tabernacle, it had a tendency to suspend memory....

So it is with man. When he enters a body of flesh, his spirit is so compressed and contracted in infancy that he forgets his former existence....[16]

Paganism Revived

To understand Mormonism it is necessary to recognize, first of all, that it represents a revival of ancient pagan myths and practices under Christian labels. This we will document. Strangely enough, rather than being ashamed of the obvious fact that Mormonism is paganism revived, leading Mormons have pointed this out themselves. They even look upon it as proof of the truthfulness of Mormonism, in spite of the fact that the Bible so clearly denounces and condemns paganism as a satanic seduction to rebellion against the only true God.

Leading Mormon authority Milton R. Hunter has written:

Mormon Prophets have continuously taught the sublime truth that God the Eternal Father was once a mortal man, who passed through a school of earth life similar to that through which we are now passing. He became God—an exalted being—through obedience to the same eternal Gospel truths that we are given opportunity today to obey.

The Mystery Religions, pagan rivals of Christianity, taught emphatically the doctrine that "men may become Gods."

Hermes declared: "We must not shrink from saying that a man on earth is a mortal god, and that God in heaven is an immortal man."

This thought very closely resembles the teachings of the Prophet Joseph Smith and of President Lorenzo Snow.[17]

So Mormonism openly aligns itself with what its own leaders identify as "pagan rivals of Christianity." It even boasts that its gospel of men becoming gods is an ancient pagan belief. How then can Mormons claim to be the only true Christians upon earth? Simply because Joseph Smith said so. How do they know he told the truth? By a feeling called the "burning in the bosom," which is the Mormon's ultimate criterion for judging truth:

> But behold, I say unto you that you must study it out in your own mind; then you must ask me if it is right, and if it is right I will cause that your bosom shall burn within you; therefore you shall feel that it is right.[18]

This subjective "feeling" that could be produced by suggestion and the desire to experience it convinces Mormons by the millions that Joseph Smith was a true Prophet (regardless of his many false prophecies); that the Mormon Church is the only true Church; and that whatever its top leaders say must be accepted without question no matter how obviously wrong or contradictory of what the Bible, the Book of Mormon, or even earlier LDS Prophets have said.

The central belief both in Mormonism and paganism is the ancient dream that men can become gods. This universal and popular delusion began with Satan's impossible and self-contradictory ambition to be equal with God: "I will be like the Most High!"[19] How many Most Highs can there be? Satan lured Eve into joining his mad rebellion against the one true God by promising that she too could become a god. Evidence that this story in Genesis 3 is not myth but history is found everywhere.

Like Mormonism, Hinduism embraces and unites numerous pagan traditions, teaching that humans are gods who have always existed and have "forgotten" who they really are. The purpose of Yoga is "self-realization"—to realize one's rightful godhood through religious practices and rituals (which, as we shall see, is the secret function of Mormon Temples). Scientology, which is a combination of Hinduism and psychology, is based upon a similar belief that we are uncreated gods called Thetans, who have forgotten our true identity. It offers a psychotherapeutic process while connected to an "E-meter" that allegedly enables individuals to peel off "engrams" picked up in prior lives and eventually return to the realization and experience of their true "Thetanhood." The similarity between pagan religions and Mormonism cannot be explained away as coincidence, but is evidence of a common source of inspiration.

One of the most primitive forms of paganism is animism—the fear that even inanimate objects are inhabited by spirits and thus are alive. In keeping with much pagan mythology, Joseph Fielding Smith, who became the tenth President of the Mormon Church in 1970, taught that the earth is a living creature. The late Apostle Bruce R. McConkie affirmed this basically Hindu-occult concept that attributes life and intelligence to the entire universe, including inanimate things:

> ... This earth was created first as a spirit, and it was thereafter clothed upon with tangible, physical element ... [and] is passing through a plan of salvation.[20]

Paganism, Mormonism, and the Fall of Man

Jesus called Satan "a liar and the father of it"[21]—i.e., the father of *the* lie. No greater lie could be conceived than that humans could become gods. Eve was deceived by the Serpent's seductive offer of godhood. Adam wasn't deceived, but he nevertheless joined the rebellion instigated by Eve's seducer because he didn't want to lose his wife.[22] The Bible makes it clear that this sin of disobedience destroyed both Adam's and Eve's relationship to God, thereby bringing instant spiritual death and eventual physical death upon them and all of their descendants.[23] None of us can complain, however, because we have each rebelled against God in our own way, and we deserve the penalty: "The wages of sin is death."[24]

In contrast to the consistent teaching of the Judeo-Christian Scriptures, pagan/occult traditions consider the seduction of Eve to be a blessing in disguise. This allegedly made it possible for Adam and Eve to have children and unlocked the door to godhood for them and their descendants. Here again in the interpretation of the fall of man we have another connection between paganism and Mormonism.[25] The similarities are too many and too close for coincidence. Sterling W. Sill, Assistant to the Council of the Twelve Apostles, expressed Mormonism's agreement with pagan/occult mythology when he wrote:

> Adam fell, but he fell in the right direction ... toward the goal ... he fell upward.[26]

It is astonishing how thoroughly Mormonism has embraced Satan's promise of godhood! In LDS doctrine the ancient lie that destroyed the human race has metamorphosed into the central truth. On the afternoon of

June 8, 1873, preaching from the pulpit of the Mormon Tabernacle in Salt Lake City, President Brigham Young declared:

> The devil told the truth ... I do not blame Mother Eve.
>
> I would not have had her miss eating the forbidden fruit for anything in the world. ....
>
> They must pass through the same ordeals as the Gods, that they may know good from evil. ... [27]

The belief that Satan told the truth and that Adam and Eve did the right thing in following him instead of God comprises the very heart of Mormonism. This is only one of many ways that Mormon doctrine takes what the Bible says and turns it inside out. However, since Mormonism isn't based upon the Bible, hardly anyone notices the glaring contradictions. Embracing the lie is not an innocent mistake of theology hidden away in some obscure teaching. It is loudly trumpeted by the Mormon General Authorities again and again. Former President Joseph Fielding Smith stated it in these words:

> The fall of man came as a blessing in disguise. ... I never speak of the part Eve took in this fall as a sin, nor do I accuse Adam of a sin. ....
>
> We can hardly look upon anything resulting in such benefits as being a sin. ... [28]

It seems unbelievable that the highest authorities of the Mormon Church would not only praise Adam and Eve for disobeying God by eating the forbidden fruit, but would base Mormonism upon the "truth" with which the Devil seduced Eve! The Bible makes it crystal clear that Adam's sin brought banishment from the Garden and death upon the entire human race, necessitating the eventual death of Jesus Christ upon the cross in payment of sin's penalty. Yet no Mormon would be concerned about such obvious and serious contradictions between Mormonism and the Bible, because Mormon doctrine and practice is not based upon the Bible or even the Book of Mormon. It is based instead upon whatever the Prophet who happens to be alive at the time declares to be the "truth" that everyone must believe.

Having accepted the fall of man as necessary and beneficial, both Mormonism and paganism honor the lie that seduced Eve and avidly pursue the "godhood" which the Serpent promised. The central purpose in occultism is to achieve mastery of various psychospiritual techniques (meditation, Yoga, formulas, rituals, mediumship, etc.) that lead to "realization" of the godhood that the Serpent promised. Mormonism has its own formula, but it is basically derived from the same ancient Luciferian pagan traditions. Again, as we just remarked a page earlier, the rituals and formulas for the deepest secrets of Mormonism are given their reason for existence by Lucifer himself at the start of the LDS Temple ritual . . . that we may be gods and goddesses.

The Mormon path to godhood involves secret rituals introduced by Joseph Smith that must be performed repeatedly in the Mormon Temple. This is the very heart of Mormonism; yet *no one* is allowed to know what it involves until he has committed himself blindly to it. In his interview in the film *The God Makers,* Dr. Harold Goodman, former Brigham Young University professor and then President of the Mormon Mission in England, declared:

> As one of our great prophets and President of the Church has indicated, "As man is, God once was; and as God is, man may become."

> So you can see why the Temple is so important to the LDS [man]: because if he is worthy to go into the Temple and there receive the sacred ordinances and covenants and keep them, he can eventually grow into becoming a god himself.

Mormonism, Mythology, and Evolution

No one explained better than early Apostle Orson Pratt Mormonism's teaching about the preexistence of humans as eternal, uncreated intelligences that have gone through an endless cosmic evolutionary process. The terms he used left no doubt concerning the intimate relationship between Mormon doctrine and pagan mythology's ancient occult traditions. Pratt's explanation is still foundational to the most basic Mormon beliefs. The Mormon variation on Hinduism's doctrines of karma and reincarnation involves the transmigration of uncreated intelligences that existed from eternity in the form of "particles of spirit" composed of the "same materials of which our spirits are composed. . . ." Apostle Pratt explained:

> A transmigration of the same particles of spirits from a lower to a higher organization is demonstrated . . . growing out of the earth in the shape of grass, herbs and trees. . . . these vegetables become

food for celestial animals and these same particles . . . [move up to] form the spirits of animals.

Here then is apparently a transmigration of the same particles of spirit from an inferior to a superior organization. . . .

Who shall set any bounds to this upward tendency of spirit . . . who shall say that it will not progress until it shall gain the very summit of perfection?[29]

There is a clear relationship between this Mormon doctrine of preexistence and the theory of evolution, which also has existed in various forms in paganism since the beginning of time. When modern science in the early nineteenth century began seriously to seek fossil evidence to substantiate the myth of evolution, it was one of the first indications that science was at last returning full circle to its ancient occult roots. The attempt to ascend the scale of cosmic evolution through one's own efforts by achieving higher states of consciousness and the dream of a quantum leap to godhood are as old as occultism itself. One of the foremost experts in occultism, Manly P. Hall, has said:

The occultists of the ancient world had a most remarkable understanding of the principle of evolution. They recognized all life as being in various stages of *becoming*. They believed that grains of sand were in the process of *becoming* human. . . .

The ancients . . . maintained that the universe was a great [living] organism not unlike the human body, and that every phase and function of the Universal Body had a correspondence in man. . . .

Greek mystics believed that the spiritual nature of man descended into material existence from the Milky Way—the seed ground of souls—through one of the twelve gates of the great zodiacal band.[30]

The mythologies of almost every culture, along with the occult traditions preserved around the world by numerous secret societies, from Greece and Rome to Africa and the South Pacific, embellished the core of evolutionary doctrine with wondrous tales of a multiplicity of gods, all of whom had once been mere men and had earned their right to godhood. Here again, Mormonism faithfully follows this ancient tradition. Apostle Pratt wrote,

> If we should take a million of worlds like this and number their particles, we should find that there are more gods than there are particles of matter in those worlds. The Gods who dwell in the heaven have been . . . exalted also, from fallen men to Celestial Gods to inhabit their Heaven forever and ever.[31]

This has been the consistent teaching of Mormonism since Prophet Smith first publicly proclaimed it more than 150 years ago; and it is the very essence of Mormonism today. In 1974, former Mormon President Spencer W. Kimball declared:

> In each of us is the potentiality to become a God—pure, holy, true, influential, powerful, independent of earthly forces. . . . We were in the beginning with God. . . .
>
> Man can transform himself. . . . He has in him the seeds of Godhood that can grow. He can lift himself by his very bootstraps.[32]

4

UP TO GODHOOD

In Mormonism, contradictions and surprises abound. Transforming oneself into a god turns out to be rather more complicated than former President Kimball made it sound. Somehow the "seeds of godhood" that are supposed to be in every human by virtue of being a literal son or daughter of the god of this earth just don't "grow" without considerable time being spent in secret Mormon Temple rituals. And in spite of Kimball's statement that any man "can lift himself [into godhood] by his very bootstraps," the fine print says it can't be done alone, but only in partnership with a spouse to whom one has been married in the Temple "for eternity." This is discouraging for dedicated bachelors, though not nearly as much so as the declarations by Joseph Smith and Brigham Young that only polygamists could become gods.[1]

Kimball has emphasized that no one becomes a god without a special Temple marriage for eternity, no matter how valiantly he pulls on his bootstraps. Says Kimball: "Only through celestial marriage can one find the strait way, the narrow path. Eternal life cannot be had in any other way. The Lord was very specific and very definite in the matter of marriage."[2] Of course, the "Lord" never said anything of the kind in either the Bible or the Book of Mormon; this was a "revelation" that Joseph Smith received from the Lord of Kolob, the "Heavenly Father" of Mormon preexistence. When asked about it, Jesus declared that marriage is only for earth, and not for heaven.[3] Nevertheless, the Mormon is obligated to believe whatever Mormonism's Prophet, Seer, and Revelator living at the time says, no matter if it contradicts the Bible or even Joseph Smith. On camera, Dr. Harold Goodman, LDS Mission President in England at the time, said this about eternal marriage:

> ... With our intellect and with our discipline ... we can continually grow and develop and become a god *if* we have received in the house of the Lord the sacred ordinances as man and wife.

> This [achieving godhood] has to be done by companions. It is not an individual pursuit.

The Strange Fruits of Eternal Marriage

Strangely enough, it is the doctrine of eternal marriage itself that is causing so many divorces among Mormons. Achieving the coveted godhood is the consuming goal for every Latter-day Saint. Since this can't be accomplished alone, but only with a marriage partner, any zealous Mormon whose spouse's interest in becoming a god or goddess wanes must get divorced so that another "eternal marriage" can be performed in the Temple with someone who is willing to do whatever is necessary to reach this goal. Jolene described the heartbreaking tragedy of her divorce:

> He was raised a Christian and I was raised a Mormon. We had a beautiful relationship and two small children; but it always came back to Mormonism, and the fact that I had to convert him. ...

> After two-and-one-half years of trying very hard, it was clear that I would never be able to persuade him.

> I loved my husband Greg very much ... but I couldn't give up my goal of Temple marriage. I went through a very emotional time of inner turmoil.

> Greg and I both cried and cried during those months of struggle ... but the lure of a Temple marriage and the godhood it promised helped me block out my love for him.

> My family was happy with my decision. They were very strong Mormons and convinced me that my love for the Church could overpower my love for my husband.

> I went to my bishop and he advised me that it would be best to get a divorce. ...

Greg considered the ambition to become a god both an impossible, ridiculous dream and an affront to the one true God. As much as he loved Jolene, there was no way he could pretend to believe that anything as obviously pagan as Mormonism was really Christian, much less join Jolene's absurd grasping after godhood. The destruction of his family, in spite of the love they had for each other, seemed like a nightmare. As Greg relates:

> Jolene came to me and said she wanted a divorce. She said that either I drove her to her mother's or she would walk, but she was leaving.

> So I took my wife, seven months pregnant at the time, and my little boy, and drove them to her parents' home. It was almost more than I could do to leave them there.

> As I drove away, weeping convulsively, and praying to God that somehow in His mercy he would bring us back together again, I struggled to comprehend the incredible contradiction.

> Here was a Church that boasts of the family togetherness it stands for . . . and yet it was this Church that had destroyed our marriage!

Born in Germany, where she was raised in a Christian home, when Erica moved to Utah, she thought the Mormons were Christians. That was what they claimed to be. It was too late to escape tragedy when she discovered the truth. Erica is a beautiful and talented singer. The Mormon Church, whenever possible, keeps its members so busy that they have no time to think for themselves. At first Erica felt like a celebrity, singing all over Utah, sometimes with some of the Osmond family:

> I met and fell in love with a wonderful Mormon man, convinced he was a Christian. I didn't know Mormon beliefs . . . but my new Mormon friends accepted me and literally loved me into their Church.

> After we were married and I was in the Church, I began to realize that Mormonism was entirely different from Christianity.

> They have a different God, a different Jesus . . . in fact, almost every Mormon belief is very different from what the Bible teaches. I was shocked!

We did have a wonderful marriage. In fact, everyone thought we had the perfect marriage. My husband and I were very compatible. We had the same interests and we had a wonderful life together.

Wanting to be obedient and respect his religious beliefs, I continued to go with him to the Mormon Church, even though I felt an uneasiness there and an emptiness.

I even went to the Temple with my husband to prepare for our sealing for eternity. That was too much. I couldn't believe what went on in there. I hadn't thought that Christians would do such things. I was so horrified that I told my husband I would never go back in there again.

As I began to understand things better, I realized that I was standing in the way of his becoming a god. This made me feel so sorry for him that I could hardly bear it.

Finally he asked me, "Why don't you leave the Mormon Church?"

"Do you really mean it?" I replied, surprised he would even suggest it.

"Yes, I wish you would!" he insisted.

So I had my name removed from the Church roles.

As soon as I did that, he divorced me so he could pursue his goal of godhood.

Horror Stories—Unbelievable But True

In the film *The God Makers,* Brian Grant, LDS Publications Director for Great Britain, assures us that a Mormon Bishop would never counsel couples to divorce except in extreme cases. Critics of the film have pointed out that many Mormons have nonmember spouses and their marriages seem to be happy. That is true. However, as soon as the nonmember spouse becomes a Christian, the relationship is almost always doomed, in spite of the fact that Mormons claim to be Christians. The evidence for this seeming paradox is overwhelming.

Many of those who have experienced the breakup of their families because of the doctrine of eternal marriage are still afraid to have us use their real names. There is "Scott," whose unforgivable mistake was to become a born-again Christian. Although he had never become a Mormon, the marriage had gone well. With no conviction of his own, Scott had allowed his wife to raise their son in the LDS Church. After becoming a Christian, Scott tried to share with his wife and son the joy and wonder of knowing Jesus Christ personally as Savior and Lord, and the good news that they could receive eternal life as a free gift of God's grace. There had been no problem while Scott was an agnostic; but when he became a Christian, his Mormon wife began to talk of divorce. One sad night he came home to an empty house. His wife, son, and furniture had all disappeared, with the help of zealous Church leaders. It took several years of prayer, frustration, and mounting legal fees to find his son in Utah.

"Steven" also came home one day to an empty house. His Mormon wife and two children had vanished with the help of Church members. That was over 20 years ago. He hasn't seen them since. All he has left is one faded picture of his little son, who would now be 28.

"Bill's" wife became a Mormon after they had been happily married for years and had several children. When he wouldn't convert to Mormonism, the local LDS leaders assisted "Diane" in divorcing and relocating in Utah, where she was quickly married to a "righteous" LDS widower. When attempts by both the husband and Diane's family were made to see the missing children, the LDS family disappeared to Alaska.

"Chuck" was a typical Mormon with a gang of children and a busy wife. The whole family was enthusiastic and active in the Mormon Church. Then he discovered that there was a group of Christian men where he worked, who met weekly for Bible study. Joining in, he soon discovered that the Bible disagreed with almost everything the Mormon Church had told him was true Christianity. One day Chuck opened his heart and received as his personal Lord and Savior the Jesus of the Bible, who was definitely not the Jesus of Mormonism. Everyone noticed the change after Chuck was born again. The Bishop overseeing his local chapel demanded that Chuck sign an agreement not to listen to Christian radio programs, not to attend the Bible study or meet with Christians, and not to read his Bible outside Mormon gatherings. When Chuck refused, the local Mormon Elders came one day when he was at work and emptied the house of everything, taking furniture along with his wife and children. Of course, she divorced him in order to remarry a worthy

Mormon working his way to godhood. In the beginning of the film, the actor standing in for him expresses Chuck's thoughts:

> I think the worst thing for me has been the way they turned my own beautiful children against me....

> You know, the brainwashing techniques of this organization are incredibly effective!

It Sounds Like Science Fiction

It was hundreds of tragic stories like these, coming by letter and phone from all over the world, that motivated Ed Decker and Dick Baer to consult a leading Los Angeles law firm about filing a class-action suit on behalf of the victims. Having suffered through similar experiences themselves, Ed and Dick had some understanding of the heartache involved. Ed tells the lawyers:

> There is no doubt that my motivation in all of this stems partly back from my own personal experience.

> I look back on my own life, seeing a Bishop counsel me to divorce my wife, being separated from my five children, whom I raised in the Mormon Church, and spending all these years just trying to reestablish those relationships....

Dick and Ed didn't know the law, but were confident that somewhere within the American legal system there had to be a remedy for those who had suffered so much. It was extremely difficult, however, for them to get the attorneys to believe what was happening, notwithstanding the mountains of evidence. The lawyers found it too much to believe that intelligent, educated people in the space-age 1980's could really be serious about attaining godhood.

"Gods and goddesses... it sounds like Von Daniken [*Chariots of the Gods*] or science fiction," remarked the younger attorney with an uncomfortable laugh. From the twinkle in his eyes and the tone of his voice, it was apparent that he was having difficulty taking these two ex-Mormons seriously. After giving it further thought, he added with a resigned sigh, "Gods and goddesses just won't fly in the jury room, gentlemen. Juries feel a responsibility to be skeptical. You need to feed them information that has a taste of truth to it. And what you're telling us... I really don't think they're going to swallow it, do you?"

Ed and Dick were in for a long day. As difficult as it was to get the attorneys to take the Mormon goal of godhood seriously, it was no easier to convince them that brainwashing was involved. The Mormon Church has not only brainwashed its own members, but almost everyone else into viewing the Church as just another middle-class fundamentalist Christian denomination. Yet in actuality Mormons never refer to themselves as Christians but take pride in using the term "Saints," believing themselves to be far superior in enlightenment, truth, and knowledge to those Christians lost in deep apostasy.

Joseph Smith, Foundation of the Mormon Church

It's not too hard to understand that Mormons would be willing to surrender their minds to Church leaders in exchange for the coveted prize of godhood. This is why the Mormon dare not flinch in his loyalty to the Mormon Church, its founder Joseph Smith, and his successors who now control it.

Jesus never offered godhood to anyone. Instead, He called His disciples to deny self and take up the cross to follow Him.[4] No wonder Joseph Smith is more popular among Mormons than Jesus Christ Himself.

Many former Mormons tell how strange it now seems that for years they never noticed that the testimonials in the regular "Testimony Meetings" are always about the Mormon Church and Joseph Smith; almost never is there even a mention of Jesus Christ, except as part of the name of their Church. As it is with every ordinary Mormon, so it is with famous Mormons, such as the Osmonds. Their published "testimonial" is not about Jesus Christ, but is all about their Church. And that Church is founded entirely upon Joseph Smith's claim that he is the Prophet through whom god-men chose to "restore" true Christianity to planet Earth. Mormonism rests upon the "revelations" which Smith allegedly received from visiting humanoid space travelers from "Kolob."

In spite of the name of Jesus Christ being on the Church letterhead, it is to Joseph Smith that the Mormons look for their redemption. He, not Jesus, holds the key to the eternal destiny of every person now upon earth. Former Mormon President Joseph Fielding Smith made that clear when he wrote:

> [There is] no salvation without accepting Joseph Smith. If Joseph Smith was verily a prophet, and if he told the truth when he said that

he stood in the presence of angels sent from the Lord, and obtained the keys of authority, and the commandment to organize the Church of Jesus Christ once again upon the earth, then this knowledge is of the most vital importance to the entire world.

No man can reject that testimony without incurring the most dreadful consequences, for he cannot enter the kingdom of God.[5]

It is therefore not surprising that the Mormons' praise and testimony centers upon Joseph Smith and the Church he founded. Not only are Mormons taught that without Joseph Smith's approval no one can enter heaven, but also that Joseph Smith will be in charge on this earth once again "dictating plans and calling forth his brethren...."[6]

In the Melchizedek Priesthood manual for 1984, titled *Come Unto Christ* (see pages 126-32), it was really Joseph who the members were to come unto:

If we get our salvation, we shall have to pass by him [Joseph Smith]; if we enter our glory, it will be through the authority that he has received. We cannot get around him.

Joseph Fielding Smith was only affirming what Brigham Young, second President of the Mormon Church and Joseph Smith's successor, had earlier declared:

... No man or woman in this dispensation will ever enter into the Celestial Kingdom of God without the consent of Joseph Smith.

From the day that the priesthood was taken from the earth to the winding-up scene of all things, every man and woman must have the certificate of Joseph Smith as a passport to their entrance into the mansion above where God and Christ are—I with you and you with me.

I cannot go there without his consent. He holds the keys to rule in the spirit world and He rules there triumphantly, for he gained full power and a glorious victory over the power of Satan while he was yet in the flesh.[7]

The Christian praises God and testifies to his faith in Jesus Christ, but the Mormon praises Joseph Smith, who sits among the gods, his sacrificial blood to "plead our cause" above. This is the message of several popular Mormon hymns, which offer the glory and honor to Joseph Smith that the

Bible says belongs only to God. One of the favorites includes the following lines:

> Praise to the man who communed with Jehovah!
> Honored and blest be his ever great name!
> Great is his glory and endless his priesthood.
> Earth must atone for the blood of that man.
> Hail to the Prophet, ascended to heaven!
> Mingling with Gods, he can plan for his brethren;
> Death cannot conquer the hero again. . . .
> Long shall his blood which was shed by assassins
> Plead unto heaven while the earth lauds his fame."[8]

In the same hymnal, in the hymn "Joseph the Seer" he is given the status of savior:

> He pleads their cause in the courts above . . . He died, he died for those he loved . . . He reigns, he reigns in the realms above . . . Unchanged in death with a Saviour's love, he pleads their cause in the courts above . . . The Saints, the Saints, his only pride, for them he lived, for them he died.

The Living Oracles

Next to the Temple in Salt Lake City is the fabulous Tabernacle, home of the world-renowned Mormon Tabernacle Choir. Twice each year, from all over the world, Mormons stream in through the gates of Temple Square and hurry to their seats inside their beloved Tabernacle for the crowded, exciting sessions of another General Conference. With eager anticipation they look forward to hearing something new and inspiring about the kingdom, something they may be able to share in reverent awe as firsthand witnesses. For it is here that the top echelon of the Mormon hierarchy, known as the General Authorities, regularly deliver revelations from their "God" to his "chosen people." President Harold B. Lee confirmed the eternal significance of the LDS General Conference when he declared during the general session on April 8, 1973:

> If you want to know what the Lord has for this people at the present time, I would admonish you to get and read the discourses that have been delivered at this conference; for what these Brethren have spoken by the power of the Holy Ghost is the Mind of the Lord, the Will

of the Lord, the Voice of the Lord, and the Power of God unto Salvation.[9]

President Joseph Fielding Smith made it clear that "at every General Conference of the Church" the speakers are giving forth Scripture that is equal to anything in the Book of Mormon or the Bible. "It is just as much Scripture as anything you will find in any of . . . the standard works of the Church."[10] These men at the top of the Mormon Church are not ordinary religious leaders exhorting and teaching from the Mormon scriptures. They are the Living Oracles of Mormonism, the First Presidency and the Apostles of God, affectionately referred to by the masses as The Brethren. The eternal destiny of every listener depends upon absolute obedience to what these men proclaim. Of course, the people "may accept or reject what the Lord offers to them." However, "Acceptance brings salvation; rejection brings damnation."[11] President Heber C. Kimball made it crystal clear that the obedience required is blind and unreasoning, when he said in an address to the Priesthood:

> . . . Learn to do as you are told, both old and young; learn to do as you are told for the future. . . .
>
> If you are told by your leader to do a thing, do it. None of your business whether it is right or wrong.[12]

Speaking before the student body of Brigham Young University at a BYU devotional held at the Marriott Center assembly hall on February 26, 1980, and broadcast live on station KBYU-FM, President Ezra Taft Benson, who briefly succeeded President Spencer W. Kimball as Prophet of the Church, made it clear again that the "Living Oracles" wield absolute authority over every faithful Mormon: ". . . Keep your eye on the President of the Church. If he ever tells you to do anything, and it is wrong, and you do it, the Lord will bless you for it." Titled "Follow the Prophet," his address with its 14 points emphasized that the utterances of the President of the Church, who is Prophet, Seer, and Revelator, take precedence over all else, including the Bible and Book of Mormon and whatever past Prophets, even Joseph Smith, may have said. As evidence that this has long been the official position of the Mormon Church, Benson said:

Brigham Young took the stand and took the Bible, the Book of Mormon and the Doctrine and Covenants and laid them down. Brother Brigham said:

"When compared with the Living Oracles, those books are nothing to me; those books do not convey the word of God direct to us now, as do the words of a Prophet or a man bearing the Holy Priesthood in our day and generation.

"I would rather have the Living Oracles than all the writing in these books."

Brother Joseph said to the congregation, "Brother Brigham has told you the word of the Lord, and he has told you the truth."[13]

Christians consider the Bible to be the final authority in everything. Even among Christian groups that believe in prophecy for today, it is recognized that God does not contradict Himself, so anything that purports to be a "revelation" from God must be in harmony with what genuine prophets in the past have said under inspiration of the Holy Spirit in the Bible. Concerning those who claim to be speaking for God, the great Hebrew prophet Isaiah gave this warning:

To the law and to the testimony: if they speak not according to this word, it is because there is not light in them.[14]

The Mormons, however, are unwilling to apply this standard test to their Prophets. The Mormon "God" is free to contradict himself; and the Latter-day Saints have been brainwashed to accept this as quite normal. For example, at a Brigham Young University fireside meeting on May 5, 1974, when Elder S. Dilworth Young, an LDS General Authority (one of the Living Oracles), was asked to define modern revelation, he responded:

Modern Revelation is what President Joseph Smith said, unless President Spencer W. Kimball says differently.[15]

Joseph Smith and his successors have stacked the deck so that not even the Bible can call them into question. Mormons are taught to parrot the LDS Eighth Article: "We believe the Bible to be the Word of God as far as it is translated correctly." How does one know where it is not "translated correctly"? By very definition, that is wherever the Bible conflicts with Mormon doctrine (which is almost everywhere), in which case the latter is followed.

This places Mormons at the complete mercy of The Brethren who rule them. It is not to the written Scriptures that these men point for authority, but to themselves as the sole representatives and spokesmen for their God. They are the God-speakers, whose utterances must be accepted as the latest words of God Himself, even though contradictory to what "God" supposedly said yesterday. President Wilford Woodruff explained that "the Bible, the Book of Mormon and Doctrine and Covenants . . . would scarcely be sufficient to guide us for 24 hours. . . . We are to be guided by the Living Oracles."[16] During the April 1961 General Conference, President Marion G. Romney declared:

> This Church is the literal Kingdom of God in the earth. We did not come to argue, to jockey for position, to compromise differences and establish policies.
>
> We came here to hear and learn the Word of God as he has and does now reveal it through his appointed servants, and to take it back and teach it to our people.[17]

If you look at this in context, to the member there is nothing to test Mormonism against except itself. And any questioning is considered a sign of weakness, a lack of testimony that will quickly separate the inquirer from the fellowship of those who hold the keys to truth and heaven. None but the most desperate are willing to take the chance.

Joseph the Greatest

Here again, in the absolute authority which the "Living Oracles" wield, Mormonism betrays yet another connection with paganism. Although the God of the Judeo-Christian Bible has always spoken through chosen prophets, the moral responsibility of every individual is always kept intact. A prophet is to be obeyed if and only if his message 1) fits into and agrees with what proven prophets of God have previously said, and 2) does not contradict God's witness in the individual conscience. In paganism/occultism, however, the "revelations" of the spirit medium, fortune-teller, medicine man, witch doctor, shaman, Living Master, or guru are independent of and thus may contradict both conscience and other prophets.

One of the marks of pagan cults is the fear and bondage which absolute authority and contradictory revelation breed. The spiritist is elated or in deep depression, depending upon what the "spirits" have most recently uttered through the medium; the believer in astrology is at the mercy of the stars and planets and those who interpret them; millions of secretaries, businesspeople, scientists, teachers, and politicians base life's decisions upon which way the tarot cards or yarrow sticks in I Ching have just fallen. In like manner, the faithful Mormon must blindly follow the latest dictates of The Brethren.

In keeping with thousands of years of pagan tradition, Joseph Smith established himself as the sole authority over all those who were willing to let him interpret "truth and the will of God" for them. Mormons obtain a "testimony," not that Jesus Christ is their personal Savior and Lord, but that Joseph Smith was a true Prophet of God and that the Mormon Church is the only true Church upon the earth. This Mormon "testimony" is not based upon reason, conscience, or agreement with the Bible, but upon a subjective feeling called the "burning in the bosom." When anyone accepts this feeling as the evidence of authenticity, he automatically thereafter accepts whatever Joseph Smith or his successors said or say.[18] On this basis, Joseph Smith was able to convince his faithful followers that he was even greater than Jesus Christ. He said:

> I have more to boast of than ever any man had. I am the only man that has ever been able to keep a whole church together since the days of Adam. A large majority of the whole have stood by me.
>
> Neither Paul, John, Peter, nor Jesus ever did it. I boast that no man ever did such a work as I!
>
> The followers of Jesus ran away from Him; but the Latter-day Saints never ran away from me yet.[19]

It is upon this astonishing boast that Mormonism was founded and either stands or falls today. Every faithful Mormon must believe that the work which Jesus established failed and had to be "restored" in the last days through Joseph Smith, whose work will not fail. Joseph, not Jesus, holds the "keys" to the "last dispensation." It is *this* Church, founded by Joseph Smith, that will continue in the fullness of the exclusive authority he possessed until the millennial reign of Christ. The Church of Jesus Christ of Latter-day Saints will allegedly be the mechanism through which Christ, in apparent partnership with Joseph Smith, will govern the world during His 1000-year reign. The LDS people must believe that Mormonism *is* the kingdom of God, and that it is through the administration of this kingdom "restored" under the authority of Joseph Smith that every righteous Mormon who attains perfection will be exalted to godhood.

The Mormon Path to Godhood

As it was with Jolene and Janet when they were still part of the Church of Jesus Christ of Latter-day Saints, so today the fond hope and ambition of every "righteous" Mormon is to become a god or goddess ruling over a new planet Earth. On each of these new earths there will be another Adam and Eve, another Lucifer and Jesus (who are spirit brothers), another fall, another redemption, another round in this process of god-making that has been going on from eternity past and will never end. Mormonism is but one more variation of an ancient pagan theme, another mythology faithfully echoing thousands of years of occult tradition that has preserved this ancient myth since it was first recited to Eve.

Within pagan traditions down through the centuries, many secret rites have been developed as the means of achieving godhood. So it is in Mormonism. For Latter-day Saints to realize this fantastic goal, there are a great many complex rules and secret rituals that are faithful to the core of pagan traditions. Among the most important are secret ceremonies in the Mormon Temples. These will be described in detail later.

The Mormon path to godhood is administered by the First Presidency and Apostles of God—The Brethren—who sit at the top of an elaborate Mormon hierarchy of power and wealth. No Mormon can become a god without complete and unquestioning submission to these leaders. This has been proclaimed again and again, such as when President Brigham Young leaned over the pulpit not long after the Tabernacle had been completed, and boasted:

> I know just as well what to teach this people and just what to say to them and what to do in order to bring them into the Celestial Kingdom as I know the road to my office....
>
> I have never preached a sermon and sent it out to the children of men that they may not call Scripture....
>
> The people have the oracles of God continually.[20]

The Ward teachers' (now called home teachers) lesson for June 1945 dealt with the subject "Sustaining the General Authorities of the Church." It explained that while no one is forced to obey the authorities, to disobey brings damnation. This lesson, which was taught in Mormon homes around the world by the home teachers, declared:

> Any Latter-day Saint who denounces or opposes, whether actively or otherwise, any plan or doctrine advocated by the "prophets, seers and revelators" of the Church is cultivating the spirit of apostasy. One cannot speak evil of the Lord's anointed and retain the Holy Spirit in his heart.
>
> It should be remembered that Lucifer has a very cunning way of convincing unsuspecting souls that the General Authorities of the Church are as likely to be wrong as they are right. . . . He wins a great victory when he can get members of the Church to speak against their leaders and to do their own thinking. What cunning!
>
> When our leaders speak, the thinking has been done. When they propose a plan, it is God's plan. When they point the way, there is no other which is safe. When they give direction, it should mark the end of controversy.
>
> God works in no other way. To think otherwise, without immediate repentance, may cost one his faith, may destroy his testimony, and leave him a stranger to the kingdom of God.[21]

There are many gurus who, like the Mormon leaders, demand total submission and blind obedience from their followers, and offer godhood in exchange. In Mormonism it is The Brethren who occupy this position, holding absolute control over the lives of the faithful. They are accountable to no one but themselves, and everyone else is accountable to them. No one among the nearly ten million Mormons who hopes to become a god dares question the authority of The Brethren . . . for they are *The God Makers*.

5

THE MORMON DILEMMA

At the cost of about 12 million dollars (small change for a Church with annual income of about $6 billion and $30 billion in assets),[1] the Mormon Church ran a series of advertisements in the *Reader's Digest* that presented a picture of Mormons as almost angelic in perfection. The portrayal of "have-it-all-together" families comprising a uniformly happy, godly, and triumphant membership living ideal lives was more than misleading. The hidden truth about Mormons and what Mormonism really represents is a far cry from what one sees in magazine ads and television commercials or at the Visitor's Center at Salt Lake City's Temple Square.

Jerald and Sandra Tanner are former Mormons who have established an international reputation for their research into early Mormon writings. Based in Salt Lake City, for more than 30 years they have been searching out, reproducing, and publishing historic documents that Mormon leaders have hidden in a desperate effort to suppress the truth about Mormonism's past. The Tanners' work has demonstrated beyond any reasonable doubt that an astonishing number of extremely embarrassing skeletons are buried in the closet of Mormon history. Jerald and Sandra have been largely responsible for bringing international attention to the fact that the Mormon Church has deliberately hidden the diaries of its early Church leaders and has engaged in an elaborate cover-up of its history that has even included the extensive alteration of its early publications. Sandra Tanner declares:

> Mormon leaders are deliberately keeping from Church members the
> true history of their religion, because they know that the members

would have a hard time believing that it is from God if they saw how it really was all put together.

It's obvious that God's hand couldn't be in it, because the leaders have had to go back and rework, rewrite, cover up, change, delete, and add all the way through on all their books. Everything has been reworked.

They suppress their diaries, because these things show the confusion and the man-made nature of the theology and the religion.

I believe that some of the strongest "anti-Mormon" literature, if you want to call it that, is some of the early publications of the Church.

If the average Mormon were able to look at these things, it would destroy his "testimony."

We will explore the murky depths of Mormonism's past in due time. First of all, however, there are many skeletons in the closet of the present that need to be brought out into the open in the interest of a truthful evaluation of this explosively growing organization that wields an influence far out of proportion to its size.

"All Is Well! All Is Well!"

These words from the popular Mormon hymn "Come, Come Ye Saints" represent an attitude that is created and nourished in Mormons by what can only be described as a brainwashing process par excellence. It is essential not only to live a "righteous" life to achieve godhood, but equally necessary to keep a positive attitude in representing Mormonism to outsiders. At all cost, non-Mormons must see Latter-day Saints for what Joseph Smith said they are: members of the only true Church on earth, who live holy and pure lives that cause them to stand out in an otherwise-corrupt world. Blemishes must be covered over and truth must be suppressed in the interest of spreading the "restored gospel." When one is convinced that he is really a god-in-embryo, denial of human weaknesses becomes an unconscious habit. It is extremely difficult for a person who is building his future godhood upon his own worthiness to admit that he is a lost sinner, no matter how obvious that is to other people.

Something radical and hard-to-describe takes place in one's self-image when he believes he is destined to become a god and rule over an entire universe that he will someday manufacture out of an apparently inexhaustible storehouse of self-existent matter and intelligence. It is no less transforming to the Mormon woman to believe that she may eventually become one of the many goddess wives of a new "god." In this exalted motherhood she will be privileged to bear millions and perhaps billions of her god-husband's "spirit babies," who will eventually gain bodies to people the new earths that he will busy himself planning and forming. Whether in a male or a female body, just to believe that one has always existed as an eternally progressing uncreated intelligence brings an awesome sense of one's own proud heritage and infinite potential.

A large percentage of Mormons have been lifetime members. Many come from families with four and five generations of Mormon tradition behind them. To the LDS, their proud Mormon heritage is as much a way of life as it is a religion. As the very foundation of everything they think and do, as well as the only permanent reality in a changing world, their Mormon faith molds their character, determines their social outlook and attitudes, gives them their prejudices, and to a remarkable extent insulates them from the influence of the world around them. Truth is synonymous with the teachings of The Brethren guiding the Church; error is all else. There is an ironclad understanding that no science or knowledge of any kind exists that could call into question the dogmas of the only true Church. Its President is the very oracle of God; when he speaks, God has spoken. Work and play, family activities, and life itself all center in and revolve around the Church. Even those who have become inactive, called "Jack Mormons," are still bound to Mormonism as though it were bred into their very blood.

The twelfth child in a family of six boys and six girls, Gwen Meyer is an example of how deep and influential Mormon roots can be. Her mother was the fifteenth child of a woman in a polygamous marriage. Her grandfather was one of the original pioneers that came to Utah. His wife, who was 30 years younger than he and a convert from Wales, followed in one of the handcart companies. As one of the many former Mormons interviewed for the film, Gwen began on-camera by reminiscing about her youth:

> When I was a child, we lived in a town that was nearly all Mormons.
> I can only think of two families that weren't LDS.

> I really felt that people who didn't belong to the Mormon Church
> were a completely different species . . . like we would think today of
> somebody from another planet.
>
> I was very shy and afraid to be around these people.

To the "Gentiles," as the Mormons call the outside world, LDS people proudly and carefully project an image of wholesomeness, industry, and happiness that most people automatically associate with Mormons. There is a built-in feeling of superiority that comes with the name "Latter-day Saint," a subtle arrogance deserving of gods-in-embryo, an urgency to excel in order to gain "exaltation" and prove to the world around them who they really are. For they are *the* people, the only true Christians, the salt of the earth; and they grow up feeling responsible to do their Mormon heritage proud. In spite of the assurance in that favorite Mormon hymn, however, all is *not* well in Zion.

A Corrupting Seduction

The proud ambition to be a god turned one of the most beautiful and powerful angels in God's heaven into Satan. It is not surprising, then, that those whom the Serpent seduces by this same selfish dream are corrupted and eventually destroyed by it. Grasping after godhood breeds pride and arrogance, and warps one's thinking in a multitude of subtle ways. Though it sounds godly, the ambition to become a god is merely a "Saintly" expression of the same basic human selfishness that lies at the root of all evil. The devastating effects of this corruption of the will are at work just beneath the seemingly unblemished complexion of the face that Mormonism turns to the outside world. Mormonism's religious self-centeredness produces the same sins that plague secular society.

In 1980 the State of Utah, which is about 70 percent Mormon, ranked thirteenth in child abuse among the 50 states.[2] The Church wields such wide political control and has so often engaged in cover-ups to maintain its shining image that there is reason to suspect many other cases of child abuse that have never become part of the statistics.

"It is contrary to the teachings of the Church to artificially curtail or prevent the birth of children."[3] Beyond this official Mormon statement on birth control, LDS couples are encouraged to produce as many children as possible for reasons already explained. Utah's family size is twice the national average.[4] Certainly the pressure to marry young and have large families to provide bodies for the many spirits out there in the premortal state waiting to come to this earth could cause tensions in growing families that would contribute to child abuse and many other conflicts.

The June and July 1983 *Utah Holiday* magazine carried a two-part series titled "Sexual Politics." Dealing in depth with the frightful crime of sexual child abuse, the authors contended that the involvement of LDS Church officials was often counterproductive to justice. The Church continually sought to protect the male offender if he was a Mormon in good standing.

Sometimes a cover-up is impossible, but even then justice is perverted. For example, Mormon radio host Lloyd Pond, a highly visible spokesperson for the Mormon Church who decried the decay of family values and the evils of sexual abuse on his nationally syndicated radio show, pled guilty to molesting a 14-year-old girl and resigned on November 22, 1996.

The terrible details are compounded by the fact that Pond walked out of the court after two counts of first-degree forcible sodomy were amended to one count of second-degree forcible sexual abuse. He was given adult probation and parole and then released on his own recognizance. Attorneys explained his behavior as a form of midlife crisis. Once again, an LDS "Elder" walked away from sexual child abuse in Utah.

Less Than Candid

Elder Price, a retired Air Force colonel serving with his wife as a missionary guide to the Hawaii Temple, was less than candid in explaining the goals of Mormonism to our film crew: "We believe that we are here to work out our salvation," he told us, "to learn, to grow, to develop the talents that God has given us. And if we are faithful and diligent in doing these things, then we will receive the appropriate reward."

When asked to explain the "appropriate reward" for ultimate achievement in the Mormon Church, he still was evasive: "The Bible tells us that we are to become perfect, even as the Father in heaven is perfect. That's what we're working toward—to become more Christlike in everything that we do."

The Bible doesn't tell us to *become* perfect, but to *be* perfect, which would indicate that whatever this "perfection" is, it can be had immediately and is not something that is eventually attained in a future state. Jesus and His apostles made it clear that the Christian's Christlikeness comes not from developing a potential perfection inherent within himself but from having received Jesus Christ as Savior and Lord into this heart and then allowing Christ to take charge in every area of his life.

When God tells us to be perfect, He isn't demanding that we become God, which is impossible. A perfect man isn't a god any more than a perfect plant or a perfect animal would be. "Perfection" in man is simply being what God expects of us as humans. This is described in the Bible as a "perfect heart"—that attitude which sincerely wants to be all that God wants us to be, and accepts by God's grace the life of Christ and power of the Holy Spirit to accomplish in us what we cannot do ourselves. The Christian life is not a struggle for self-improvement, but the denial of self and a surrender to Jesus Christ that allows Him to live His life in and through us.

For most Mormons, the constant battle to become worthy of godhood is an eternal and hopeless struggle that they never seriously intend to pursue. Knowing that as a consequence they will have to settle for second-class citizenship in heaven, about 70 percent of Mormons have never qualified to enter the Temple to begin the secret rituals that are prerequisite to becoming gods. This is a startling fact that outsiders would never suspect from the less-than-candid image which the Mormon Church presents to the outside world.

An outsider cannot begin to comprehend the depth of despair that Mormons often go through, knowing that their best is always less than perfection. For those few Mormons who do feel worthy to become gods (and that number makes up a strange minority), a great difficulty comes in knowing that an imperfect wife or husband will not be there in celestial exaltation with them. That fact creates an alienation that pulls the "good one" out of the path of perfection unless he or she divorces the spouse and marries another worthy Mormon to join the quest for godhood.

The Disappointments of Do-It-Yourself Godhood

While the promise that a person can become a god is extremely inspiring to some people at first, the gradual realization that godhood must somehow be earned becomes understandably discouraging. The Bible offers eternal life to everyone who is willing to admit he can't earn it, and accepts it as a free gift of God's grace made possible because Christ paid the full price for our sins through His death upon the cross in our place. In contrast, Mormonism teaches that eternal life is exaltation to godhood and must be earned by the good works of those who thereby prove they are worthy. As Dr. Harold Goodman told us:

> The goal of every Latter-day Saint is to be married as a family unit in the house of the Lord and there receive these sacred blessings that will allow us eventually, if we're worthy, to dwell and be in the presence of our heavenly Father.
>
> A person has to be worthy; he has to receive a satisfactory interview from his Bishop and from his Stake President.
>
> That is the only way that we can be with Him [our heavenly Father] to rule and reign with Him. Otherwise, we could not be in His presence.

For the average Mormon, the strain of keeping several thousand commandments in order to prove his worthiness of exaltation to godhood becomes a burden too great to bear. For example, only 50 percent of the approximately ten million Mormons are considered active members by Church standards. According to Church statistics, only half of those who are active have ever been through the LDS Temple ritual,[5] the most important step in the Mormon plan of "exaltation." Moreover, of those who have made it to that plateau of worthiness, only about half remain worthy enough to continue their secret Temple rituals for the dead that are an essential part of Joseph Smith's Mormon gospel. Even more revealing is the fact that only an inner core of this worthy few actually continue more than briefly to participate in the Temple work that is so necessary for their own righteousness and final exaltation into godhood.[6]

These are more than mere statistics. They reflect the heartache and frustration of real people who are trapped by loyalty to a "Prophet" whose "restored" gospel eventually proves to be anything but the good news it is supposed to be. A hopeless dilemma confronts the more than 90 percent of Mormons who finally admit—but usually only to themselves in rare moments of honesty regarding their religion—that it is beyond their ability to reach the prescribed level of perfection through righteous obedience to the many laws and ordinances that distinguish Mormonism from Christianity. Afraid to abandon Prophet Smith and the Church he founded, because his endorsement is essential for entrance into heaven, the Mormon finds himself at the same time unable to prove himself worthy of what Mormonism offers. Thus the Mormon dilemma: Outside the Church is no salvation,[7] yet inside the Church there is no hope either, for no one who is honest with himself could ever pretend to meet its impossible standards of personal righteousness.

It is therefore not surprising that Mormonism, in spite of the bright smiles and happy image projected in magazine ads and TV commercials, creates a growing feeling of guilt and frustration that festers just beneath that manicured façade. There are sad and seemingly surprising statistics that dredge up hidden reality and expose it to the light. For example, suicide is the third-highest cause of death in Utah, and teen suicide is consistently above the national average. Wife-beating and child abuse are serious problems. A major portion of clinical psychiatry is devoted to the LDS woman. Half of all Utah births are by teenage mothers; seven out of ten of these births are conceived out of wedlock, and abortion is a serious problem. Recently, in a conversation with a young girl who had just graduated from high school in a small Utah town, we learned that one-third of the girls in her graduating class had been pregnant and unmarried. Salt Lake City has twice as many reported rapes as other cities its size across America.[8]

Mormon Women

In Hinduism, the woman has the opportunity to build up enough good karma to be reincarnated as a man and after that to reach godhood. In Mormonism, however, the woman doesn't have that opportunity. She can never become a god, only a goddess, eternally bearing children as one of many wives to a god-husband. That may be why so many young Mormon women opt for childbearing as their career here and now. A 1978 survey showed that only 30 percent of the women entering Brigham Young University finished, whereas 80 percent of the men completed their four years. After marriage, however, they soon find it necessary to get a job in spite of their growing families and the fact that in Utah during the 1980s the working woman was paid 53.5 cents for every dollar a man earns for the same job.[9] Utah still has a high incidence of scams and bankruptcies, and one of the lowest per capita incomes of any of the 50 states. So although the Church clearly and emphatically teaches that the Mormon woman's place is in the home, out of apparent necessity more than 50 percent of the women in Utah work outside the home, which is above the national average.[10]

The pressure from the Church and Mormon doctrine upon the LDS woman is staggering. Until the recent changes in the LDS Temple ritual, each Mormon woman was required to swear an oath of total obedience to her husband in the Temple. She must be perfect. Each wife who has been through the Temple has a secret name that only her husband and she know. He uses this to call her out of the grave on the day of resurrection; and there seems to be no remedy for her if he purposely or forgetfully fails to do so.

Ed Decker was once a guest on a popular radio talk show in a major city. The phone lines were so jammed with calls from intrigued listeners that the host kept him on for another hour. That ran until a program featuring a busy psychiatrist in that city was to come on the air. He was so interested in the lively call-in discussion that he invited Ed to share his program also. Everything was going smoothly until a particular call caused Ed to turn to his host and ask him about depression among Mormon women.

The reaction was sudden and startling. Silently and swiftly the psychiatrist signaled the technician to cut the microphones and go to a station break. As soon as the mikes were dead, he confided in Ed that it would destroy his large practice if such a subject were discussed. Most of his patients were Mormon women, he explained. By the time the station break was over, Ed had been gently but firmly removed from the broadcast room.

The oppression of Mormon women and the many problems arising as a result don't exist in only a few isolated cases, nor is this something dreamed up by fanatical activists. It's real, alive, and prevalent all over Utah. Articles such as "Loving in Violence—The Betrayal of Battered Wives"[11] and "Mormon Women and Depression"[12] have only scratched the surface of problems that the Mormon Church is unwilling to admit and face.

An Exploding Church

In spite of the many problems that Mormonism's pagan doctrines and practices (and dictatorial control over lives and minds) eventually generate, multitudes are being drawn into the Church of Jesus Christ of Latter-day Saints. For those who haven't yet learned its dark secrets, the Mormon Church with its social and welfare programs and emphasis upon wholesome family living seems an ideal place to make friends and raise a family. And even if the goal of becoming a god or goddess seems a bit farfetched at first, after a few years of brainwashing it begins to make sense to most Mormons, even to some of the very well-educated and sophisticated.

At the time of the publication of this book, the Mormon Church is one of the fastest-growing religious groups in America, as well as one of the wealthiest business corporations. From log cabins to massive skyscrapers, from handcarts to jumbo jets, the LDS Church is now exploding across the globe. It took 117 years for the Mormon Church to reach one million members, 19 years to add a second million to worldwide membership, nine years to add the third million, and a mere five years to add its fourth million. In 1984, it had climbed quickly to a membership of 5.2 million, with the expectation that it would now be doubling in size every ten years.

From 1984 to 1997 the LDS Church grew to approximately ten million members worldwide, the growth of Mormonism in the United States, where this book and the film peeled back the LDS veneer of deceit, is now of less than three percent per year. Obviously we cannot credit all that to this work, but *The God Makers* book and film were surely a catalyst that launched a strong ex-Mormon movement that swept across the country for an entire decade. Today there are scores of books and films on the subject.

The greatest growth rate of the Church is in those countries where the wholesome image of the missionaries is readily observed and a serious lack of apologetics materials is present. Today, with the Internet crossing every worldwide communications barrier that existed 20 years ago, the documentation to deal with Mormonism is exploding in nations everywhere. Just in May of 1997, Ed's website, http://www.Saintsalive.com, had almost 30,000 pages of information downloaded in over 50 countries!

Projections by Rodney Stark, University of Washington sociologist, indicate that "in about 83 years, worldwide Mormon membership should reach 260 million."[13] To accommodate this phenomenal growth, new Church buildings (Mormons call them chapels) are being constructed at the rate of nearly two each day around the world.

A major factor in this exponential expansion is the vast missionary training program that sustains an international proselytizing campaign built on the motto "Every member a missionary." In actual fact, however, only about 20 percent of the young Mormon men (and even fewer of the young women) ever go on the traditional mission.[14] Yet this produces a formidable missionary force far beyond anything created even by much larger churches, such as the Southern Baptists, who by comparison have 14 million members but only about 7000 missionaries worldwide. In 1983 the LDS Church operated about 190 missions with approximately 28,000 full-time missionaries. Very few of these are supported by the Church, in spite of its vast wealth. All expenses during the "mission" are met by the individual missionary, his family, or other members.

Until recently, each missionary was called to the field for a period of two years. Skyrocketing mission expenses due to inflation placed an increasing load upon the missionary and his family at a time when President Spencer W. Kimball, head of the Mormon Church, was calling for a substantial increase in the missionary force. Consequently, the former two-year mission period had been reduced to 18 months in order to induce more young Mormons to respond. Young ladies, who had formerly been quietly "accepted" in the mission field, are now actively encouraged to seek a mission calling, as are retired couples. In addition to the full-time missionaries, scores of thousands of local Church members are organized as "stake"[15] or part-time missionaries, working at their calling evenings and weekends. Under current Mormon President Gordon B. Hinckley, expansion of missionary effort and financial investment outside the United States has been greatly accelerated, and the missions term moved back to two years.

Mystery of the Missing Missionaries

In spite of the promised glory of godhood and increasing pressure from The Brethren which filters down through the Mormon hierarchy, at first the Church had fewer missionaries proportionately than before the new program. The actual count in 1984 was down to about 26,500 from well over 30,000 a few years earlier.[16]

By 1995, however, when the Church established a flat monthly cost that made the experience a lot less difficult for the average Mormon family, the count resurged past 50,000. Yet, even among Mormons, the once-shining image of an army of invincible missionaries has been tarnished by the disillusioning fact that about 25 percent of the missionaries are abandoning their mission before the end of their term.[17] In spite of such a revealing rate of loss, however, the missionary program is a substantial statistical success. The Church estimates that the general conversion rate is seven converts per missionary year,[18] a rate high enough to more than compensate for even the hypothetical loss of every missionary sent out.

A high percentage of returning missionaries enroll at Brigham Young University, which has a student body of 26,000, a second campus in Hawaii, and study centers in such far-flung places as London, Jerusalem, New Zealand, and Samoa. At the entrance to "the Y," as most Mormons call BYU, the visitor is greeted by the slogan "The Glory of God Is Intelligence." As one drives through the campus, the perfectly groomed lawns and equally groomed students create an atmosphere of respectful awe. One walks around the campus speaking and even thinking in a library whisper. There is not so much as a piece of paper out of place. That is the outward image of BYU which the Church cultivates and which it expects its students to represent to the "Gentile" world.

The Pagan Connection Again

As C.S. Lewis and a number of other experts have concluded, there are only two religions in the world: Christianity and Hinduism (paganism).[19] One teaches that we are separated from the one true God by sin, and God became a man to die for our sins; the other declares that men are not separated from God, but that each person has within himself the power to overcome evil and thus to become God or at least a god. Hinduism or paganism embraces and absorbs everything except biblical Christianity, which is its only genuine rival. Although it uses Christian language to disguise its paganism, Mormonism is less Christian than it is Hindu. The basic dilemma faced by every Mormon is a direct result of its Hindu roots. In the Baghavad-Gita, Krishna declares that he comes forth to save the righteous and to condemn the sinners.[20] This is just the opposite of the biblical Christ, who came to save sinners.[21] The great complaint of paganism and all secret occult societies is that whereas one must be "worthy" to join them, Christianity deliberately embraces the unworthy.

Ed was speaking at a church when a local Mormon official stood during question-and-answer time and proclaimed that Ed was doing the Church a service by getting rid of its dead wood, those who could not live up to the standards of the Church. "You are just getting our refuse, our garbage," he shouted. "Who would want them anyway?" Ed answered, "I want them, and so does Jesus." While the church was excited with the answer, it went right over the head of the Mormon official. He had absolutely no concept of grace.

In Mormonism there is a constant struggle to prove one's worthiness. Like Krishna, the Mormon Jesus saves only the righteous. Mormon doctrine declares that without righteousness, there is no forgiveness of sin; and without forgiveness of sin, there is no personal salvation.[22] This places the Mormon squarely on the horns of the same dilemma that occupies the pagan in endless rituals that never bring real peace—for it is sinners, obviously, who need salvation. Jesus said, "I came not to call the righteous, but sinners to repentance."[23] In Mormonism, however, sin is overcome by gritting one's teeth and living righteously—a task that the Bible says is impossible: "For there is not a just man upon the earth that doeth good and sinneth not."[24]

Jesus declared, "None is good, save one, that is, God."[25] The Mormon is taught, however, that he can become a god by living up to the standards of perfection and righteousness set forth in the Mormon "restored gospel." Pulling oneself up by one's bootstraps, however, proves as impossible in the spiritual realm as it so obviously is in the physical.

The Tragic Dilemma

Thousands of Mormon families seem among the finest in America. They live entire generations with hardly a visible blemish to tarnish the accepted image of the perfect home life and Church. However, as Ed Decker and Dick Baer became known, a flood of information began pouring in to them as overwhelming evidence that the Mormon Church is full of hurting people who are smiling on the outside but sobbing and dying on the inside. We were not made to become gods. There is only one true God, and beside Him all gods are pretenders who are grasping after godhood but can never reach it. That is why Mormonism simply doesn't work, and why those who struggle to prove their worthiness either develop a hard shell of blind pride or else become so frustrated that they want to give up but can't. So they stay, entangled in the web of deceit set out for them by those same personages of light, those demons of darkness that reached out and laid hold of Joseph Smith 150 years ago.

According to a number of reliable sources, psychiatrists in Salt Lake City and throughout Utah are kept busy working with Mormons who know that Mormonism isn't true and want to get out but can't escape. It isn't easy to leave the Mormon Church, especially in Utah; yet keeping one's real feelings inside for fear of the consequences that would result if the Church found out what one is thinking can become a horrible burden. Mormons are warned against having a personal relationship with Jesus Christ, so they have no one else they can confide in except a psychiatrist. At least doctors won't betray confidences to The Brethren. Mormons sometimes confide in ex-Mormons, knowing they would understand. It is not unusual for Mormons to slip into the home of Jerald and Sandra Tanner in Salt Lake City to share their disillusionment. Sandra told us:

> In Utah it's very hard for someone to leave the Church and make it public. There is, first of all, the threat for one's job. He may have a Mormon employer and this could seriously threaten his work position.
>
> Many of the people I see work for the Church itself, and are afraid of losing their positions. Some are afraid of divorce.
>
> I know people in high positions who don't believe Mormonism. I've talked to a Mormon Bishop who told me he didn't believe Mormonism at all.
>
> The motivation for many of them is that Mormonism is a nice way to raise your family. It's the easy road. If you're already here and you're already in it, then why upset things?

This is the tragic dilemma that many Mormons face. It isn't easy to keep up that saintly façade when inside you hate yourself for being a hypocrite. But to tell the truth is so costly that many Mormons find themselves trapped by circumstances and fear. Jim told us:

> Recently, the husband in a Mormon family we know began asking me questions.
>
> Then he called one night and said, "I know that what you're saying is true. There's no doubt in my mind. I can't punch any holes it in.
>
> "But I'm scared to death," he added, "that I'm going to lose my wife and children and my business. . . .
>
> "If I let out what I really believe now, what I've discovered . . . I'll lose it all!"

There are thousands of people like this, and they need help desperately. One of the best things we can do is to show them that the situation is even more tragic than they realize. It isn't just a question of mind control by The Brethren, false prophecies, misrepresentation, and heresy. There is something deeper involved, and understanding that deeper issue is the only thing that compels these hurting people to do what needs to be done.

6

AN ASTONISHING
LEGACY

At the very center of the LDS faith are the Temples with their secret pagan ceremonies. While Mormons believe that the "Prophet" is the link between man and God, the Temples are the link between man and godhood. Only in the Temple can the Mormon gain the secret knowledge and perform the occult rituals that allegedly bridge the chasm from human finiteness to eventual godhood. Strangely enough, these magnificent sanctuaries are used mainly "to redeem the dead"; and they stand as monuments honoring Satan's lie that death is neither real nor final.

God warned Adam and Eve that the penalty for rebellion is death. Mormonism teaches that its reward is godhood. The Bible clearly teaches that death is final, and that those who die have no further chance to be saved: "... It is appointed unto men once to die, but after this the judgment."[1] We learn why this must be so from the story that Jesus told of the rich man who died and went to hades. The tormenting thirst he experienced there as a result of his separation from God was so great that it would have been impossible for him to respond rationally to God's love and the gospel. He was so obsessed with getting out of the horrible place that it was now too late for him to be able to make a decision based solely upon truth.

For those who die without having received Christ as Lord and Savior, it is forever too late to be saved. Jesus said, "If ye believe not that I am he, ye shall die in your sins ... [and] *whither I go ye cannot come.*"[2] Blatantly denying this, Mormonism teaches that, just as the Serpent told Eve, "You won't really

73

die." In Mormonism, those who die aren't really dead but can still communicate with the living and join the Mormon Church beyond the grave.

Mormonism, thus, contradicts not only the Bible but its own scriptures. Another of the great ironies of Mormonism is that their scripture declares just the opposite of this second-chance-after-death doctrine. The Book of Mormon clearly lays this out:

> And now, as I said unto you before, as ye have had so many witnesses, therefore, I beseech of you that ye do not procrastinate the day of your repentance until the end; for after this day of life, which is given us to prepare for eternity, behold, if we do not improve our time while in this life, then cometh the night of darkness wherein there can be no labor performed. Ye cannot say, when ye are brought to that awful crisis, that I will repent, that I will return to my God. Nay, ye cannot say this; for that same spirit which doth possess your bodies at the time that ye go out of this life, that same spirit will have power to possess your body in that eternal world.

> For behold, if ye have procrastinated the day of your repentance even until death, behold, ye have become subjected to the spirit of the devil, and he doth seal you his; therefore, the Spirit of the Lord hath withdrawn from you, and hath no place in you, and the devil hath all power over you; and this is the final state of the wicked (The Book of Mormon: Alma 34:33-36).

A further irony is found in the fact that very little of Mormonism's peculiar doctrine comes from the Book of Mormon. Most of it comes from additional "revelations" received by Joseph Smith and his successors. These are found in such books as *Journal of Discourses, Doctrine and Covenants, Teachings of the Prophet Joseph Smith,* and others.

A Church for the Dead

Mormon Temples are among the most beautiful and awe-inspiring buildings in existence. No expense is spared in making each Temple a showplace of beauty and elegance. For most Mormons, the Temple is so sacred that anything said or done within its walls must be of God. What many Mormons themselves don't realize is that most of the Temple rituals are performed for disembodied spirits.

The ordinances practiced in Mormon Temples are of two types: those for the living, and the identical rituals done by proxy for the dead. The latter allegedly enable those who have been waiting in "spirit prison" for the millennium to become Temple Mormons. If the departed spirits choose to accept the proxy rituals, they are then allowed (contrary to the Book of Mormon) to go to the place called "Paradise," the home of all worthy Mormons who have died. The central importance of these ceremonies in Mormonism is emphasized in LDS scriptures. For example:

> And now, my dearly beloved brethren and sisters, let me assure you that these are principles in relation to the dead and the living that cannot be lightly passed over, as pertaining to our salvation.
>
> For their [the dead's] salvation is necessary and essential to our [the living's] salvation. . . .[3]

Although the Bible specifically warns us to avoid genealogies,[4] the Mormons are obsessed with them. President Joseph Fielding Smith declared: ". . . The greatest commandment given us and made obligatory, is the Temple work in our own behalf and in behalf of our dead."[5] This hardly agrees with what Jesus said. When asked, "Which is the greatest commandment in the law?" the Lord replied: "Thou shalt love the Lord thy God with all thy heart, and with all thy soul, and with all thy mind. This is the first and great commandment."[6] Yet the most important part of Mormonism concerns the dead. Joseph Smith said: "The greatest responsibility in this world that God has laid upon us is to seek after our dead."[7]

Faithful to Joseph Smith and in direct disobedience of biblical warnings to avoid genealogies, the Mormons operate the largest genealogical center on earth. Located in Salt Lake City, it is staffed with more than 600 trained experts, who sort and catalog incoming census rolls, church registers, wills, and deeds gathered from all over the world. This information is transferred to microfilm and stored in an underground vault deep inside the towering granite Wasatch Mountains 20 miles south of Salt Lake City. These bomb-proof vaults have the capacity to store the equivalent of 26 million volumes of genealogical material.

The Mormon Genealogical Library in Salt Lake City contains the family tree records for more than one billion names. In addition, it is linked with a worldwide network involving about 400 branches containing further records of the dead. While genealogy is a hobby for the many "Gentiles" who use LDS facilities for research, it is serious business to the Temple Mormons. Their very salvation depends upon it.

Heber J. Grant, seventh President of the Mormon Church, once stated: "I am deeply interested in genealogical work. . . . I have in my employ a sister who devotes all her time to the preparation of genealogical records . . . pertaining to the families to which I belong in direct descent and through marriage."[8]

Typical of the stories that are circulated among Mormons in order to arouse their diligent attention to this vital subject is the following about a Mrs. Triptow:

> . . . One day last month . . . she found the names of four new ancestors for whom she had searched 15 years.
>
> She spotted their names and christening dates in the Bedlington (England) parish register printout at the Genealogical Society library.[9]

Another Pagan Connection

While making it clear that "after death comes judgment" without hope of salvation, the Bible contains one verse that does refer to baptism for the dead. Pointing to this, Mormons say, "The Bible teaches baptism for the dead, and we baptize by proxy for the dead in our Temples. This proves that the Mormon Church follows the Bible and all other churches don't, so it must be the only true Church." Reading this verse in context, however, it becomes clear that baptism for the dead was not practiced by Christians, but by pagans. The fact that Mormons baptize for the dead is one more link in the long chain of the pagan connection.

In 1 Corinthians 15, Paul uses the pronouns "we" and "us" for 28 verses in speaking of and to Christians. Then in verse 29 he suddenly changes the pronoun to "they" when he says, "Else what shall *they* do who are baptized for the dead? If the dead rise not at all, why then are *they* baptized for the dead?"

It is quite evident that Paul is not referring to Christians but to the non-Christian pagans of his day, because he refers to them as "they," indicating some group other than the Christians to whom he has been speaking and addressing as "we" or "us." In verse 30 he changes the pronoun back again when he says, "And why stand *we* in jeopardy every hour?" Clearly the "they" in verse 29 refers to someone other than the "we" in verse 30. Since the latter, as is clear from the context, obviously includes himself and the Christians he is writing to, the former must refer to non-Christians—i.e., the pagan worshipers of Paul's day. Clearly, Paul is using the fact that the mystery religions practiced baptism for the dead as evidence that even the pagans believed in life after death, which is what he now begins to argue for by other examples. Far from teaching baptism for the dead, the Bible points out that it is a pagan and not a Christian practice.

In our modern world, it is the Mormons' well-intentioned though pagan program for evangelizing the dead and performing secret rituals by proxy for them that is one of the major distinctives between Mormons and other religious groups. Indeed, the Mormons often point to this with pride. John Taylor, third President of the Mormon Church, stated: ". . . We are the *only* people that know how to save our progenitors. . . . We in fact are the *saviours of the world*, if they ever are saved. . . ."[10] Mormons themselves have admitted the pagan connection by implying that their seeking after the dead is very much like ancestor worship. At the 146th General Conference of the Church, Adney Y. Komatsu of the First Quorum of Seventy stated:

> . . . A young couple who were members of the Church in Japan . . . joined with others in seeking out their ancestors and in planning to have the temple work done for them.
>
> The girl searched diligently through shrines, cemeteries and government record offices, and was able to gather 77 names. . . .
>
> As this young couple joined their family members . . . they displayed their book of remembrance . . . [and] discussed with those relatives assembled their ancestral lines and the importance of completing the genealogical research.
>
> It was difficult for their non-member families to understand the reasons for a Christian Church teaching principles such as "ancestral worship," for this was a Buddhist teaching and tradition. . . .
>
> Through genealogical research and through doing temple work for their progenitors, and especially with a Temple now becoming available in Tokyo, members can so live that the gospel will yet be embraced by many more in the Orient.[11]

During the April 1982 General Conference, Elder W. Grant Bangerter, a General Authority in the First Quorum of the Seventy, emphasized the importance of LDS Temple work for the dead. At the same time he reinforced the Mormon acceptance of the idea that there is no death when he said, "Temple work is for the redemption of the dead.... And may we always remember that we perform the temple ordinances for people and not for names. Those we call 'the dead' are alive in the spirit and *are present in the temple.*"[12] Not only do Mormons seek their dead, as Joseph Smith taught them, but their dead allegedly seek them and even gather in the Mormon Temples to encourage those performing the rituals to carry on in their behalf. Wilford Woodruff, fourth President of the Mormon Church, declared:

> The dead will be after you, they will seek after you as they have after us in St. George [Temple]. They called upon us, knowing that we held the keys and power to redeem them.
>
> I will here say before closing, that two weeks before I left St. George, the spirits of the dead gathered around me, wanting to know why we did not redeem them.[13]

Prisoners at Large

One of the strangest things about the Mormon Temples' functioning for the dead is the fact that these dead are supposed to be in a Mormon purgatory called the "spirit prison." It seems rather odd that spirits confined to a prison could at the same time be present in Mormon Temples, seeking the living and calling upon them to save them. Supposedly, the spirits of Mormons who have died are in Paradise awaiting the resurrection, and in the meanwhile they journey in the spirit world as missionaries to this "prison" to preach the Mormon gospel to the inmates there. Accepting this gospel, however, would hardly seem the basis for releasing or even paroling anyone from spirit prison to attend Mormon Temples and appear to Mormons elsewhere to assure them that the Mormon Church is the only true Church. At least on the basis of statements by leading Mormons it would seem that confinement in this prison continues until the end of the millennium. President Joseph Fielding Smith declared:

> It is decreed that the unrighteous shall have to spend their time during this thousand years in the prison house prepared for them

where they can repent and cleanse themselves through the things which they shall suffer.[14]

Apostle Heber C. Kimball, a Mormon General Authority and member of the First Presidency under Brigham Young, called this "prison" hell. Its purpose is apparently to torture the wicked in payment of their sins, and there is no indication that this process can be shortened by believing the Mormon gospel. In spite of the similarity between the Mormon "spirit prison" and Catholic purgatory, there is nothing in Mormonism comparable to Catholic "indulgences" for shortening the time of punishment. On the contrary, it isn't believing the Mormon gospel but enduring the necessary punishment that brings eventual release from the "spirit prison." Apostle Kimball declared:

> That is loving the wicked, to send them there to hell to be burnt out until they are purified.
>
> Yes, they shall go there and stay there and be burnt, like an old pipe that stinks with long usage and corruption, until they are burnt out, and then their spirits may be saved in the day of God Almighty.[15]
>
> You have often heard me speak about my kindred. . . . Will they be saved? Yes, they will, but . . . they will first go to hell and remain there until the corruption with which they are impregnated is burnt out. . . .
>
> The day will yet come when they will come to me and acknowledge me as their savior, and I will redeem them and bring them forth from hell to where I live and make them my servants; and they will be quite willing to enter into my service.[16]

It all sounds confusing. In Mormonism there is no hell, and yet there is one after all; but it isn't really hell—it's a "spirit prison" where the dead pay for their own sins, although the Bible says that only the death of Christ could pay that penalty. Equally strange, while the spirits are confined to this "prison" they are somehow able to visit their Mormon relatives on earth and call upon the living to "save" them. While suffering in the Mormon "hell," they are nevertheless mysteriously at large and able to attend Mormon Temples to observe the pagan rituals that are being performed for them there. One would expect that since the most important work that Mormons have to do involves "saving" their dead, they would have worked out some more consistent teaching on the subject. The finite details of this important doctrine remain buried in a sort of fuzzy folklore that brings an aura of mystery and intrigue, making the members nervous enough to avoid a detailed study of the facts in the matter.

Mormon Necromancy

Although two apparent exceptions are given,[17] the Bible teaches that the spirits of the dead are either in hell or heaven and cannot return to earth to communicate with the living. This is also clearly taught in the Book of Mormon, which says:

> And there is a place prepared, even that awful hell . . . wherefore the final state of the souls of men is to dwell in the Kingdom of god, or to be cast out. . . .
>
> . . . Ye cannot suppose that such [sinners] can have place in the Kingdom of heaven; but they shall be cast out, for they are the children of the Kingdom of the Devil. . . .[18]

If the spirits of the dead are either in heaven or hell, then appearances in Mormon Temples, as in seances, can only be demons impersonating the dead to foster belief in Satan's denial of death.[19] This is why attempted communication with the dead, which is called necromancy, is absolutely forbidden in the Bible.[20] Here again, in open rejection of the Word of God, Mormonism not only encourages but boasts of alleged contact with the spirits of the dead. At the same 1982 General Conference mentioned above, Elder A. Theodore Tuttle, another General Authority, proudly declared:

> On the third of April 1836, one week after the dedication of the Kirtland Temple, the monumental event occurred—the Savior appeared and accepted the Temple!
>
> Moses and Elias also came. Then, Malachi's prophecy was fulfilled, for Elijah the prophet stood before them. . . .[21]

In an LDS Sunday school lesson comparing the lives of "Two Great Men," Joseph Smith and John Wesley, Elder Paul L. Harmon remarked: "As Latter-day Saints we have the highest regard for the integrity and courage of John Wesley. We sing many hymns written by him and his brother, Charles. We believe John Wesley was in the group of fifty eminent men who appeared, along with the signers of the Declaration of Independence, to President

Wilford Woodruff in the Saint George Temple in 1877 and requested that baptism be performed in their behalf."[22] Mormons glory in the tales of such spirit appearances, which they consider to be irrefutable evidence that theirs is the only true Church. (Similar phenomena are common among various occult and satanic groups.)

Numerous books have been written on the subject, chronicling everything from divine aid in doing genealogy to visitations of spirit people right in the Temples themselves. Joseph Heinerman's book *Temple Manifestations* (Salt Lake City: Magazine Printing and Publishing, 1974) and its companion, *Spirit World Manifestations* (Salt Lake City: Magazine Printing and Publishing, 1978) are most notable among such publications.

Describing this gathering of the dead in his own words, President Woodruff said:

> These were the signers of the Declaration of Independence, and they waited on me for two days and two nights.
>
> . . . I straightway went into the baptismal font and called upon brother McCallister to baptize me for the signers of the Declaration of Independence, and fifty other eminent men, making one hundred in all, including John Wesley, Columbus and others. . . .
>
> I then baptized him for every President of the United States, except three; and when their cause is just, somebody will do the work for them.[23]

Stories of such spiritual visitations are common in the oral tradition or folklore of the Mormon Church. Many times it is alleged to be a dead relative who appears to a Mormon, to state that he or she has converted to Mormonism in the spirit world. The demonic apparition will often declare that "the Mormon Church is the only true Church," and ask to have its genealogical work completed on its behalf in the Temple so it can join the Mormon Church "on the other side." This was the case when a demon appeared in the form of the great-grandmother of Joanna and convinced her by this "sign" that Mormonism was true.[24] These appearances are very real and extremely convincing, and usually accomplish the satanic deception intended.

The many references to "light" in the stories about these apparitions that circulate among Mormons seem especially significant in view of what the Bible says about Satan transforming himself into an "angel of light."[25]

Moroni, the key messenger who "restored" truth for Joseph Smith, is usually described as an "Angel of Light."[26] Interestingly enough, the reference for "Angel of Light" in the late LDS Apostle/scholar Bruce McConkie's encyclopedic work on Mormon doctrine reads "See Devil." Moreover, the "Personages of light" that brought revelations to Joseph Smith (later identified as the heavenly Father and His Son) are reminiscent of the "being of light" that convinces the "clinically dead" that they aren't really dead and that there is no judgment but only acceptance and love. The similarity between this idea and Satan's lie to Eve that she wouldn't really die is clear.

During the dedication of the Mormon Temple in Manti, Utah, personages of light, halos and circles of light, auras of light about the speakers, strange melodious music, and other manifestations from the "spirit world" were noted and considered signs that the Lord had accepted the Temple.[27] One of the most common kinds of Temple stories involves the alleged repeated appearances of Christ, very much like appearances of the Virgin to Catholics. For example, LDS President Lorenzo Snow claimed that, at the time he was President of the Council of the Twelve Apostles, Jesus appeared to him in the Salt Lake Temple. He told how on September 2, 1898, Jesus stood three feet off the floor, floating on a plate of solid gold, and spoke to him. This was supposedly in response to the secret signs of the Mormon Priesthood made by President Snow as he stood in the Temple dressed in his Priesthood robes.[28]

Although it is the living who perform the occult rituals, Mormon Temples are primarily Temples of the dead. There the living must take upon themselves the oaths of the dead in order to "redeem" them. Thousands of pagan ceremonies are performed each day in Mormon Temples around the world for the dead, so that they too can receive the benefits of Mormonism. The Latter-day Saints are encouraged to have encounters with the alleged spirits of the dead in and out of the Temple. It is their belief that these encounters, though absolutely forbidden in the Bible, are the most sacred evidences that Mormonism is the only true religion.

"Mormo" and the Mormons

Not only Mormons, but many others also, in defense of these "good moral people," sincerely object to any attempt to show a satanic inspiration behind Mormonism. It is often insisted that the considerable evidence for this is circumstantial only. That is the reaction Ed Decker and Dick Baer meet from the attorneys in the film *The God Makers*.

Opening a copy of Anton LaVey's *Satanic Bible* to the page listing "Infernal Names," Ed says, "Look at this. The god of the ghouls* is named 'Mormo.' His followers would be Mormons."

"That's just the kind of conclusion we can't jump to!" retorts the older attorney sharply. "It could be just a coincidence."

"Except for the fact," adds Ed, "that Mormons are obsessed with genealogies and Temple rites and rituals for the dead, who they believe can visit the living, and who can convert to Mormonism even in the grave."

Dick Baer cuts in to reinforce what Ed is saying. "In Chinese, *Mormon* means 'gates of hell.' That's why the Mormon missionaries seem to have some problems in Hong Kong, for instance. They have to avoid using the word *Mormon* in trying to convert the Chinese."

The lawyers are becoming increasingly uncomfortable. "That could be just another coincidence!" is the instant and irritable response of the older attorney.

He is almost scolding Dick and Ed at this point for offering what he considers to be the flimsiest of circumstantial evidence. When one examines Mormonism carefully, however, the proof of satanic inspiration becomes overwhelming.

More Than Circumstantial

As would be expected, Mormons take great offense at any suggestion that Satan could have influenced Joseph Smith in any way. It is an insult to them that such a possibility would even be raised. There is no escaping the fact, however, that a surprisingly pagan and anti-Christian influence is woven like a web through Mormonism, leaving a legacy of doctrines and practices that bear the unmistakable fingerprints of Lucifer himself. This is a common denominator in almost all of the mystery religions; and Mormonism (which boasts of its similarities to them) is no exception.

A major portion of the secret rituals that take place in Mormon Temples is called the Endowment. Part of it involves a "creation drama" that puts most Temple patrons (those going through the ceremony) to sleep. This is

---

* An evil being obsessed with the dead.

followed by a reenactment on film or stage of events in the Garden of Eden. After he and his wife, Eve, have been expelled from the Garden into the "lone and dreary world," Adam builds an altar and cries out, "O God, hear the words of my mouth!"

When he has repeated this three times, an arrogant voice responds off-stage, "I hear you!" Lucifer then enters the scene. Sauntering over to Adam, he asks, "What is it you want?"

"Who are you?" demands Adam in surprise.

"I am the god of this world," replies Lucifer.

Strangely enough, when confronted with the fact that there are trillions of gods in Mormonism (even more than in Hinduism, which has only about 300 million), the average Mormon will invariably try to deny the polytheistic nature of his religion by insisting, "But we only worship 'the God of *this* world.'" Of course, he doesn't intend to admit that Lucifer, who identifies himself as "the god of this world," is his "god" when he says that.

However, the very multiplicity of Mormon "gods," who allegedly exercise dominion over innumerable earths, necessitates identifying the "god" that Mormons worship as "the god of this world." The beliefs that Joseph Smith left his followers force them to identify their "god" with the very title that the Bible gives to Satan.[29] This is only part of an astonishing Luciferian legacy that permeates Mormon beliefs and practices. It is just another spiritual hook awaiting the unwary.

Lucifer's Power and Priesthoods

Earlier in the Garden of Eden sequence, Mormons going through the Temple (i.e., the Temple patrons) watch the unfolding drama as Lucifer instructs Adam and Eve that there is no way for them to gain the knowledge to become "as gods" except to disobey "Father" and eat of the forbidden fruit.[30] In Mormonism, Lucifer is not a fallen angel, as the Bible teaches, but the literal (though rebellious) son of God and the actual *brother* of Jesus. As we have already seen, Mormonism also teaches that Satan told Eve the truth, that Adam and Eve didn't sin in disobeying God, and that the "fall" was really a "blessing in disguise" that opened the door to godhood for the human race. At this point in the Temple ceremony, the Luciferian legacy is reinforced by a fascinating sequence of events.

Lucifer has appeared on the scene wearing an embroidered apron very similar to the one Masons wear in their secret rituals. Partaking of the forbidden fruit and having now become "wise," Adam notices Lucifer's apron and asks him what it means.

Satan then replies, "It is the emblem of my power and priesthoods."

Having said that, Lucifer directs Adam and Eve to fashion similar aprons for themselves. He excitedly and slyly cries, "See, you are naked. Take some fig leaves and make you aprons. Father will see your nakedness. Quick! Hide!"

In this flurry of activity, the unwary Temple patron may miss the subtle truth just revealed. The very emblems that Lucifer claims are the emblems of his power and priesthoods are sewn into the Temple undergarment that each patron is now wearing under all the Temple clothing, sewn to the navel, knee, and breasts of this "magic underwear" acquired in the washing-and-anointing ritual in the basement of the Temple.

As obedient to Satan as they were disobedient to God, Adam and Eve follow the instructions of "the god of this world." What follows after that is so astonishing as to be unbelievable. Yet it is repeated thousands of times in Mormon Temples around the world, confirming again and again the Luciferian legacy. As soon as Adam and Eve have tied their Luciferic aprons about them, the ceremony narrator instructs the Temple patrons to place their own fig-leaf aprons (part of the Temple costume brought with them or supplied) over their beautiful Temple clothing.

As obedient to Satan as Adam and Eve have been, each Mormon going through the Temple solemnly puts on the fig-leaf apron. In contrast, the Bible indicates that God refused to accept Adam and Eve's fig-leaf aprons as a covering for their nakedness. Instead, He clothed them in the skins of animals that He had sacrificed for them as a symbol of the sacrifice Christ would one day make upon the cross for the sins not only of Adam and Eve but of the whole world.

With this emblem of Lucifer's "power and priesthoods" covering the elaborate pleated robes of the Mormon Priesthood they are wearing, the patrons proceed through the entire Endowment Ceremony that is so sacred and important on the Mormon path to godhood. Astonishing as it may seem, Temple Mormons are married and buried in this fig-leaf apron that their own doctrine identifies as the symbol of Lucifer's "power and priesthoods." This is only part of the fascinating legacy that Lucifer has succeeded in bequeathing to the Mormon Church.

Ed was in Fairbanks, Alaska, teaching a seminar series at a civic center a few years after this book was first released. As he relates this story, you will see the chilling reality of what this Luciferian ritual is really all about.

> I was sharing about how I used to stand at the veil at the conclusion of the ritual, with my arms inserted into the slits in the veil that matched the slits in my undergarment as I embraced the man portraying the Lord on the other side. As I would stand there, foot to foot, knee to knee, hand to back, mouth to ear, I would whisper, "Health in the navel, marrow in the bones, strength in the loins and sinews, power in the Priesthood be upon me and my posterity. . . . "

> As I reached that point in my narration, it suddenly dawned on me for the very first time that in this Temple ritual I had been up to my armpits in the *very same* emblems that were on Lucifer's apron in the Garden of Eden scene at the beginning of the Temple ceremonies. They were the same emblems that were on the sacred garments I would wear under my clothes! Yet Lucifer had clearly said that these were the emblems of *his* power and *his* priesthoods!

> It was like the scales finally came off my eyes. I realized that the "power in the priesthood" that I had received as a Mormon at the veil was not the power of the Melchizedek priesthood as I had always thought. I already had that power or I couldn't even have gotten a Temple recommend. *It was Lucifer's power and priesthood!* Not only did I have my arms stretched through these Luciferian emblems, but those same emblems were on my breast as I was going "breast to breast" with the Temple worker on the other side of the veil (who also had the same emblems on his "garment"). Further, I was pronouncing this Luciferian power over my posterity—my children and my children's children!

> As quickly as I could get out of the meeting, I hurried to a phone and called my wife, Carol, in Seattle. "You won't believe what happened to me 45 minutes ago!" I exclaimed. She cried back, "You won't believe what happened in this house here 45 minutes ago!"

> It seemed that at the same time I discovered this heinous spiritual trap that I had fallen into as a Mormon, my two sons, Jason and Joshua, began to go

into something like convulsions, rolling on the floor in a fetal position, vomiting and crying.

"What did you do?" I asked my wife. She replied that she had stood over them and commanded the demons that were attacking them to leave them and the house and our property immediately, in the name of Jesus. Our children immediately calmed down and were now in bed, sleeping quietly.

I realized then the awful power of the dark side of Mormonism. I flew home the next day and we prayed as a family to break those spiritual ties to the occult power of Satan that I had been bound to in the LDS Temple ritual.

What God Is This?

The Mormon "god" Elohim comes upon the scene (in the Temple drama) and discovers that Lucifer has beguiled Adam and Eve. He is shocked and outraged, in spite of the fact that He not only knew in advance of this plan to entrap Adam and Eve into mortality, but also helped arrange it. After all, in Mormonism this was all necessary and good, for without the prearranged "fall," humans could neither have children nor reach godhood. Strangely enough, Elohim says nothing about the fig-leaf aprons that His creatures are wearing. And equally strange, Mormon Temple patrons by the thousand go through these pagan ceremonies again and again without ever questioning why they all do it clothed in the symbol of Lucifer's power and priesthoods. Having clothed Adam and Eve and the participating Mormons in fig-leaf aprons, Lucifer is clearly in charge of the proceedings.

Thundering with rage, Elohim curses Lucifer to crawl on his belly, eat dust forever, and have his head crushed—but He remains silent concerning the symbol of Satan's power and priesthoods that all of His creatures now wear in obedience to "the god of this world," whom they clearly follow. Unimpressed by Elohim's dire pronouncements, Lucifer arrogantly defies the Mormon "God" to His face, vowing to "reign with blood and horror on the earth." He then goes about his business, apparently unaffected by Elohim's curse, since he never changes his conduct or bodily functions. One can only wonder who "Elohim" really is, since His rebellious son, Lucifer, is obviously so much stronger than He.

Rather than being a coincidence, as the attorneys believed, it seems instead to be quite in keeping with the above that "Mormo" is the god of the ghouls in the *Satanic Bible*. This is the kind of slyly perverse evidence that

Satan would leave of the Luciferian legacy he has bequeathed to Mormonism. Nor is this all. Mormonism denies the existence of hell, but in Chinese, *Mormon* means "gates of hell." Here we have another perverse twist that is consistent with Satan's character. There is still more. Joseph Smith was reported to have said: "Hell is by no means the place this world of fools suppose it to be, but on the contrary, it is quite an agreeable place. . . . "[31]

Having taught that hell is agreeable, Smith described heaven as a place of everlasting burning where the throne of God is encompassed in flames.[32] This reversal of biblical truth is the classic attempt by Lucifer to switch places with God that is found in all Luciferian/occult religions.

Elaborating upon Joseph Smith's remarkable teachings about heaven and hell, early Mormon Apostle John A. Widtsoe wrote: "The meanest sinner will find some place in the heavenly realm. . . . In the Church of Jesus Christ of Latter-day Saints, there is no hell. All will find a measure of salvation. . . . The gospel of Jesus Christ has no hell. . . . "[33] Yet at the same time, the Book of Mormon itself identifies this belief as yet another Luciferian legacy, for it declares that Satan is the one who will lead the unsuspecting into hell by denying that it exists:

> And others will he pacify, and lull them away into carnal security, that they will say: All is well in Zion, yea, Zion prospereth, all is well . . . and thus the Devil cheateth their souls and leadeth them away carefully down to hell.
>
> And behold, others he flattereth away, and telleth them there is no hell . . . and thus he whispereth in their ears, until he grasps them with his awful chains from whence there is no deliverance.[34]

The Classic Shell-Game Switch

It should be abundantly clear by now that Mormonism is based upon neither the Bible nor the Book of Mormon. At the very heart of Mormon doctrine is the teaching that there is no hell; thus death is not final, and the "dead" can repent and be baptized into the Mormon Church in the spirit world. Not only is this contrary to what the Bible teaches, but the Book of Mormon (as we have seen) also explicitly declares that there is absolutely no chance to repent and be saved once a person has died. Indeed, the Book of Mormon teaches that it is Satan himself who deludes people into thinking they will have another chance after death.

For behold this life is the time for men to prepare to meet God . . . for after this day of life which is given us to prepare for eternity, behold . . . there can be no labor performed.

Ye cannot say, when ye are brought to that awful crisis, that I will repent, that I will return to my God. Nay, ye cannot say this. . . .

For behold, if ye have procrastinated the day of your repentance even until death, behold, ye have become subjected to the spirit of the devil, and he doth seal you his; therefore, the Spirit of the Lord hath withdrawn from you, and hath no place in you, and the devil hath all power over you; and this is the final state of the wicked.[35]

If, as the Book of Mormon itself teaches, Satan is luring unsuspecting souls into hell by saying it doesn't exist and that they will be able to repent and join the Mormon Church even after they die, then it is clear that Mormonism, which teaches this, is Satan's religion. If Mormonism doesn't tell the truth about hell, can its teachings about heaven be trusted? What about the Mormon "heaven"? Here the Luciferian legacy becomes even more astonishing.

The lie that there is no death is intimately linked with the next thing Satan said to Eve, that she could become a god. These two lies were the theme of Joseph Smith's famous "King Follett Sermon" preached before 20,000 of his followers in April 1844, which Mormons consider to be "his greatest sermon and one of the greatest sermons ever delivered by mortal man."[36] In it Joseph Smith's description of heaven sounds suspiciously like hell.

. . . And you have got to learn how to be Gods yourselves . . . the same as all Gods have done before you . . . from exaltation to exaltation, until you attain to the resurrection of the dead, and are able to dwell in everlasting burnings. . . .

How consoling to . . . know that although the earthly tabernacle is laid down and dissolved, they shall rise again, to dwell in everlasting burnings . . . [as] a God and ascend the throne of eternal power the same as those who have gone before.[37]

Is the Mormon god really Lucifer, and as a consequence is the "heaven" that Mormons are working so hard to gain really hell? Such a diabolical twist would seem very much in character for Lucifer, who has every right to claim Mormons as his own, since they so willingly and proudly wear the special emblem of his power and priesthoods in life and in death.

7

Myths, Zion, Mecca, and Magic

Mormons have held some very strange beliefs. Brigham Young taught that the spirits of the wicked would be "thrown back again" into some primitive state "like brother Kimball's old pottery ware, to be ground up, and made over again."[1] Apostle Orson Pratt taught that each vegetable and animal "has a living intelligent spirit capable of feeling, knowing, and rejoicing" and existed in the premortal state and will be redeemed and resurrected;[2] and that a "transmigration of (their) particles of spirit from a lower to a higher" form and onto eventual "godhood" takes place similar to the transmigration of souls in Hinduism.[3] Joseph Smith taught that when "Gentiles" were baptized into the Mormon Church, their Gentile blood was literally taken out of their veins by "the Holy Ghost" and replaced with Jewish blood. This is why Jews are called "Gentiles" in Mormonism, and Latter-day Saints of whatever nationality are considered to be the real "Jews." As Joseph Smith said:

> ... The effect of the Holy Ghost upon a Gentile is to purge out the old blood, and make him actually of the seed of Abraham.[4]

The founding Prophet of the Mormon Church also declared that the moon was inhabited by people about six feet tall who dressed like Quakers and lived to be a thousand years old.[5] Smith's successor, Brigham Young, came forth with an even more amazing revelation—that the sun is also inhabited.[6] Many Mormons shrug off these absurdities by saying that Smith and Young were really not speaking as Prophets when they made these statements, but only venturing their personal opinions. Other Mormons, however, even well-informed ones, seriously say that our astronauts didn't explore the entire moon and that there may be things we don't know yet about the sun— a form of doublethink that allows them to remain loyal to both science and their religion. One's loyalty to Prophet Smith and a "testimony" that he founded the only true Church must be retained at all cost.

In a classic mishandling of truth and fantasy, Brigham Young declared:

> We are the smartest people in the world . . . the best people that ever lived upon the earth. . . . I do not say this boastingly, for I believe that this truth is evident to all who are willing to observe for themselves.

> I want you to . . . tell all the great men of earth, that the Latter-day Saints are to be their redeemers. . . .

> Believe in God, believe in Jesus, and believe in Joseph his Prophet and in Brigham his successor. And I add, if you will believe in your heart and confess with your mouth that Jesus is the Christ, that Joseph was a Prophet, and that Brigham was his successor, you shall be saved in the kingdom of God.

> Every spirit that confesses that Joseph Smith is a Prophet, that he lived and died a Prophet and that the Book of Mormon is true, is of God, and every spirit that does not is of anti-Christ.[7]

The Myth-Makers

The gullible belief in such myths as inhabited suns and moons was quite general among early Mormons. Joseph's brother Hyrum taught that "every Star that we see is a world and is inhabited . . . the Sun and Moon are inhabited, and the Stars . . . are inhabited the same as this Earth."[8] There were even commonly accepted fantasies among the early Mormons about taking trips to these other worlds out in space. Oliver B. Huntington claimed that Joseph Smith's father had prophesied over him at Kirtland in 1837 that he would preach the Mormon gospel "to the inhabitants of the moon. . . ."[9] A record has been found of a December 15, 1836, blessing that Joseph Smith, Senior, gave to Lorenzo Snow (who later became President of the Church):

> Thou shalt have power to translate thyself from one planet to another; and power to go to the moon. . . .[10]

Although these marvelous journeys never occurred, the early Mormons took such ideas quite seriously. It is therefore not surprising that they had little trouble believing Joseph Smith's story about being visited by god-men from a distant planet near a giant star called Kolob, or that these extraterrestrials had ordained him to restore true Christianity to this earth. Joseph Smith claimed numerous visits from "glorious Personages," including: "God the Father and His Son Jesus Christ, John the Baptist, Peter, James, John, Moses, Elijah, Elias [Joseph Smith mistakenly thought that these were two separate prophets, because of the difference between the Hebrew and Greek spellings in the Old and New Testaments], Michael, Raphael, Nephi, Moroni, Mormon and possibly others."[11] Even though, as his mother and others attested, Joseph Smith had always been an unusually talented teller of tall tales, at least some of his visions of heavenly beings may have been as real as the apparitions in haunted houses and Mormon Temples, and from the same demonic source.

Moon Trips and Gold Plates

A group of people who believed that their missionaries would soon be preaching the Mormon gospel on the moon and distant suns would have little difficulty accepting Joseph Smith's tale that he had discovered golden plates with hieroglyphics on them or that he had translated this ancient language with a "seer stone." What about the 11 men who claimed to have seen and handled those mysterious plates of gold? Doesn't that give the story credibility as an actual event? That the tale of the gold plates fits in with the other myths is evident from the statement of the "witnesses" that the ancient history recorded in gold was "shown unto us by the power of God. . . . An angel of God came down from heaven, and he brought and laid before our eyes . . . the plates. . . ."[12] Later LDS scriptures claim that the plates were "seen by faith."[13] It is clear that they were not bearing witness to an actual physical seeing and handling of the gold plates, but to a mythical event of the same kind as visions of angelic beings and visits from god-men.

The further testimony of one of those "witnesses" to the gold plates (a staunch supporter of Joseph Smith from the start named Martin Harris) is very significant in understanding the nature of this event. Harris claimed "that he had actually visited the moon" and explained that it "was only the faithful who were permitted to visit the celestial regions."[14] Like visiting the moon, there were only a select few of the faithful who were permitted to see the fabled gold plates. One can only assume that the visit of the angel from heaven, who showed the "witnesses" the mysterious gold plates, was of the same nature as Harris's visit to the moon.

By originating their own myths, Joseph Smith and the other early Mormon leaders took the most strategic and effective steps possible to found a new religion. Had Mormonism been merely an aberrant form of Christianity, it would probably have remained very small or dwindled to almost nothing, as scores of other heresies that have come and gone. With its own mythology, however, the Church of Jesus Christ of Latter-day Saints has given its members a basis for feeling that they are completely different from historical Christianity and all the churches around them.

Joseph Smith told tales so fantastic that in order to believe them it took a definite leap of faith, a solid commitment to him as a "Prophet." Having taken this specific step, not on the basis of Scripture or reason but of a subjective feeling called the "burning in the bosom," the convert is not likely to turn back.

The Mormon "Zion"

Strangely enough, Salt Lake City, headquarters of Mormonism, is not the most sacred place to Latter-day Saints. Nor is it in North Carolina, where official Mormon publications have claimed that Noah built his ark. It is found in Jackson County, Missouri, where Joseph Smith declared that the Garden of Eden was located. This is despite the fact that the Bible says four rivers flowed out of Eden, one being the Euphrates; that one of the other rivers flowed into Ethiopia and another into east Assyria,[15] all of them an ocean and a continent away from Missouri. Discrepancies such as that were never a problem to Joseph Smith, nor apparently to his followers. As proof of his "revelation," Smith pointed to some rocks near Spring Hill, Missouri, and declared them to be remnants of a stone altar upon which Adam had offered a sacrifice to God after being expelled from the Garden of Eden!

There isn't one non-Mormon archaeologist or historian who would consider that idea anything but fantasy. Yet this wild claim that locates Eden 10,000 miles from the Euphrates region is still devoutly believed by Mormons today, because they have a "burning in the bosom" that proves Joseph Smith was a true Prophet of God. This holy Mormon site is known as

Adam-Ondi-Ahman to the LDS, who believe Joseph Smith's "revelation" about it recorded in their scriptures:

> It is the place where Adam shall come to visit his people, or the Ancient of Days shall sit, as spoken of by Daniel the Prophet.[16]

Prophet Smith declared that at His second coming, Jesus Christ would return to Independence, Missouri, in spite of the clear statement in the Bible that He will come back to the Mount of Olives outside Jerusalem.[17] The Bible makes it clear that Jerusalem is Zion. That didn't sway Joseph Smith, however, who stuck by his "revelation" that "Zion" is really Independence, Missouri. Unfortunately, the site that Prophet Smith "divinely chose" for the Zion Temple that must be built prior to Christ's return is owned by the Church of Christ—Temple Lot. This is only one of approximately 100 rival splinter groups that have come out of Joseph Smith's Mormonism.

In view of this, the self-righteous accusation by Mormons that the many denominational differences among Christians prove them all wrong seems hypocritical at best. However, the many Mormon denominations are united on at least three points: They all believe that 1) Joseph Smith was a true "Prophet" who "restored" true Christianity; 2) they all accept various writings of Joseph Smith as extrabiblical scripture; 3) each one claims to be the "only true Church" and accuses all the others of being apostates.

Claiming to be the only true followers of Prophet Smith, the Temple Lot Church is hardly likely to sell the site to those nicknamed the "Brighamites" or "Utah Mormons"—those who followed Brigham Young instead of Joseph Smith's son after Joseph Smith's death. An original historic document has recently come to light which makes it clear that Mormonism's founding Prophet passed on his "authority" to his son Joseph Smith III, whom he named as his successor. This substantiates the claimed authenticity of the Reorganized Church, whose Prophets have all been descendants of Joseph Smith—and it adds great significance to the rebaptism and reordination of his followers that was carried out by Brigham Young.[18]

In part the handwritten document dated January 17, 1844, and signed by Joseph Smith just five months before his death declared:

> Blessing given to Joseph Smith III by his father Joseph Smith, Junior.... Blessed of the Lord is my son Joseph who is called the third.... For he shall be my successor to the Presidency of the High

Priesthood; a Seer, and a Revelator, and a Prophet, unto the Church;
which appointment belongeth to him by blessing, and also by right.

From the evidence, it would appear that the followers of Prophet Young
have no priesthood authority, because they broke the line of succession from
Prophet Smith, who allegedly obtained this "restored authority" from heavenly visitors. Nevertheless, under Brigham Young's dynamic leadership the
"Utah Mormons" quickly outstripped all rival groups in size and influence.
Today the word *Mormon* has come to mean the Utah-based Church, which
claims that its Prophets and Apostles are the true successors of Joseph Smith,
in spite of the rebaptisms under Brigham Young.

The Mormon Mecca

From every one of the 50 states and from scores of foreign countries, a
continual parade of about two million visitors a year converges upon Salt
Lake City's impressive Temple Square. Most of these are faithful LDS on peri-
odic pilgrimages to Mormonism's Mecca. Walking through the beautifully
landscaped, expansive grounds to view the impressive monuments inside
those high, impenetrable brick walls and huge iron gates, one has the peculiar feeling of having stumbled upon an ancient monastery cloistering some
mystical order of monks. This unique place, with its haunting sense of history, has become an international attraction that draws like a magnet from
the ends of the earth more tourists than even the Grand Canyon.

Pausing thoughtfully nearly anywhere in the Square, one can almost
hear the distant echo of Brigham Young's prophetic words spoken in 1847.
Travel-weary and half-dead from tick fever, he raised himself up on his bed
on that far-off rocky promontory overlooking the desolate Valley of the Great
Salt Lake and inspired his band of trusting followers with the long-awaited
declaration: "*This* is the place!"

Visitors to Temple Square, eager to learn early American history, unwittingly become captive audiences for the sharp Mormon guides, whose
canned presentations are cleverly intertwined with soft-sell persuasions calculated to convince unwary listeners that the only true Church is the Mormon Church. Any questions to which an honest answer would be
embarrassing to the Mormon Church are skillfully turned aside. The one
place that every tourist would like to see is inside the Temple. That
mysterious sanctuary, however, is closed to all visitors, including most

Mormons. Only that small, select number who have been declared "worthy" may enter.

Classic Tourist Trap

Mormondom's Mecca is a classic tourist trap where visitors are propagandized and come away with more than they intended. Typical of the "historical" pamphlets that one somehow acquires in going through Temple Square is one featuring a large picture of the Christ statue located at the Visitor's Center. In bold print that almost jumps from the page, the greatest historical event in centuries, according to Mormonism, is announced: "IN 1830 THE ALMIGHTY GOD RESTORED HIS CHURCH TO EARTH AGAIN." On the facing page this bold declaration continues:

> The restored church is known as The Church of Jesus Christ of Latter-day Saints, with headquarters in Salt Lake City.
>
> It possesses the divine priesthood of God. It is headed by prophets and apostles as was the church in the days of Peter and Paul.
>
> It invites all men to receive its message, for it is a message of salvation for everyone, whether Jew or Gentile, bond or free.[19]

Everything in Temple Square is carefully calculated to give the impression of truth supported by legitimate history. Knowing well, however, that much of the Church "history" it spends millions to promote runs the full range from sly half-truths to outright lies, the Mormon hierarchy closely guards early diaries and other documents that would reveal the sordid facts:

> In the past few years the hierarchy has taken a series of repressive steps designed to crack down on Mormon scholars who weren't afraid to follow the truth.... [Dr. Leonard J.] Arrington, the first independent professional to fill the office of church historian, was replaced and his successor appointed from among the ranks of church authorities. Important church archives were sealed.[20]

Time recently reported:

> In 1993 the church capped a harsh campaign of intellectual purification... with the excommunication of D. Michael Quinn, a leading historian whose painstaking work documented Smith's

involvement with the occult and Church leaders' misrepresentation
of some continued polygamy in the early 1900s.[21]

As Lawrence Foster, historian and Mormon-watcher from Georgia Tech, puts it: "The extent of the Mormon hierarchy's control over its adhering society seems without parallel in U.S. history."[22] Leading Mormon liberal Sterling McMurrin says:

> ... The Mormon religion is tied to Joseph Smith. You ask will it ever free itself? Not in the foreseeable future.
>
> They don't want to. They'd rather distort history.[23]

The impression that one gets in Temple Square and in the literature handed out at the elaborate Visitor's Center is that everything is aboveboard, fully substantiated by legitimate scholarship. Nothing could be further from the truth.

As we have observed the ever-changing face of the Temple Square Visitor Center over the years before and since *The God Makers* and other books and videos were released, we have noticed that many of the blatantly heretical presentations have either been removed or been softened. Most seem to be tied to an effort to make Mormonism look as Christian as possible to the unwary visitor.

On one trip we noticed that many of the guides were attractive young women dressed in casual, comfortable clothes. One of our friends accidentally dressed like a Mormon going to church. He asked one of the few older gentlemen what was going on. "Why are there these young women out here and just what has happened to some of these displays?" he asked.

The man responded that The Brethren had decided to remove much of what the average Christian considered controversial, and to bring in the young ladies to change the atmosphere to one considered more comfortable. "We get more referrals now in a month than we used to in a whole year," he confided with a grin.

The Visitor Center is still touting Meso-America as the center of the Book of Mormon lands. Although archaeologists within its ranks confess that not one shred of evidence has been found to support the Book of Mormon, the Mormon Church persists in the fraudulent claim that archaeology substantiates it as a true history of early America. Recognized as an expert on pre-Colombian civilizations in the Americas by the Smithsonian Institute, archaeologist Michael Coe has said:

> ... There is not one professionally trained archaeologist, who is not a Mormon, who sees any scientific justification for believing the [Book of Mormon] to be true, and ... there are quite a few Mormon archaeologists who join this group. ...

> The picture of this hemisphere between 2000 B.C. and 421 A.D. presented in the book (of Mormon) has little to do with the early Indian cultures as we know them, in spite of much wishful thinking. ...

> The bare facts of the matter are that nothing, absolutely nothing has ever shown up in any New World excavation which would suggest to a dispassionate observer that the Book of Mormon, as claimed by Joseph Smith, is a historical document relating to the history of early migrants to our hemisphere.[24]

The Myth-Defenders

Mormonism would gain a measure of respectability if only some credible evidence could be found to support at least one of Joseph Smith's claims. Since the Book of Mormon is supposed to be an actual history of real people, places, and events on the North and South American continents, archaeology would seem the best hope for establishing Smith's credibility. Although events in the Bible go back much further in time than most of the Book of Mormon, the world's great museums contain huge quantities of evidence uncovered by archaeologists that verify biblical history to the minutest detail. Yet not one pin or coin or piece of pottery has ever been found related to the Book of Mormon.

The Mormon Church is to be commended for financing, beginning in 1952, "the largest and most ambitious archaeological project ever funded by a religious institution (including the Vatican). ..."[25] Known as the New World Archaeological Foundation, its first field directors were non-Mormons. As a result of the work sponsored by this foundation, much valuable evidence has been uncovered that has increased knowledge about the early history of the Americas—but none of it comes even close to verifying anything related to the alleged peoples, places, or events recounted in the Book of Mormon.

In spite of this, Mormon missionaries around the world continue to spread the myth that the authenticity of the Book of Mormon has been established on the basis of archaeological evidence. Some of the most popular speakers at Mormon "Firesides" around the country are amateur archaeologists showing slides and giving lectures about "scientific proof" for the Book of Mormon. This is great stuff for bolstering the faith of the average Mormon, and though not always actively encouraged by the Church leaders, it is rarely discouraged.

John C. Sorenson, chairman of Brigham Young University Anthropology Department, has called such "faith-building" pronouncements by amateur "experts" "worse than useless."[26] He described some of the most popular books among Mormons on the subject of archaeology and geography (by Dewey and Edith Farnsworth, Jack West, and Paul Cheesman) as "naïve," as "harmful," and as "cut-and-paste" efforts. His further comments in this particular article are significant:

> All this criticism may be too narrow. There is plenty of evidence that the Latter-day Saints are gullible on many subjects, not just this one.

> President Harold B. Lee expressed impatience with the rumor-mongering which is endemic among Mormons. The too-generous standing ovations at BYU are becoming legendary.

> Salt Lake City has earned a nationwide reputation as a center for stock fraud, and Douglas Stringfellow beguiled Utahans for years.[27]

The Brokers of Fraud

While gullible enthusiasm for archaeological "evidence" within the Church remains high, fanned frequently by stories about "new finds," professional archaeologists, geographers, and historians within the Church have become discouraged about ever substantiating the Book of Mormon. Many of them are convinced it is a fraud. Those with professional integrity admit the facts, though often only in private. Referring to the ongoing propaganda within the Church about "evidence" for the Book of Mormon, J.N. Washburn, a Mormon writer, has said, "Much that is cited as evidence is, in my mind, wishful thinking."[28] Joseph E. Vincent gives some insight into the problems this myth has created:

At one time when I was a member of a ward bishopric, one of the counselors said to me: "Why is it we have accurate maps of Palestine and not of the Book of Mormon lands? Why do we know so well where Jerusalem, Bethlehem and Nazareth are and do not know where Zarahemla, Bountiful and Cumorah are? Does that mean that actually those places are fictitious as the non-Mormons say they are?"[29]

Vincent tried to assure this man that "all is well in Zion," but it wasn't easy. Respected Mormon archaeologist Professor Dee F. Green has said:

> The first myth we need to eliminate is that Book of Mormon archae-ology exists. . . . If one is to study Book of Mormon archaeology, then one must have a corpus of data with which to deal. We do not.
>
> . . . No Book of Mormon location is known with reference to modern topography. Biblical archaeology can be studied because we do know where Jerusalem and Jericho were and are, but we do not know where Zarahemla and Bountiful (nor any location for that matter) were and are.
>
> . . . A concentration on geography should be the first order of busi-ness, but we have already seen that twenty years of such an approach has left us empty-handed.[30]

The admission by Mormon archaeologists and anthropologists that no one knows the location of even one Book of Mormon city or geographical site, including the famous Hill Cumorah, is absolutely fatal to the claims of the Mormon Church and exposes The Brethren as brokers of fraud. The Hill Cumorah is allegedly the location where at least a half million warriors died in the last great Book of Mormon battle; where Moroni buried the fabled gold plates; and where Brigham Young claimed that inside the hill was a huge cav-ern filled with wagonloads of gold plates. Yet the small hill near Palmyra, New York, which the Church identifies as Cumorah, has never yielded so much as one scrap of evidence of this great battle, nor has anyone ever been able to unearth even one gold plate (which would be one of the world's great-est archaeological finds and would prove the Book of Mormon).

Though divided on much, most (if not all) Mormon archaeologists agree on one thing: The real Cumorah, if there ever was one, definitely was *not* located where Joseph Smith claimed he discovered the gold plates. If the

Book of Mormon events took place anywhere, it could only have been in the Yucatan Peninsula of Central America. That is where Mormon archaeological activity has been centered for years. Yet The Brethren continue to sponsor the annual pageant in Palmyra that draws huge crowds to the misnamed hill with its monument and huge lettering along the hill's entire side identifying it as "Cumorah."

The Book of Mormon contains a photograph of this alleged Hill Cumorah. If it indeed is Cumorah, then The Brethren should stop sponsoring archaeological teams searching for it in the Yucatan or anywhere else. If it is not Cumorah, then to continue to represent it as such with thousands of photographs and the annual pageant is the most blatant fraud conceivable. Yet Mormon missionaries continue to sell Mormonism door-to-door around the world based upon this kind of misrepresentation.

The Dilemma of Disillusionment

The Brethren are caught in a trap from which there is no escape except repentance. If Joseph Smith was a true Prophet, why did he mistakenly identify the wrong hill outside Palmyra, New York, as Cumorah? And how did the gold plates get *there* when they were buried by Moroni (if this was a real event) in the Yucatan? Mormonism stands or falls with Joseph Smith, and we need no further evidence than Cumorah that he was an impostor and that The Brethren are the modern brokers of his pitiful fraud.

Strangely enough, the obvious fact that the Book of Mormon is a fraudulent document seldom causes those who know this to leave the Church. Even Professor Green has said:

> I find that nothing in so-called Book of Mormon archaeology materially affects my religious commitment one way or the other, and I do not see that archaeological myths so common in our proselytizing program enhance the process of true conversion. . . .[31]

The founder of the Church-supported New World Archaeological Foundation was another highly respected Mormon scholar, Thomas Stuart Ferguson. At one time known among LDS as one of the staunchest defenders of the Book of Mormon (having written three books on the subject), Ferguson surprised Jerald and Sandra Tanner with a visit to inform them that after "25 years of trying to prove Mormonism, [he] had finally come to the conclusion that his work had been in vain. He said that his training in law had taught him how to weigh evidence and that the case against Joseph Smith was absolutely devastating and could not be explained away."[32] Under pressure from the Mormon hierarchy to affirm his loyalty, Ferguson wrote a letter in which he said, "My relationship and membership with the Church has never been terminated."[33] However, he has lost his confidence in Mormonism as a religious faith.

Why would anyone continue on as a member of the Mormon Church if he was convinced that Joseph Smith was a fraud? Unfortunately, most Mormons have been brainwashed into believing that all other churches are false, so when they discover that the real fraud is Mormonism itself, they can't believe there's anything else out there that might be true. Having been deceived so badly once, it is understandable that disillusioned Mormons are afraid to try anything else. This is pretty much expressed by Ferguson in another letter dated December 3, 1979:

> I lost faith in Joseph Smith as one having a pipeline to Deity—and have decided that there has never been a pipeline to Deity—with any man....
>
> I give Joseph Smith credit as an innovator and as a smart fellow. I attend, sing in the choir and enjoy my friendships in the Church.
>
> In my opinion, it is the best fraternity that has come to my attention.[34]

Strange Explanations

Some Church leaders have come up with ingenious explanations for the complete failure to find any evidence supporting the Book of Mormon. In a March 25, 1964, address, Fletcher B. Hammond said: "... The Gentiles have not yet received the Book of Mormon by faith ... and until they do ... it appears that empirical facts will not be allowed to come forth as evidence of the truthfulness of the Book of Mormon...."[35] At the 109th Annual Conference, Antoine R. Ivins suggested:

> Faith to me is the greatest thing in life, and God purposely, I believe, covered up in antiquity the history of this people and the story of the Book of Mormon so that ... it would have to rest upon faith ... that could be given to us only by God Himself.[36]

One wonders, then, why God allowed literally tons and mountains of evidence to remain in verification of the Bible. Church leaders have become very concerned by the questions being raised due to the absence of evidence, and the fact that descriptions of cities, rivers, mountains, and journeys in the Book of Mormon cannot be correlated at all with topography and geography. To quiet these questions, for which The Brethren have no answers, an article was published in the Church Section of the *Deseret News* cautioning Church members about putting too much importance upon facts and evidence:

> The geography of the Book of Mormon has intrigued some readers of that volume ever since its publication. But why worry about it?
>
> Efforts to pinpoint certain places from what is written in the book are fruitless.... Attempts to designate certain areas as the Land Bountiful or the site of Zarahemla or the place where the Nephite city of Jerusalem sank into the sea "and waters have I caused to come up in the stead thereof" can bring no definitive results. So why speculate?
>
> To guess where Zarahemla stood can in no wise add to anyone's faith. But to raise doubts in people's minds about the location of the Hill Cumorah, and thus challenge the words of the prophets concerning the place where Moroni buried the records, is most certainly harmful. And who has the right to raise doubts in anyone's mind?
>
> Our position is to build faith, not to weaken it, and theories concerning the geography of the Book of Mormon can most certainly undermine faith if allowed to run rampant.
>
> Why not leave hidden the things that the Lord has hidden? If He wants the geography of the Book of Mormon revealed, He will do so through His prophet....[37]

That kind of blind faith in a "prophet" is the primary mark of a cult. When a Church is founded upon beliefs that are beyond any objective verification and rest upon a "burning in the bosom," its members have surrendered to tragic deception. The Mormon Church was established upon the most blatant fraud, and it is maintained today because its members are blinded to the obvious by their devoted submission to whatever the Church says, no matter how absurd.

Joseph the Glass-Looker

Long before Joseph Smith allegedly was led by the angel Moroni to the ancient gold plates, he had already established a wide reputation as a "seer" who, in the words of his mother, Lucy, "possessed certain means by which he could discern things invisible to the naked eye."[38] Joseph's mother related that because of this remarkable talent, a certain "Josiah Stoal [sic] came from Chenango county, New York, with the view of getting Joseph to assist him in digging for a silver mine."[39] The Mormon writer Hyrum L. Andrus said, "Joseph could also have had the seer stone at this time...."[40] Mormon historian B.H. Roberts says of Stowell:

> Having heard of Joseph Smith's gift of seership, he came to the Smith residence to employ him.... Joseph [Smith] hired out to Mr. Stoal [sic]... and for something like a month they vainly sought to find the "hidden treasure."... Joseph continued for some time in his employment.[41]

A local citizen of the area at that time, W.D. Purple, relates:

> In the year 1825, we often saw in that quiet hamlet Joseph Smith, Jr....[living with] the family of Deacon Isaiah Stowell...[who had] a monomaniacal impression to seek for hidden treasures, which he believed were hidden in the earth....

> Mr. Stowell... heard of the fame of...Joseph, who by the aid of a magic stone had become a famous seer of lost or hidden treasures.... He with the magic stone was at once transferred from his humble abode to the more pretentious mansion of Deacon Stowell.

> Here, in the estimation of the Deacon, he confirmed his conceded powers as a seer, by means of the stone which he placed in his hat and by excluding the light from all other terrestrial things could see whatever he wished, even in the depths of the earth.

> In February 1826, the sons of Mr. Stowell, who lived with their father, were greatly incensed against Smith, as they plainly saw their father squandering his property in the fruitless search for hidden treasures... and caused the arrest of Smith....[42]

W.D. Purple was present at the trial, and his careful notes of the entire proceedings were later published in *The Chenango Union* of May 3, 1877. In his *History of the Church*, Joseph Smith admitted working for a Josiah Stowell in connection with a silver mine, but said nothing about his arrest. Mormon apologists rejected W.D. Purple's account as spurious and tried to deny that their founding Prophet, at the same time the angel Moroni was allegedly appearing to him annually in preparation for leading him to the buried golden plates, was hiring himself out to locate buried treasure by means of a "seer stone" that he used like a fortune-teller's crystal ball. After spending 20 pages trying to discredit the idea that Joseph Smith had ever been arrested for "glass-looking," Dr. Hugh Nibley, dean of Mormon apologists, conceded:

> ... If this court record is authentic, it is the most damning evidence in existence against Joseph Smith ... the most devastating blow to Smith ever delivered. ...[43]

The devastating blow fell July 28, 1971, when Wesley P. Walters and Fred Poffarl together discovered in a mildewed box in the darkest part of a basement storage room beneath Chenango County jail the records of Judge Albert Neely and Constable Philip M. DeZeng.[44] These proved once and for all that Joseph Smith had indeed been arrested and found guilty on March 20, 1826, of pretending to find buried treasure by "glass-looking." Although the court in enforcing the laws took a dim view of this superstitious practice and found Joseph Smith guilty of fraud as an "imposter," this was a very common occupation at the time. Four years before Joseph's arrest, the local newspaper in his hometown of Palmyra, New York, in a article about money-digging, explained that it was widely practiced in that area, and stated:

> We could name ... at least five hundred respectable men, who do in the simplicity and sincerity of their hearts verily believe that immense treasures lie concealed upon our Green Mountains; many of whom have been for a number of years most industriously and perseveringly engaged in digging it up.[45]

One year before Smith's arrest, the newspaper in a nearby town carried this lament:

> We are sorry to observe even in this enlightened age, so prevalent a disposition to credit the accounts of the Marvellous.
>
> Even the frightful stories of money being hid under the surface of the earth, and enchanted by the Devil or Robert Kidd, are received by many of our respectable fellow citizens as truths. ...[46]

A few days since was discovered in this town, by the help of a mineral stone (which becomes transparent when placed in a hat and the light excluded by the face of him who looks into it, provided he is fortune's favorite), a monstrous potash kettle in the bowels of old mother Earth, filled with the purest bullion.

Some attempts have been made to dig it up, but without success. His Satanic Majesty, or some other invisible agent, appears to keep it under marching orders; for no sooner is it dug on to in one place, than it moves off like "false delusive hope" to another still more remote. But its pursuers ... [have] driven a steel ramrod into the ground directly over it, to break the enchantment. ...

By the rust of the kettle, and the color of the silver, it is supposed to have been deposited where it now lies prior to the flood.[47]

The Making of a Prophet

It was in this setting that Joseph Smith and his father operated as money-diggers. Young Joseph Smith had found this "seer stone" while on a dig. It was brown and about the size of an egg, and is still held by the Mormon Church, safely locked away.[48] There is no record that Joseph Smith ever actually recovered any buried treasure, but many reports that he and the other "glass-lookers" located all manner of valuable finds that kept "sinking deeper" in the earth as the diggers pursued them. There was always an "explanation" about some enchantment or spirit that prevented the treasure from being taken, and there were always enough superstitious people who believed this sort of nonsense to keep Joseph Smith and numerous other "glass-lookers" in business during those mad years.

Here was the making of the Prophet. Upstate New York was filled with people who were ready to believe almost any tale, the taller the better. Buried treasure, especially anything gold, had irresistible appeal. And if engraved on the gold were mysterious hieroglyphics giving the history of the ancient inhabitants of this land, the story was all the more enticing. How could the strange writing be deciphered? Why, of course, Joseph Smith had a magic stone that he looked at in his hat and on which he could see anything—even the translation of ancient languages.

So it came to pass that the mysterious gold plates were "found." This time the "spirit" guarding them was an angel who led Joseph Smith to the priceless treasure; and after preventing him supernaturally during several abortive attempts, at the end of four years the angel allowed him to take this ancient record because he had been chosen to restore true Christianity to earth. On a few occasions the plates were said to be under a blanket in the room nearby (no one could look upon them except Joseph) while the lengthy "translation" was in process. Joseph Smith didn't need to look at the plates, however; he looked into his hat, and there, shining on the "seer stone," were the hieroglyphics on one line and the translation just below. Usually the priceless plates were kept "hidden in the woods," for they were of little importance in the process. It was the "seer stone" that did it all, just as it had been doing so many marvelous things for Joseph for so long.

From the many accounts of eyewitnesses, family, friends, neighbors, Mormons, and non-Mormons, it is clear that Joseph Smith used his "seer stone" (and other "magical objects") as a divination device—something that is absolutely forbidden in the Bible.[49] In the beginning it may all have been just an overactive youthful imagination caught up in the hysteria of money-digging that was so prevalent in that part of America at the time. However, as he continued to play the game, either pretending that the stone and he had miraculous powers or attempting to develop such powers, young Smith opened himself increasingly to demonic influences until he was caught in the web of strong delusion. We will document this in detail later, but there is no question that Joseph Smith became very heavily involved in the occult, and that its grip upon him strengthened after he became the founding "Prophet" of a new Church.

The Mysterious Masonic Talisman

We can trace the steps downward as young Joseph became first a "Prophet" and then a "magician" with a Luciferic commitment for which he received in exchange the power over other people that he prized so highly. We have already seen in part that a Luciferian legacy forms the foundation of the Mormon Priesthoods. The secret ceremonies in the Temples, which we will reveal further in a later chapter, are related to ritual magic. In his presidential address before the Mormon History Association on April 20, 1974, Dr. Reed Durham (at that time director of the LDS Institute of Religion at the University of Utah) disclosed some startling information about Joseph Smith that confirms our appraisal and almost cost Dr. Durham his membership in the Church:

> ... I should like to initiate all of you into what is perhaps the strangest, the most mysterious, occult-like esoteric, and yet Masonically oriented practice ever adopted by Joseph Smith....

> All available evidence suggests that Joseph Smith the Prophet possessed a magical Masonic medallion, or talisman, which he worked during his lifetime and which was evidently on his person when he was martyred....

> ... Purchased from the Emma Smith Bidamon family, fully notarized by that family to be authentic and to have belonged to Joseph Smith, [it] can now be identified as a Jupiter talisman. It carries the sign and image of Jupiter and ... in some very ... mysterious sense ... [it] was the appropriate talisman for Joseph Smith to possess.

> I wasn't able to find what this was ... [until] finally in a magic book printed in England in 1801 ... how thrilled I was when I saw in his list of magic seals the very talisman which Joseph Smith had in his possession at the time of his martyrdom....

> In astrology, Jupiter is always associated with high positions, getting one's own way.... So closely is magic bound up with the stars and astrology that the term astrologer and magician were in ancient times almost synonymous.

> The purpose of the Table of Jupiter in talismanic magic was to be able to call upon the celestial intelligences, assigned to the particular talisman, to assist one in all endeavors. The names of the deities which ... could be invoked ... were always written on the talisman.... Three such names were written on Joseph Smith's talisman....

> When properly invoked, with Jupiter being very powerful and ruling in the heavens, these intelligences—by the power of ancient magic—guaranteed to the possessor of this talisman the gain of riches and favor and power and love and peace ... and anyone who worked skillfully with this Jupiter Table would obtain the power of stimulating anyone to offer his love to the possessor of the talisman, whether from a friend, brother, relative, or even any female.[50]

Considering the power he obtained, his control over so many other people, and the dozens of wives he acquired in his short life, Joseph Smith probably had a lot of faith in that talisman. If Joseph Smith had sincerely desired to "restore" true Christianity, he would have followed the Bible. Instead of that, however, he sought to revive under Christian terminology something that he must have known had nothing whatever to do with Christianity, but was in fact its pagan rival. There is ample evidence that Joseph Smith knew exactly what he was doing. From early childhood he and his family had been dabbling in divination, necromancy, and various forms of ritual magic. Smith believed in and practiced occultism until his death. This is the secret foundation of the Mormon Church he established.[51]

D. Michael Quinn, a devout Mormon and a history professor at Brigham Young University, was voted Outstanding Teacher at BYU for 1986. He is also the author of an exceptional work *Early Mormonism and the Magic World View.* Quinn's book was the first major effort by a Mormon scholar to deal with the *magical* roots of his faith. It was not written as an anti-Mormon attack; instead, it was written by a scholar to reveal the true roots of Joseph Smith's visions and the birth of Mormonism.

Quinn cites a comprehensive study of the magic arts from the 1700s and notes that all three distinctive forms of ritual magic are represented in the account of Smith and the gold plates: necromancy, transformation or shape-shifting, and theurgy or divine communication (page 133). In short, Smith's encounter upon Hill Cumorah was a classic textbook case of sorcery!

Quinn is no longer a Mormon and no longer a professor at BYU. His reputation among Mormons is in the cellar because of his search for factual truth, yet his the book stands as a beacon of truth and solid evidence that the Smith family was deeply involved in various forms of occultism.

8

THE WORLD'S
MOST PERFECT BOOK?

In 1843, about 13 months before Joseph Smith's death at the hands of the mob that stormed the jail where he was being held for treason and riot, there was sudden excitement among the Mormons due to a great archaeological find. During the excavation of a mound near Kinderhook, Illinois, at the end of April, six bell-shaped, thin brass plates with strange hieroglyphics engraved on them were uncovered at a depth of about 11 feet. Appearing to be of ancient origin, the "Kinderhook Plates" (as they came to be known) were displayed briefly in public and then sent to Joseph Smith because of his alleged ability to translate unknown languages.

Upon receiving and inspecting the plates, Joseph Smith declared that the "writing on them was similar to that in which the Book of Mormon was written" on the gold plates, and "he thought that by the help of revelation he would be able to translate them."[1] About a year later, the *St. Louis Gazette* reported that the Prophet was

> ... busy in translating them [the Kinderhook Plates]. The new work which Jo. is about to issue as a translation of these plates will be nothing more nor less than a sequel to the Book of Mormon.[2]

There is no question that Joseph Smith regarded these plates as genuine. His "translation" thereof is probably locked in the Church archives in Salt Lake City along with a great many other embarrassing documents. Reflecting the growing excitement among Latter-day Saints at the time, the Mormon publication *Time and Seasons* boasted: "Why does the circumstance of the plates recently found in a mound in Pike County, Illinois by Mr. Wiley...

go to prove the Book of Mormon true?—Ans. Because it is true!"[3] In his diary for May 1, 1843, a month before he was murdered, Joseph Smith wrote:

> I insert fac-similes of the six brass plates found near Kinderhook....
>
> I have translated a portion of them, and find they contain the history of the person with whom they were found. He was a descendant of Ham, through the loins of Pharaoh, king of Egypt, and that he received his kingdom from the Ruler of heaven and earth.[4]

Unfortunately for the credibility of Mormonism's founding Prophet, the plates were a deliberate hoax carefully manufactured and planted in a mound to be "discovered." This was confessed by the three men responsible about a month after Joseph Smith's death and subsequently confirmed after examination by a number of experts.

For example, University of Chicago Egyptology Professor James H. Breasted reported some years later in a letter:

> The "Kinderhook Plates" are, of course, childish forgeries, as the scientific world has known for years.
>
> What does this all add up to? Does it merely mean that one of the "finds" which the Latter-day Saints believed supported the Book of Mormon does not support it, and that there is no real blow to the prophetship of Joseph Smith? Not at all, for as Charles A. Shook well observed ... "Only a bogus prophet translates bogus plates."
>
> Where we can check up on Smith as a translator of plates, he is found guilty of deception. How can we trust him with reference to his claims about the Book of Mormon? ...
>
> Smith tried to deceive people into thinking that he had translated some of the plates. The plates had no such message as Smith claimed....
>
> Smith is thus shown to be willing to deceive people....[5]

A Scam That Got Out of Hand

There is no question that Joseph Smith became an accomplished and extremely successful deceiver, and that he had some accomplices and was also greatly aided by the ignorance and gullibility of most of the early Mormons. To anyone except a Mormon who makes an impartial investigation, the evidence seems overwhelming that Mormonism, in spite of the undoubted sincerity of millions of people involved in it today, began as a deliberate scam that got out of hand and mushroomed into something beyond the imagination of its original designers. Although it is impossible today to know every detail of what happened then, many of the steps along the way can be traced accurately. Oliver Cowdery (who baptized Joseph and was the Prophet's scribe as he read off the "translation" he saw on the "seer stone" in his hat) and Sidney Rigdon (who was undoubtedly the brains behind later theological innovations) were probably coconspirators. Yet they (and perhaps Joseph Smith himself at times) were also deceived to some extent.

At the front of the Book of Mormon is first the testimony of the "Three Witnesses" and then of the "Eight Witnesses." A logical question is, Why these two separate groups? The "Eight" seem to have been an afterthought. A "revelation" of March 1829 made it clear that there were to be *only* three witnesses: ". . . Three of my servants, whom I shall call and ordain . . . shall know of a surety that these things are true . . . and to *none else* will I grant this power, to receive this testimony among this generation. . . ."[6] Ether 5:2-4 also makes this clear. Changes and contradictions are common enough in Mormon "revelations" as necessity requires. In this case, the necessity may well have arisen from questioners asking why the "Three Witnesses" only saw the plates in the hands of an angel in a *vision*,[7] and why they went into the woods to have an angel "reveal" to them "by the power of God" gold plates that Joseph Smith was still "translating" and had in his possession.[8] In order to quiet such questions, it may have become necessary to have "witnesses" see something more tangible. That could have been easily arranged with a little careful preparation.

Like the other "Three," the "Eight Witnesses," who claimed they had seen and handled said plates "which have the appearance of gold . . . [with] engravings thereon all of which has the appearance of ancient work . . ."[9] were gullible, untrained, and uncritical observers, eager to believe, who probably did see and handle *something* that convinced them. This would explain why the five of the "Eight" who eventually left the Church (only the three Smiths out of the 11 "witnesses" remained in Mormonism) apparently never denied seeing *something* that looked like ancient engraved gold plates. How was the deception pulled off? It would have been easy enough for Oliver Cowdery, a former blacksmith who allegedly turned counterfeiter, to contrive

something like the Kinderhook Plates that would have deceived the "Eight."
Or Joseph Smith might have done it on his own.

Ideally Suited Witnesses

All 11 of the "witnesses" were astonishingly unstable and unreliable.
Oliver Cowdery, David Whitmer, and Martin Harris, the "Three Witnesses"
who saw the plates "by faith" in an angelic vision, each subsequently had
other "visions" that convinced them of contrary religious beliefs. In one of
his visions, Whitmer claimed "God" spoke to him in an audible voice and
told him to separate himself from the Mormons.[10] Hiram Page, one of the
"Eight," acquired his own "seer stone" and began "to receive revelations,
often contrary to those received by Joseph Smith."[11] Both Cowdery and Whitmer were led astray by Hiram Page's "peep-stone." Cowdery, who with
Joseph Smith allegedly received the first "Priesthood" at the hands of John
the Baptist, was excommunicated from the Church for accusing the Prophet
of adultery.

Martin Harris, one of the "Three," not only "traveled to the moon," but
"saw" Jesus standing beside Joseph Smith in a meeting, though no one else
present except the "Prophet" saw him. On that occasion Prophet Smith laid
his hand approvingly upon Martin's head and said, "Martin, God revealed
that to you. Brothers and sisters, the Savior has been in your midst. I want
you to remember it. He cast a veil over your eyes for you could not endure to
look upon Him."[12] Yet Harris, who *could* "look upon Him," was later
described in a Mormon publication as mad, demonic, and deranged, ". . . flying from one thing to another, as if reason and common sense were thrown
off their balance."[13] Indeed, Martin Harris did go from one thing to another,
changing his religious beliefs no less than 13 times. Mormonism had been
about number six on the list.

From all that we know about the "witnesses" to the Book of Mormon,
they would seem to be strange choices for divine appointment to this great
honor and responsibility. Today they are still described in Mormon publications as fine and honorable men, whose testimony "proves" the story of the
gold plates. Yet Joseph Smith called all eight defectors liars and cheats "too
mean to mention," and accused Cowdery and Whitmer of being part of a
"gang of counterfeiters, thieves, liars and blacklegs."[14]

To get an idea of just how bad things were, we need to look at how Joseph Smith handled each of the three main witnesses to the authenticity of the Book of Mormon. Remember that The Brethren send out the Mormon missionaries to hand out copies of the Book of Mormon to their investigators, citing the testimonies of these men as actual evidence and asking the investigators to pray and ask God for a sign that this is true. All the while, The Brethren believe the following about these men who are raised up as the witnesses of the Book of Mormon.

Oliver Cowdery was the Church's second Elder, often called the "Second President." The early-day companion of Joseph Smith, he was the scribe for the Book of Mormon, present at the "Restoration of the Priesthood" and as close to the real truth as any man.[15]

However, in 1838 in Kirtland, Oliver Cowdery confronted Joseph Smith with the charge of adultery with Fanny Alger, and with lying and teaching false doctrines.[16] Joseph Smith denied this charge and instead charged Cowdery with being a liar.[17] Church records now show that Miss Alger was Smith's first "spiritual wife." Oliver was telling the truth![18]

Cowdery was excommunicated for this and other "crimes."[19] Later, as a Methodist, he denied the Book of Mormon[20] and publicly confessed his sorrow and shame for his connection with Mormonism.[21]

While the Mormon Church claims that Cowdery rejoined them in the fall of 1848,[22] they also accused him later that year with trying to "raise up the Kingdom again" with the apostate William E. McLellin.[23]

Oliver Cowdery was publicly charged by Joseph Smith and Mormon leaders with stealing, lying, perjury, counterfeiting, adultery, and being the leader of a gang of "scoundrels of the deepest degree!"[24]

David Whitmer saw the plates "by the eye of faith" handled by an angel.[25] He later told of finding them lying in a field, and later still he told Orson Pratt that they were on a table with all sorts of brass plates, gold plates, the Sword of Laban, the "Director," and the Urim and Thummim.[26]

During the summer of 1837, while in Kirtland, Whitmer pledged his new loyalty to a prophetess (as did Martin and Oliver) who used a black seer stone and danced herself into "trances."[27]

It was the start of the finish for Whitmer. It ended in 1847 in his declaration to Cowdery that he (Whitmer) was to be the Prophet of the New Church of Christ and Cowdery a counselor.[28]

In the meantime, Whitmer was excommunicated and roughly put out. His and Cowdery's families were in fact driven into the streets and robbed by the Mormons while Whitmer and Cowdery were away trying to arrange a place to flee to.[29]

Cursed by leaders such as Sidney Rigdon, Whitmer was denounced by the Prophet Joseph Smith as a "dumb beast to ride" and "an ass to bray out cursings instead of blessings."[30]

Martin Harris was first a Quaker, then a Universalist, then a Restorationist, then a Baptist, then a Presbyterian, and finally a Mormon.[31] After his excommunication in 1837, he changed his religion eight more times, going from the Shakers to one Mormon splinter group to the next, and then back to the main group in 1842.[32] Yet in 1846 Harris was preaching among the Saints in England for the apostate James J. Strang.[33]

Harris testified that his testimony for Shakerism was greater than it was for Mormonism. (The Shakers' "Sacred Roll and Book" was also delivered by an angel.)[34]

His later testimony that he saw the plates by "the eyes of faith and not with the natural eyes" should eliminate him automatically as a witness.[35]

In the *Elder's Journal* for August 1838, Joseph Smith denounces Harris as "so far beneath contempt that to notice him would be too great a sacrifice for a gentleman to make. The Church exerted some restraint on him, but now he has given loose to all kinds of abominations, lying, cheating, swindling, and all kinds of debauchery."[36]

The deplorable truth concerning these three key "witnesses" to the alleged golden plates and the Book of Mormon is suppressed for obvious reasons. Clearly they were scoundrels who were part of Joseph Smith's scam from the beginning. Yet they are presented as honorable men and their "testimonies" (though later renounced) are offered as proof of the alleged miraculous origin of the Book of Mormon.

Visions, Visions Everywhere

The time and place in which Joseph Smith grew up had a great deal to do with his success in putting over such a transparent fraud. Most Mormons today naïvely imagine that Joseph Smith's "visions" of angels and assorted heavenly beings prove him to be a great Prophet and marked him out as unique. On the contrary, Mormonism was only one of a number of such new religious groups that were formed and flourished at that same time in the same general area. Some of these groups were very similar to Mormonism. James Jesse Strang "claimed that he found some plates which he translated with the Urim and Thummim. He had witnesses who claimed they saw the plates, and their testimony is recorded in almost the same way that the testimony of the 11 witnesses is recorded in the Book of Mormon."[37]

At least for a time, all of the witnesses to the Book of Mormon except Cowdery accepted Strang as Joseph Smith's successor after his death. John Whitmer wrote, "Strang reigns in the place of Smith the author and proprietor of the Book of Mormon."[38] Strang had allegedly received the following "revelation" about 14 months after Joseph Smith's death:

> The Angel of the Lord came unto me . . . and the light shined about him above the brightness of the sun, and he shewed unto me the plates of the sealed record and he gave into my hands the Urim and Thummim.
>
> And out of the light came the voice of the Lord saying: My Servant James . . . Behold the record which was sealed from my servant Joseph. Unto thee it is reserved. . . .
>
> Go to the place which the Angel of the presence shall show thee and . . . take with thee faithful witnesses. . . . And while I was yet in the Spirit the Angel of the Lord took me away to the hill in the East of Walworth against White River in Voree, and there he shewed unto me the record buried under an oak tree. . . .
>
> . . . And I beheld it as a man can see a light stone in clear water, for I saw it by Urim and Thummim. . . . [39]

Even more spectacular, though still with many similarities to the Mormons, were the Shakers, who declared: "Christ has made his second appearance on earth, in a chosen female known by the name of Ann Lee, and acknowledged by us as our blessed Mother in the work of redemption."[40] This was one of the groups that Martin Harris joined. He seems to have remained faithful to them the rest of his days, claiming "repeatedly that he had as much evidence for [the] Shaker Book as he had for the Book of Mormon . . . [and that] his testimony is greater than it was of the Book of Mormon."[41] And why not? For there were "Eight Witnesses" who certified that "We, the undersigned, hereby testify that we saw the Holy Angel standing upon the house-top, as mentioned in the fore-going declaration, holding the Roll and Book."[42] Indeed, there were more than 60 "witnesses" who had a "testimony" concerning the "Sacred Roll and Book" of Shakerism, one of the 60 having had eight different visions.[43]

The money-digging madness and enthusiasm for divination with "seer stones" were only a small part of a hysteria that pervaded much of the area in which Joseph Smith spent his first 30 years. Sensational visions of angels and other strange sights and sounds were part of everyday conversation and were accepted as normal. Religious "revivals" involving hysteria and fanaticism spread from town to town—so much so that the entire region was called the "burned-over district" of New York State.

Opening the Door to Demonic Power

Instead of joining any of these new religions, however, Joseph Smith started his own. It was only natural that its origin should be linked with the very "glass-looking" and "money-digging" that had obsessed him and his family for years. It seems probable that what began as a money-making scheme (hoping to publish and sell the "translation" of an ancient record "discovered like a treasure in the ground") gathered momentum in another direction and led to the formation of a new religion and finally to the grandiose dream of a theocracy that would one day rule the world. Merely pretending can open the door into Satan's kingdom more easily and efficiently than most people realize.

There are too many examples to be ignored of people who began with make-believe, playing with a Ouija board, crystal ball, pendulum, dowsing rod, or other divination devices (several of which were commonly used by early Mormon Apostles) without even believing in such devices, but were drawn into the occult as a result. There are cases of groups that "pretended" to have a spirit seance when sudden demonic manifestations spontaneously occurred, taking control out of their hands. A classic example is the "Phillip Group" in Toronto, Canada, comprised of skeptical parapsychologists who "pretended" to make contact via table-tipping with a make-believe discarnate spirit they named "Phillip." Rapping sounds began to come from within the table, giving Phillip's "real history." The table danced and finally flew around the room so fast that the parapsychologists had to run to keep up with it.[44] Similar phenomena were common among early Mormons.

There is no evidence whatever that such power as this has its source within the subconscious or in that 90 percent of the brain that psychologists allege is unused. This theory is pure materialist superstition. There is now a considerable and increasing volume of accumulating testimony from credible modern scientists who have themselves witnessed repeated occurrences of "poltergeist" activity. Attempting to find a materialistic explanation, these careful researchers have meticulously measured angles, intensity of force, and trajectories of flying objects, and have tested every conceivable physical theory—all to no avail.

Anthropologists acknowledge that poltergeist and other occult phenomena are identical everywhere, even among cultures that differ widely and have had no contact with each other. This clearly indicates a common source independent of human knowledge and beliefs. Almost without exception, witch doctors, medicine men, spiritists, and other shamans who repeatedly produce occult phenomena have attributed this power to "spirits." Their identity is betrayed by the fact that a consistent Luciferian philosophy is always implied by occult phenomena wherever or whenever they occur.

Satan presented four basic lies to Eve:* 1)His rejection of what Eve thought God had said denied a personal God who makes moral pronouncements and implied an impersonal Force; 2) since this Force must be in everything, one tree wouldn't kill her if all others were good for food, and therefore we don't die but are merely recycled (through reincarnation and spirit survival); 3) we can all become gods through mastery of this Force; and 4) this mastery or godhood comes about through being initiated into a secret gnosis (e.g., eating of the Tree of Knowledge). Not only are these four basic lies implied by occult phenomena, but they are often communicated audibly (though mediumship), telepathically, by some form of divination (Ouija boards, tarot cards, etc.), or by automatic writing.[45] This consistency in occult phenomena and philosophy cannot be explained away, no matter how distasteful the conclusion it forces upon skeptical materialists.[46]

The Mormon Connection

Both evidence and logic suggest that in a similar manner to the "Phillip Group," the strong desire on the part of Joseph Smith and his followers to

---

* For a more complete explanation of these four lies and their place in Satan's overall strategy, see Dave Hunt, *The Cult Explosion* (Harvest House Publishers, 1980).

believe his fantastic tales opened the early Mormons to demonic powers. We see a definite and revealing progression: First young Smith uses the "seer stone" to "divine" the location of buried treasure, and then to "translate" unknown languages; later he uses a "Jupiter talisman" for ritual magic; and finally he introduces "magic underwear" (this will be explained later) with occult, Luciferian, Masonic markings that Temple Mormons must wear 24 hours a day for protection from evil. These occult practices are specifically forbidden in the Bible. During this progression of deepening involvement in occultism, we see Smith's theological beliefs metamorphose from the fairly orthodox to the blatant paganism that embraced all of Satan's four lies to Eve, including that of multiplicity of gods and that of infinite human potential to become gods.

There were so many strange visions and so much weird behavior among the early Mormons that to explain it as merely hysteria or hallucinations is inadequate. John Whitmer, official Church Historian in Joseph Smith's time, wrote concerning occult phenomena among the Mormons: "Some had visions ... would act like an Indian in the act of scalping ... [or] slide or scoot on the floor with the rapidity of a serpent...."[47] Joseph Smith even wrote:

> Soon after the gospel was established in Kirtland ... many false spirits were introduced, many strange visions were seen ... men ran out of doors under the influence ... some got upon the stumps of trees and shouted ... [some] had the gift of tongues falsely, they would speak in a muttering, unnatural voice and their bodies be distorted....[48]

There were even phenomena similar to modern UFOs, but in a form that appealed to and could be recognized by viewers in that day. A large number of Mormons saw a huge "steamboat ... painted in the finest style ... filled with people ... [sail] steady along over the city [of Kirtland] ... right over the Temple...." One of the "witnesses" to this amazing event wrote in his journal:

> Old Elder Beamon, who had died a few months before, was seen standing in the bow of the Boat swinging his hat and singing a well known hymn.[49]

Referring to the dedication of this Temple in Kirtland, Apostle George A. Smith declared:

> That evening ... four hundred and sixteen people gathered in the house. ... David Whitmer bore testimony he saw three angels passing up the south aisle, and there came a shock on the house like the sound of a mighty rushing wind ... and hundreds of them were speaking in tongues ... or declaring visions. ..."[50]

After he left the Church, Whitmer (one of the "Three Witnesses") stated in a newspaper interview:

> The great heavenly "visitation" which was alleged to have taken place in the temple ... was a grand fizzle. [It] was promised ... a veritable day of Pentecost, but there was no visitation. No Peter, James and John; no Moses and Elias put in an appearance. ... I know that the story sensationally circulated and which is now on the records of the Utah Mormons as an actual happening was nothing but a trumped up yarn.[51]

Apparently some saw it and some didn't. What about the angel Whitmer claimed to have seen holding the gold plates? Apostle George A. Smith told how some of the Saints saw messages coming to them out of the sky and related a specific instance:

> Black Pete got sight of one of those revelations carried by a black angel, he started after it and ran off a steep bank twenty-five feet high, passed through a tree top into the Chagrin river beneath.[52]

Playing into Satan's Hands

Another Mormon writer from that time relates:

> During the latter part of February, 1831, the Prophet ... was ordaining Harvey Whitlock a high priest. ... [Whitlock] turned as black as Lyman was white. His fingers were set like claws. He went around the room and showed his hands and tried to speak, his eyes were as the shape of oval O's. ...[53]

Here again we have an obviously evil manifestation, while many others are in the same category but are not as openly demonic. The same writer tells of another occasion when such manifestations continued for hours while Joseph Smith ministered to his followers:

> Leman Copley, a very large man of 214 pounds, from his sitting position in the window turned a complete somersault in the house and settled back across a bench where he lay helplessly. . . .
>
> Then another, Harvey Green . . . began screaming like a panther. . . .
>
> These operations continued all day and into the night. . . . Levi Hancock [said], "I was so scared . . . I knew the things I had seen were not made [up]!"[54]

There were so many visions of angels, yet at the same time frightening demonic experiences, that Joseph Smith received a special "revelation" instructing the Saints in how to tell a devil from an angel or a glorified man. In shaking hands with a devil, Smith explained, one would feel nothing, whereas an angel's hand would feel normally physical, while a "glorified man" would refuse to shake hands.[55] On another occasion the Prophet felt it necessary to warn that Satan had sometimes appeared inside the Temple as an angel of light. He explained that this bad angel could be recognized "by the color of his hair . . . and by his contradicting a former revelation."[56]

The above represent only a fraction of the documented examples of demonic influence and manifestations. Most of them were accepted as genuine revelations or manifestations from God. The naïvely superstitious beliefs current among the Mormons about how to handle demons were amplified by such Mormon luminaries as Heber C. Kimball, a member of the First Presidency at the time:

> Now I will tell you, I have about a hundred shots on hand all the time—three or four fifteen-shooters, and three or four revolvers, right in the room where I sleep; and the Devil does not like to sleep there, for he is afraid they will go off half-cocked.
>
> If you will lay a bowie knife or a loaded revolver under your pillow every night, you will not have many unpleasant dreams, nor be troubled with the nightmare; for there is nothing that the Devil is so much afraid of as a weapon of death.[57]

The Keystone of Mormonism

Although Brigham Young declared that "you may leave out the Book of Mormon and the Book of Doctrine and Covenants" and just stick with the New Testament and you "will arrive at salvation,"[58] this is completely contrary to Mormon belief and practice and a perfect example of how Mormon "Prophets" contradict each other. To the question "What will be the consequences if they [the United States] do not embrace the Book of Mormon as a divine revelation?" early Mormon Apostle Orson Pratt replied, "They will be destroyed from the land and sent down to hell, like all other generations who have rejected a divine message."[59] Joseph Smith said, "Take away the Book of Mormon and the revelations, and where is our religion? We have none."[60] In one of his most definite statements on the subject, Joseph Smith said:

> I told the brethren that the Book of Mormon was the most correct of any book on earth, and the keystone of our religion, and a man would get nearer to God by abiding by its precepts, than by any other book....[61]

Obviously, Prophet Smith held the Book of Mormon to be far above the Bible, and that is still the position of the Mormon Church today. This is more than astonishing in view of the fact that over 4000 changes had to be made in the Book of Mormon since it was first published in 1830 with 3000 dollars that Martin Harris raised by mortgaging his farm to get it printed. These corrections run all the way from those necessitated by changes in Joseph Smith's beliefs to elimination of hundreds of obvious contradictions, absurdities, and childish grammatical errors.

After his initiation into the Masonic mysteries, Joseph Smith repudiated and ridiculed the Trinity, teaching that there were an infinite number of gods, each of whom had once been a sinful, fallen man, and that Father, Son, and Holy Spirit are three separate and distinct gods.[62] This required many "corrections" to the Book of Mormon. First Nephi 13:40, for example, which read in the 1830 edition, "and shall make known to all kindreds, tongues and people, that the Lamb of God is the Eternal Father and the Savior of the world" was changed to read "that the Lamb of God is the *Son of* the Eternal Father." Similar changes were made in a number of other places.[63] Strangely enough, however, the declaration in the introduction of the Book of Mormon that its purpose is to convince "Jew and Gentile that Jesus is the Christ, the

Eternal God" and the statement of the "Three Witnesses" giving the honor to the Father, Son, and Holy Ghost, "which is one God," were apparently overlooked and left unchanged.

The Most Correct Book?

Joseph Smith allegedly saw shining on the "seer stone" in his hat each character from the gold plates and beneath it the English translation, which he would read out to Oliver Cowdery, his scribe. Only when Cowdery had read it back to him correctly after writing it down would the miraculous process go on to the next character. There was no room for error. However, the errors numbered in the hundreds, and were exactly what one would expect from the pen of an imaginative but uneducated young man such as Joseph Smith. B.H. Roberts, eminent Mormon historian and General Authority of the Church, confessed in an unpublished manuscript that the evidence pointed compellingly to Joseph Smith as the book's author:

> In the light of this evidence, there can be no doubt as to the possession of a vividly strong, creative imagination by Joseph Smith, the Prophet, an imagination, it could with reason be urged, which, given the suggestions that are to be found in the common knowledge of accepted American Antiquities of the times, supplemented by such a work as Ethan Smith's *View of the Hebrews*,[64] would make it possible for him to create a book such as the Book of Mormon....
>
> ... There is much internal evidence in the book itself to sustain such a view. In the first place there is a certain lack of perspective in the things the book relates as history that points quite clearly to an undeveloped mind as their origin. The narrative proceeds in characteristic disregard of conditions necessary to its reasonableness, as if it were a tale told by a child, with utter disregard for consistency....
>
> For these absurdities in expression; these miraculous incidents in warfare; these almost mock—and certainly extravagant—heroics ... are certainly just such absurdities and lapses as would be looked for if a person of such limitations as bounded Joseph Smith undertook to put forth a book dealing with the history and civilization of ancient and unknown peoples....
>
> Could an investigator of the Book of Mormon be much blamed if he were to decide that Ethan Smith's book with its suggestion as to the

division of his Israelites into two peoples; with its suggestion of "tremendous wars" between them; and of the savages overcoming the civilized division—led to the fashioning of these same chief things in the Book of Mormon?[65]

In the original printing of the Book of Mormon there were literally scores of places where *were* was used instead of *was* ("it were easy to guard them . . . I were about to write them"), *was* was used instead of *were* ("the priests was not to depend . . . they was angry with me"), and *is* was used instead of *are* ("there is save it be, two churches . . . things which is not seen"). Another common grammatical error that betrayed Joseph Smith's authorship was the insertion of an *a* in front of verbs: "Ammon and Lamoni was a journeying . . . he found Muloke a preaching." Other common grammatical mistakes that some of the more educated Mormons found embarrassing and had to be corrected in the second printing were *arrested* being used when it should have been *wrested*; *arriven* instead of *arrived*; *fraid* instead of *afraid*; *no* instead of *any*; and numerous other mistakes familiar to any elementary schoolteacher.

King James English in America in 600 B.C.

In the process of "translating" the Book of Mormon by means of his "peep stone" from hieroglyphics on "gold plates," Joseph Smith not only plagiarized several books about early America that were popular in his day, but he also copied entire chapters of the Bible. For example, compare Isaiah 2–14 with 2 Nephi 12–24; Isaiah 48 and 49 with 1 Nephi 20 and 21; and Isaiah 50 and 51 with 2 Nephi 7 and 8. Not content with that, Joseph Smith included, in portions of the Book of Mormon allegedly written in 600–500 B.C., hundreds of quotations from the New Testament. Perhaps he was too rushed, or else it didn't occur to him to paraphrase when plagiarizing. Consequently, the hundreds of quotations from both the Old and New Testaments (without acknowledging they were copied from Joseph Smith's Bible, but as though they came from the "gold plates") are all in King James English, 1500 to 2000 years before that edition of the Bible was published.

Remarkably, these passages of Scripture which the Book of Mormon Prophets allegedly received either independently from God or from ancient sources include not only the verse and chapter divisions from the King James Bible, but even the *italics* as well. In just one chapter of the Book of Mormon,

Mosiah 14, there are 15 italicized words or phrases written exactly as they appear in Isaiah chapter 53. Isn't it a bit beyond belief that the Book of Mormon "Prophet" Nephi, who allegedly wrote during 600 to 500 B.C. in Egyptian hieroglyphics—a *picture* form of writing—could not only quote Matthew, Luke, Peter, and Paul verbatim centuries before they wrote their Gospels and Epistles, but also do it in such an exact fashion that the translator could see it in King James English as well? This can allow only one explanation: The characters in the Book of Mormon were purely fictitious, and everything they said, including quotations from the Old and New Testaments, was written by Joseph Smith, who certainly had access to the King James Bible.

In Alma 46:15, believers are called Christians in 73 B.C., where Acts 11:26 says they were first called Christians at Antioch in about 42 A.D. The title "Christ" is used in the Book of Mormon, without explanation why Jews living in the Americas would use this Greek word instead of the Hebrew word *Messiah*. Honey bees are said to be in America about 2000 B.C. in Ether 2:3, yet they were first brought to the New World by the Spanish explorers. In Ether 2:16-3:6 the Jaredites are instructed by God to build barges for the trip across the ocean to America, with holes not only in the top but in the bottom also. They are driven by a "furious wind" that "did never cease to blow" (Ether 6:5,8), yet it took them 344 days to cross the Atlantic. At only three knots per hour, they would have gone around the entire earth during this timespan. The absurdities, incongruities, anachronisms, and contradictions are too numerous to list here and have been covered by a number of authors.

Beyond the Book of Mormon

Prophet Smith repeatedly declared that this miraculously given and translated Book of Mormon contained "the fullness of the everlasting gospel" that he had been called to restore.[66] However, his "gospel" expanded to include a "god" who was once a sinful man and who is now resurrected in a physical body, who himself has a "Father God" and "Grandfather God" and on endlessly over him; that there are "three degrees of glory," a Mrs. "God" in heaven, no hell or eternal punishment, a premortal state, eternal matter, no creation, no Creator, marriage for eternity, only polygamists become gods, and a whole string of offices under allegedly "restored" Aaronic and Melchizedek Priesthoods, such as Elder, Seventy, High Priests, President of the Church, First Presidency (made up of two Presidents under the Living

Prophet), Stake Presidencies, Apostles, Bishoprics, as well as baptism for the dead, etc. It simply wasn't possible to make all of the changes in the Book of Mormon that were required in order to bring it into agreement with the evolving "gospel" of Mormonism as it developed with Joseph Smith's growing involvement in occultism.

Consequently, none of the above found its way into the Book of Mormon in its many revisions. The Book of Mormon contains almost no Mormonism and therefore makes Joseph Smith's original statements that it contained the "fullness of the gospel" look even more foolish today. Yet, the Church of Jesus Christ of Latter-day Saints continues to publish and praise the Book of Mormon because it has gone so far out on a limb in saying that the message deciphered from the gold plates is the foundation of Mormonism that it is no longer possible to back down graciously.

The Mormon Church is therefore in the uncomfortable position of having to take seriously the childishly naïve and contradictory content of the Book of Mormon and the poorly conceived mythology concerning its "discovery." The embarrassing truth about an amateur fortune-teller named Joseph Smith, who was addicted all his life to seeking buried treasure and had been convicted of working a cheap scam, has to be suppressed.

What happens if questions are raised about the absurdities, grammatical errors, the contradictions, or the complete lack of archaeological evidence? These are taken care of by a subjective feeling that conveniently overrides common sense and all facts. The "burning in the bosom" is regarded as the manifestation of the Holy Ghost mentioned in Moroni 10:4. The Mormon missionaries' suggestions that prospective converts pray for this "burning" is extremely important in perpetuating the delusion of Mormonism because it sidesteps facts and substitutes feelings. The Book of Mormon promise is that those who "ask with a sincere heart" and have "faith in Christ" will receive this "sign." No one wants to be looked upon as insincere or lacking in faith, so there is a very strong desire to have this "feeling," which the very desire itself could psychologically create.

The most important part of Mormonism—its very heart—which we will reveal, has been so secret that the inner circle of Mormon elite who practice it must swear oaths to forfeit their lives rather than reveal it. Prophet Smith claimed to have received these key "revelations" from extraterrestrials visiting him from a distant planet. A hint at the identity of the "gods" from

Kolob who inspired him is found in the fact that these "keys" to "godhood" are not unique to Mormonism as most Mormons imagine. They have been the stock-in-trade of numerous secret occult societies for centuries. One of these groups, to which Mormonism has a surprising and significant relationship, is both well-known and highly respected today. An extremely large percentage of today's world leaders have sworn its secret oaths.

9

THE MASONIC
CONNECTION

The annual convention of the Mormon History Association held in the aging, historic Nauvoo Hotel on April 20, 1974, had been pretty much routine all day like those before it: old friends meeting once again, familiar ground gone over in an attempt to find some new light that would build faith in the Prophet and strengthen testimonies of the Church. The surprise came—and what a shock it was—when Dr. Reed C. Durham, Jr., the Association's outgoing president, gave the traditional Presidential Address. As he strode to the podium with his sheaf of papers, there was prolonged applause for a popular leader who had given himself enthusiastically to the cause of establishing a faith-promoting history of the Latter-day Saints. When the applause subsided and he began to read his carefully prepared paper on the touchy subject of the relationship between Masonry and Mormonism, a few eyebrows were raised and an uncomfortable hush settled over the uneasy listeners. No one, however, perhaps even including Dr. Durham himself, suspected the explosive power of the bomb he was about to drop.

There was no question as to the facts, nor that the information had been available to everyone present. Much of it they had heard before: the close similarities between Mormon and Masonic Temple ceremonies with their secret names, aprons, penalties, blood oaths, grips, and tokens, as well as the many Masonic markings inside and outside Mormon Temples: the square, the compass, the beehive, the astrological symbols, the all-seeing eye of occultism, and the upside-down five-pointed star, symbol of Satanism. Though it was unsettling to be reminded again that absolutely nothing had been said about secret Temple rituals by Joseph Smith in the new Church's 12-year history until immediately *after* he had been initiated into Masonry, those present had been able to shrug that off before, and did so on this occasion with only slight twinges of conscience. So what else was new?

What followed near the end of Durham's talk, however, wakened with a start those who had been dozing while the lights were out for viewing his slide presentation. The audience was stunned. Why hadn't they seen this before? The connection was obvious and had always been there, clear as crystal. They just hadn't *wanted* to see it, because the implication was too devastating. But now they had no choice—Dr. Durham had forced them to look at something so incriminating that Joseph Smith's credentials as a Prophet were torn to tatters.

The Masonic Legend of Enoch

Thanks to the diligence and courage of a very few people who had brought their tape recorders, the staggering speech was soon in "underground" circulation. Typed copies surfaced almost immediately in such diverse places as Masonic Lodges and the briefcases of BYU professors. It was awesome to see how quickly the Mormon hierarchy knew what had been said and took action because of it. *The very next day* the angel with its Masonic markings that Dr. Durham had referred to in his talk was hastily removed from its Visitor's Center display in Nauvoo, Illinois, never to be seen in public again. Professor Durham himself barely escaped being removed from the Church by writing a hasty "To whom it may concern" letter reaffirming his faith in Prophet Smith and the Church he founded.

After explaining about the Jupiter talisman found on Joseph Smith at his death, the occult powers associated with it, and the fact that his mother's family identified this as "Joseph's Masonic jewel," Dr. Durham reminded his audience that he had set out to "provoke some thought and present something new" concerning the undeniable relationship between Mormonism and Masonry. "If I have not succeeded in doing that by now," he added, "please indulge me one last further attempt." They soon wished they hadn't.

He then launched into a brief summary of "a famous legend which the grand orator elaborates in lecture form in the ceremonies of the 13th, 14th and 21st degrees of Masonry... bearing remarkable similarity to Mormonism." Referring to the ancient roots of this tale in "cabalistic lore and mythology," Durham then pointed out that "the legend was in American Masonic print by 1802; and by Joseph Smith's time many publications had made the legend popularly well disseminated."[1] The summary he then gave of the legend must have stunned his Mormon audience, for it contains not only the key esoteric doctrines of Mormonism as they evolved beyond the original semiorthodoxy of the Book of Mormon, but also the major elements in Joseph Smith's story, including his role in finding and translating the alleged gold plates. In his introductory summary of the Masonic legend, Dr. Durham said:

> ...In the pre-existence, there was a special Secret Doctrine that was given by Deity... to the Earth first to Adam [who] was to carefully guard this Secret Doctrine because it contained all the Mysteries... [including] the secret name of God.
>
> Adam then bestowed it upon his son, Seth, who guarded it very carefully—only among the inner circle of believers—and then it was handed down until it came to Enoch... the central figure in the legend.

It is with Enoch that the remarkable resemblances with Joseph Smith and Mormon history become disconcertingly clear.[2]

A Devastating Comparison

The similarities between this ancient Masonic legend about Enoch, and the mythology that Joseph Smith et al. managed to establish concerning his alleged exploits in finding and translating the gold plates, are too numerous and exact to allow any other explanation than the most obvious one. As Dr. Durham said that night to his stunned audience of fellow Mormon historians, "The parallels [to the legend of Enoch] of Joseph Smith and the history of Mormonism are so unmistakable that to explain them only as coincidence would be ridiculous."[3]

In the legend, Enoch was 25 years old "when he received his call and vision," as was Joseph Smith "when he brought forth his sacred record." Enoch's vision was of a hill containing a vault prepared for "sacred treasures," on which he saw the identifying letter M; while Joseph Smith was led by an "angel" whose name began with M to a similar hill containing an underground vault (like Enoch's) filled with "sacred treasures." Part of the treasures

revealed to Enoch were gold and brass plates engraved with Egyptian hieroglyphics giving the history of the world and ancient mysteries of God, which
he preserved by putting them in the vault in the hill; similarly, Joseph Smith
recovered from a vault in a hill gold and brass plates engraved with Egyptian
hieroglyphics containing ancient history and mysteries of God. Enoch's treasure also included a metal ball, a priestly breastplate, and the fabled "Urim
and Thummim"—precisely the same objects that were found by Joseph
Smith along with the gold plates.

If the above sounds like an impossible coincidence, there is more. Joseph
Smith often referred to himself in his "revelations" as "Enoch,"[4] claiming
that he had been given this name by God. The Enoch of the legend was chosen to recover and preserve for mankind the sacred name of God; and Joseph
Smith was allegedly chosen to recover and "restore" the everlasting gospel of
God to the earth. Enoch buried the sacred record to preserve it just before a
great disaster (the Flood), foreseeing that after the deluge "an Israelitish
descendant would discover anew the sacred buried treasure." Enoch "placed
a stone lid, or slab, over the cavity into the hill," exactly as Moroni did in the
Book of Mormon when he buried his record as the only survivor of the disaster (great battle) that destroyed his entire nation. Joseph Smith, who recovered this record, claimed to be an Israelite, fitting the vision of Enoch even in
this regard.

Of course, in the Masonic legend it was "Solomon and his builders, the
Masons, while building and excavating for the Temple at Mount Moriah, who
discovered the cavern and the sacred treasure." The legend relates that, like
Joseph Smith, they were able to obtain it only after three unsuccessful
attempts. Three wicked men, however, tried to force "one of the faithful
Masons who had discovered the treasure, Hiram Abif, or Hiram the Widow's
son, to reveal the hiding place and the contents of the hidden treasure." He
would not; and as they were killing him, "Hiram, with uplifted hands, cried
out, 'Oh Lord, my God, is there no help for the widow's son?' This has since
become a general Masonic distress call." There were three faithful Masons
who pursued the villains, and cut off the head of one of them with his own
sword. Dr. Durham ended his disquieting talk by summarizing some of the
other "coincidences" involved:

> Joseph Smith had three witnesses to the Book of Mormon and the
> record itself bears witness that an archvillain named Laban . . .

[who] was thwarting the availability... of the sacred records had his head cut off by his own sword....

Now these parallels, dramatic as they seem, still do not represent the strangest part of the story. All of these aspects of the legend seem transformed into the history of Joseph Smith, so much so that it even appears to be a kind of *symbolic acting out of Masonic lore.*

But there is a point in this drama where the action goes beyond metaphor and the symbol merges into a tragic reality. This has to do, of course, with the death of Hiram Abif in the legend and the martyrdom of Joseph Smith....

Joseph Smith gave himself up to be imprisoned and on June 27, 1844 a mob stormed the little Carthage jail. Hyrum [Smith] was killed instantly and John Taylor seriously wounded.

Joseph Smith, Master Mason and widow's son, went to the window and with upraised hands, commenced giving the Masonic distress call to fraternal Masons who were present in the mob: "Oh Lord, my God . . ." He was unable to complete his plea and fell out of the window to his death.

How does a Mormon historian interpret Joseph Smith and the Masonic Enoch legend? The parallels demand an answer. Was Joseph Smith the fruition of Enoch's prophecy? . . . Did mysterious and divine, even magical, forces attach themselves to him?

Can anyone deny that Masonic influence on Joseph Smith and the Church, either before or after his personal Masonic membership? The evidence demands comments. . . . I do not believe that the Nauvoo story can adequately be told without an inquiry into Masonry.[5]

In fact, Masonry played a key role in the myths in which Joseph Smith wrapped Mormonism. As we shall see, Joseph's brother Hyrum was a member of the Mount Moriah Lodge No. 112 in Palmyra, New York. Its responsibility was the perpetuation of the Legend of Enoch, the cloth from which much of the fabric of Mormonism was formed.

The Pagan/Occult Connection Again

Although Joseph Smith claimed he was "restoring" true biblical Christianity, leading Mormons have admitted that Mormonism is actually a revival of the key doctrines of the mystery religions that Milton R. Hunter called "the pagan rivals of Christianity." Masonry likewise claims to be the restorer and perpetrator of the ancient mysteries, including the Secret Doctrine and identity of God.

There can be no doubt that Joseph Smith received a great deal of inspiration from Masonry. It is clear that this happened over a period of time. As we shall see, both the Melchizedek Priesthood and the alleged "First Vision" (which, in spite of its nine contradictory versions, is the foundation of Mormonism) show a progression in Prophet Smith's ideas that betrays a definite and growing influence from Masonry. The entire Mormon mythology about the gold plates is so similar in so many details to the Masonic Legend of Enoch that no rational person could deny the intimate connection. Clearly the Masonic Legend of Enoch inspired the story that made Joseph Smith both famous and infamous and won him the allegiance of millions of people who call him a Prophet of God.

The gradual theological metamorphosis in Joseph Smith from almost biblical beliefs (as expressed in the original printings of the Book of Mormon and Book of Commandments) to a polytheism that denied hell and promised godhood to the worthy on the basis of secret pagan Temple rituals is also consistent with the growing Masonic influence upon him. In that same talk, Dr. Durham documented the part that Masonry played and gave substantial evidence concerning its undeniable, dominating influence in the formation of Mormonism:

> I am convinced that in the study of Masonry lies a pivotal key to further understanding Joseph Smith and the Church.... The many parallels found between early Mormonism and the Masonry of that day are substantial: conferences, councils, priesthood, temples, anointing with oil, the issuance of licenses, certificates for identifying legitimate fellow workers [called Temple Recommends by Mormons], elders, high priests and even the Book of the Law... [plus] things Egyptian, the new revelations of suns and moons, governing planets and fixed stars [while] unique at that time to Mormonism were commonplace in Masonry.
>
> ... Most of the things which were developed in the Church at Nauvoo were inextricably interwoven with Masonry—in addition to the endowment, the temple and the Relief Society.... I suspect also

that the development of prayer circles and even polygamy are no exceptions.

But more importantly, I suggest that enough evidence presently exists to declare that the entire institution of the political kingdom of God, including the Council of Fifty, the living constitution, the proposed flag of the kingdom, and the anointing and coronation of the king, had its genesis in connection with Masonic thought and ceremonies. It could not be coincidence that all of these concepts had their counterparts within Masonry in the day of the Prophet Joseph Smith.[6]

By the end of his speech that night, Dr. Durham had left very little of Mormonism—at least of those peculiar elements that distinguish it from Christianity—that he had not traced back directly to Masonry as the source of inspiration. That influence began with the Enoch legend that undoubtedly inspired Smith's entire scenario of obtaining the gold plates after three unsuccessful attempts and escaping from villains who tried to steal them. It continued through the many Masons who were drawn to Mormonism (along with many members from other secret societies) and became an increasing factor as their ranks swelled within the new Church. In spite of that, however, during the first 12 years of Mormonism's history nothing of the secret inner workings of Masonry came into the Church. It can hardly be a coincidence that it was only after Joseph Smith himself became a Mason and participated in secret Masonic rituals that Masonry literally transformed Mormonism. As Dr. Durham reminded his audience:

> To begin with, Masonry in the Church had its origin prior to the time Joseph Smith became a Mason. Nauvoo was not its genesis. It commenced in Joseph's home when his older brother... Hyrum received the first three degrees of Masonry in Mount Moriah Lodge No. 112 of Palmyra, New York, at about the same time that Joseph was being initiated into the presence of God and angels and was being entrusted with the sacred gold plates.

> By the end of 1832, Joseph Smith had welcomed new brethren, along with their influences, into the Church. Men such as W.W. Phelps, Brigham Young, Heber C. Kimball and Newel K. Whitney, each of whom had been deeply involved in Masonry....

At the instigation of John C. Bennett, George W. Harris, John Parker, Lucius Scovil, as well as other Mormon Masons residing at Nauvoo, and certainly with the approval of the hierarchy of the Church, the institution of Masonry commenced.

Joseph and Sidney were inducted into formal Masonry at Sight, on the same day upon which the Illinois Grand Master Mason ... Abraham Jonas officially installed the Nauvoo Lodge. It was on March 15, 1842. On the next day, both Sidney and Joseph advanced to the Master Mason Degree.

In only a few years, five Mormon Lodges were established, several others in planning, a Masonic Temple constructed, and the total membership of Mormon fraternal brethren was over 1,366.

... Masonic influences upon Joseph in the early Church history ... were significant. However, these same Masonic influences exerted a more dominant character as reflected in the further expansion of the Church subsequent to the Prophet's Masonic membership.

In fact, I believe that there are few significant developments in the Church, that occurred after March 15, 1842, which did not have some Masonic interdependence. ... There is absolutely no question in my mind that the Mormon ceremony which came to be known as the Endowment, introduced by Joseph Smith to Mormon Masons initially, just a little over one month after he became a Mason, had an immediate inspiration from Masonry.

It is also obvious that the Nauvoo Temple architecture was in part, at least, Masonically influenced. Indeed, it appears that there was an intentional attempt to utilize Masonic symbols and motifs.[7]

The "True Masonry"

Captivated by the Masonic Legend of Enoch, Joseph Smith had taken this name for himself.[8] His entire story about finding gold and brass plates with hieroglyphics, the Urim and Thummim, etc., clearly came from this Masonic legend. In further introducing Masonry into his growing Church, however, Mormonism's founding Prophet could not go much beyond what was common knowledge. Although growing numbers of practicing Masons were becoming Latter-day Saints, these men had been sworn to secrecy upon penalty of death, so were limited in what they could divulge even to their

Prophet. In spite of having earlier denounced all secret societies,[9] Joseph Smith seems to have become increasing intrigued by Masonry's cloak of secrecy.

Whether drawn into Masonry on that account or not, soon thereafter he turned the Mormon Church into a secret society with the same tokens, signs, and horrible penalty (throat slit, heart and vitals torn out) for revealing Temple secrets (as in Masonry). Once initiated, Prophet Smith discovered in detail what he already knew only in part—that Masonry, like Mormonism, is a secret, anti-Christian mystery religion, as those who know it best have admitted:

> [Masonry is] . . . the custodian and depository (since Enoch) of the great philosophical and religious truths, unknown to the world at large. . . .[10]

> Every Masonic Lodge is a temple of religion, and its teachings are instructions in . . . the universal, eternal, immutable religion. . . .[11]

> Without this religious element it would scarcely be worthy of cultivation by the wise and good. . . .

> Freemasonry is not Christianity. . . . It admits men of every creed within its hospitable bosom. . . .[12]

> The first Masonic legislator whose memory is preserved to us by history was Buddha. . . .

> [Masonry] . . . sees in Moses . . . in Confucius and Zoroaster, in Jesus of Nazareth, and in [Mohammed] great teachers of morality and eminent reformers. . . .[13]

> All truly dogmatic religions have issued from the Kabalah [Judaic occultism] and return to it. Everything scientific and grand in the religious dreams of the Illuminati, Jacob Boehme, Swedenborg, Saint-Martin and others is borrowed from the Kabalah; all the Masonic associations owe to it their secrets and their symbols.[14]

It is clear why Joseph Smith had such a fascination with Masonry and found so much of it useful: Like Mormonism, it opposes historic Christianity. He claimed that heavenly visitors told him that all Christians were corrupt and all their creeds an abomination, and that he was to "restore" the "true" religion. Obviously Joseph Smith believed that it was closer to the truth than

Christianity was, because visitors from Kolob had allegedly told him not to join any Christian church on earth—yet he joined the Masons, a secret religious society.

Masonry's claim—that the "true religion," once pure in the mystery religions but corrupted by the world at large, was recovered by King Solomon's Masons and has since been preserved within the secrets of Freemasonry—is too close to Joseph Smith's claims concerning Mormonism's "restoration" of the gospel to be coincidence. However, Joseph Smith could not give credit to anyone except himself, for the same reason that the Mormon Church today dare not admit that most of its inner secrets are Masonic in origin. Smith was the "Prophet," and he had to keep it that way. Having joined Freemasonry, the Prophet proceeded to change its dogmas just enough so that he could take credit for them as his "revelations." He had undertaken the task of personally revising the entire Christian Bible by "revelation," and he now did the same thing with Masonry.

Just as Joseph Smith had called Mormonism the "true Christianity," so Mormonism must also be the "true Masonry," and this is what he called it. He convinced his followers of this, including those who had been Masons for years. Heber C. Kimball wrote to Parley P. Pratt:

> We have organized a Lodge here of Masons ... near 200 have been made Masons. Brother Joseph and Sidney [Rigdon] were the first that were received into the Lodge. All of the twelve have become members except Orson P. [Pratt]. . . . Brother Joseph says Masonry was taken from the Priesthood, but has become degenerated. . . . We have the true Masonry.[15]

In his speech, Dr. Durham referred to a letter written by Joseph Smith to a Mr. John Hull, a Congregational minister who had been active in Masonry "for over 40 years [and] . . . had held every office in Masonry up to and including Worshipful Master of the Lodge." Of this letter, Durham said:

> The entire two-page letter clearly demonstrates that Mormonism and Masonry were related and that Joseph used Masonry and apparently had no qualms in doing so.

> It is also clear in the letter that the Kingdom of God was thought to be the true Masonry, which, when ultimately established with a king and a president, would abolish all earthly confusion and evil and usher in the Millennium.

The whole earth was compared symbolically to a Grand Masonic Lodge, the counterpart of which was the Grand Lodge in the eternal regions of Glory; an idea quite legitimate in Masonic thought. . . .

It appears that the Prophet first embraced Masonry, and then in the process he modified, expanded, amplified or glorified it.[16]

The Pagan, Anti-Christian Mysteries "Restored"

Masonry became so popular among the Mormons after Joseph Smith and Sidney Rigdon were initiated that the Mormon Masonic Lodges were soon outgrowing non-Mormon Lodges by a very wide margin. It wasn't long before "the Nauvoo Lodge had more members than all the other Illinois lodges together."[17] If they had been allowed to continue, it appears that the Mormons would have taken over Masonry. Moreover, in the process, they were initiating subtle changes in long-established Masonic rituals under the direction of their Prophet, who was now actively engaged in "restoring" Masonry as he had Christianity. Unwilling to have Joseph Smith eventually take over as Grand Commander, the Masonic hierarchy expelled the Mormons. In justification of this move, one Masonic historian wrote:

If the [Nauvoo] Lodge had been suffered to work two years longer, every Mormon in Hancock County would have been initiated.[18]

What was happening at the same time within Mormonism is quite clear. On May 4, 1842, less than two months after he had been initiated into Masonry, Joseph Smith introduced what is known today as the Mormon Temple Endowment Ceremony. It was the Masons among the Mormons who were the first to be initiated by the Prophet into these secret rites, which can only be called Mormon Masonry. This was done in the very same room that was used for Masonic rituals by the Nauvoo Lodge. Mormon historian B.H. Roberts explained that the room "in which were instituted these sacred ceremonies" was not only used as the first Mormon Temple (before construction of the Nauvoo Mormon Temple), but "it was also the place of meeting for the Nauvoo Lodge of Free Masons."[19]

Thus were originated the secret functions of the "power and priesthoods" of Lucifer, which form the very core of Mormonism. No honest investigator can deny that this all came out of Masonry's mystery religion heritage. The Prophet accepted this pagan source and even claimed to "restore" its original purity by "revelation" from God. Jesse C. Little testified: "The Angel of the Lord brought to Mr. Joseph Smith the lost key words of several [Masonic] degrees, which caused him, when he appeared among the brotherhood of Illinois, to work right ahead of the highest and to show them their ignorance of the greatest truth and benefits of Masonry."[20] At about the same time, Joseph Fielding wrote in his diary:

> Many have joined the Masonic Institution. This seems to have been a stepping stone for preparation for something else, the true origin of Masonry. This I have also seen and rejoice in it.

> There has been great light poured out upon the Saints of late, and a great spirit of hearing. I have evidence enough that Joseph is not fallen.

> I have seen him, after giving, as he said before, the origin of Masonry, the Kingdom of God on the earth, and am myself a member of it.[21]

These were exciting days among the Mormons, for they saw the introduction for the first time into Mormonism of those secrets that now form its very heart. In a letter to Orson Pratt, Heber C. Kimball wrote:

> We have received some precious things through the Prophet on the Priesthood which would cause your soul to rejoice. I cannot give them to you on paper, for they are not to be written. So you must come and get them for yourself.[22]

These secrets that Joseph Smith began to introduce out of Masonry's mysteries he declared "were to be discerned, unlocked, unraveled, and appropriately unfolded unto the Church, line upon line, by the one who holds the keys [Smith himself] of the Holy Priesthood." Commenting upon this, Durham said, ". . . If Masonry in reality contained any of the true ancient Mysteries, it would have been necessary for Joseph to accept it."[23] Thus Dr. Durham, along with other Mormon leaders, in attempting to justify Joseph Smith's borrowing from Masonry, acknowledges that the "truth" that Mormonism is founded upon is not the Bible, but "the true ancient Mysteries" of pagan occultism. Reinforcing this point, Dr. Durham told his audience:

The philosophic and more reflective Masonic scholars have always believed that the symbols embodied in Masonry were indeed the ancient Mysteries coming from remote antiquity.

The Mysteries were said to be traced back through the Hermetic Philosophers, through Plutarch, the Cabala, the Pythagoreans, the Magi of Media, to Babylon, to Chaldea, and Egypt.

And as these Mysteries came down into the modern institution of Masonry—the 12th and 13th centuries A.D.—they had experienced so many progressive alterations that there remained only an imperfect image of their original brilliancy.

My assumption is that Joseph Smith believed he was restoring Masonry's original pristine brilliancy, and that he was recreating the Mysteries of the ancient Priesthood.[24]

The Mystery: Lucifer's Power and Priesthoods

Certainly "the ancient Priesthood" that Durham suggests Joseph Smith "restored" first to Mormon Masonry and then to Mormonism itself was not a biblical priesthood, but a pagan one preserved within the mystery religions. That this is the Luciferic priesthood is equally clear. Freemasonry teaches that the earliest traditions have passed on the knowledge that the demons forbade Adam to eat of the Tree of Knowledge, but that the Angel of Light (Lucifer, the Light-bearer) helped Adam to eat of the forbidden fruit for his own enlightenment. This is too similar to the teachings of Mormonism to be mere coincidence. Many Mormons are not aware of Mormonism's real teachings, because they are not considered "worthy" to be initiated into its secrets. It is interesting to see what Albert Pike, a leading Masonic authority, said about this technique of deliberately keeping the uninitiated in ignorance:

> Masonry, like all the religions, all the Mysteries, Hermeticism and Alchemy, conceals its secrets from all except the Adepts and Sages, or the Elect, and uses false explanations and misinterpretations of its symbols to mislead those who deserve only to be misled; to conceal the Truth, which it calls light, from them. . . . Truth is not for those who are unworthy. . . .[25]

> The Blue Degrees are but the outer court . . . of the Temple. Part of the symbols are displayed there to the [lower] Initiate, but he is

intentionally misled by false interpretations. It is not intended that he shall understand them, but it is intended that he shall imagine he understands them.[26]

In its highest form, for those who have attained to the secret knowledge of the mystery, Masonry is a Luciferic religion. Similarly, we have already seen Luciferic secrets in the Mormon Temple ceremonies. Like Masonry, after which its innermost secrets are patterned, Mormonism is designed to mislead those who are part of it but haven't yet been initiated into its dark secrets.[27]

Why is there in Masonry this deliberate design in the symbols both to mislead the uninitiated and yet at the same time to provide sufficient hints of the "truth" for those who are "worthy" to understand it? As in Mormonism, the answer is that the "mystery" is too shocking to be revealed to those at the lower levels. What is this "mystery" that only the very few at the highest levels of Masonry (and Mormonism) are intended to understand? Manly P. Hall, one of the world's foremost experts in occultism, explains:

> When the Mason . . . has learned the Mystery of his craft, the seething energies of Lucifer are in his hand and before he may step onward and upward, he must prove his ability to properly apply [this] energy.[28]

In *Morals and Dogma*, Masonic Grand Commander Albert Pike wrote:

> LUCIFER, the Light-bearer. Strange and mysterious name to give to the Spirit of Darkness. Lucifer, the Son of the Morning. Is it *he* who bears the *Light*, and with its splendors intolerable blinds feeble, sensual, or selfish Souls? Doubt it not![29] (emphases in original).

Is Pike for or against Lucifer? We are not to doubt that Lucifer blinds; but he does it with the "Light," and only to the "feeble, sensual, or selfish." So Pike, far from slandering Lucifer, is complaining against those who have given the name "Spirit of Darkness" to the one who is the true "Light-bearer . . . the Son of the Morning." Pike writes in a way that only initiates will understand. However, when he addressed the leaders of World Freemasonry, then he reportedly spoke plainly:

> To you, Sovereign Grand Inspectors General, we say this, that you may repeat it to the Brethren of the 32nd, 31st and 30th degrees—

The Masonic Religion should be, by all of us initiates of the high degrees, maintained in the purity of the Luciferian Doctrine.

If Lucifer were not God, would Adonay whose deeds prove his cruelty, perfidy and hatred of man, barbarism and revulsion for science, would Adonay and his priests calumniate him?

Yes, Lucifer is God, and unfortunately Adonay is also god . . . for the absolute can only exist as two gods. . . .

Thus, the doctrine of Satanism is a heresy; and the true and pure philosophical religion is the belief in Lucifer, the equal of Adonay; but Lucifer, God of Light and God of Good, is struggling for humanity against Adonay, the God of Darkness and Evil.[30]

Adonay is a Hebrew title translated "Lord" in the Old Testament and used only when referring to Jehovah, the one true God of Israel, who is also the God of Christians. Masonry has taken the anti-God philosophy of the mystery religions that reverse what the Bible teaches, turning Lucifer (Satan) into God and God into Satan. This is the religion that Joseph Smith and about 1500 early Mormons embraced enthusiastically before they were expelled from Masonry. According to no less an authority than Dr. Reed Durham, this is also the religion that determined almost every major doctrine and practice in Mormonism.

10

SACRED OR
SECRET?

Housing various depictions of Mormon history presented in a way that is calculated to win converts and avoid any embarrassing details, Visitor's Centers are to be found adjacent to most Mormon Temples around the world. Salt Lake City's Temple Square boasts two such propaganda centers. The North Visitor's Center houses the giant statue of Christ, "large murals of Bible scenes, and displays about Mormon history and beliefs."[1] The South Center contains information "about the Book of Mormon, Christ's visit to ancient America, and why Mormons build temples."[2] In addition to artistic representations of Mormon beliefs, each such center around the world offers a series of pamphlets distributed to visitors without charge to persuade recipients that the Church of Jesus Christ of Latter-day Saints is the only true Christian church on earth.

In his 1974 Mormon History Association speech, Dr. Reed C. Durham's reference to the angel with Masonic markings caused its hasty removal from its South Visitor's Center display in historic Temple Square. However, something else that belonged in the secret archives with the Masonic angel and other embarrassing memorabilia was housed in the very beautiful North Visitor's Center adjacent to the Salt Lake City Temple, at the time of this book's release. The piece of art in question was an impressive bronze statue depicting Adam and Eve kneeling in an act of worship as they face an altar between them.

The very primitive altar depicted was built of stones piled carefully on top of each other, and probably represented that fabled sacrificial site just

145

outside the Garden of Eden that Joseph Smith claimed to have discovered in Missouri. Ignoring that peculiar idea, the statuary portrayed a message that was extremely revealing to anyone who has studied the mystery religions and occultism.

Quenching the Flaming Sword

We are told that when Adam and Eve were expelled from the garden paradise because of their sin, it was to keep them and their descendants from eating of the Tree of Life and living forever. Clearly, God didn't want to allow man to perpetuate himself in a fallen state of rebellion that has brought increasing evil and suffering upon the human race as humans have multiplied across the earth. Not only would it not have been kind or wise to do so, but God had in mind something better. He promised that the Messiah, "the Seed of the woman"[3] (i.e., virgin-born), would one day come and deal the Serpent a deathblow.

That God cannot reverse the *consequences* of sin by simply waving a magic wand of forgiveness is taught again and again in the Bible, as well as by history and human experience. Something so deep within man has gone so horribly wrong as a result of his self-willed rebellion that education, semantics, personal determination, or psychological techniques can never solve the basic problem. Nothing less than the death of the rebels—and out of death the creation of new beings—can return man to fellowship with God. This is the clear message of the cherubim that God stationed with a flaming sword to guard the Tree of Life when he expelled Adam and Eve.[4]

God was not saying that man would never taste the fruit of that tree, which symbolizes eternal life. In the last chapter of the Bible, man is back in Paradise and freely eating of the Tree of Life.[5] The message in Genesis 3 is consistently echoed throughout the Bible: that in order to get to the Tree of Life, men must pass the flaming sword of judgment which brings the death that God pronounced as the penalty for sin. Rejecting the Serpent's lie that death is unreal, humans must admit that, having sinned, they deserve to die. We must confess that sin is so horrible that God's judgment of the death penalty is just.

Unfortunately, humanity continued to rebel by complaining against the death penalty that God imposed. Our primary instinct is self-preservation. We flee from that sword and try every device to escape the just penalty we deserve for our sin. We have good reason, for we recognize that the death required by justice would be eternal.

In His mercy and grace, God had a plan to save us from the eternal separation that justice demanded. Since He is infinite, God could pay that infinite debt to justice. In order to do so righteously, however, He had to become as one of us, a member of the human race. This He did through the virgin birth. As the "Seed of the woman," Jesus Christ the Son of God never ceased to be God, and He will never cease to be man. As the sinless Lamb of God, He could die for our sins; having paid that infinite debt, death could not hold Him. He resurrected and is now alive, having conquered death for us. He offers to give eternal life to all who will receive Him as Savior and Lord, and He does this by coming to live in each heart and life that opens to Him.

Here the symbolism of the flaming sword and the Tree of Life is fulfilled. In contrast to all other humans—who fled that sword of judgment and death—Jesus walked up to it and took it in His heart for us. Thus he became the Savior, the way to life for all who will accept Him as "the way, the truth, and the life" that He claimed to be. Some unknown poet put it beautifully:

> His blood that flaming sword must quench,
> His heart its sheath must be.

Followers of Cain

In expelling Adam and Eve from Paradise, God stripped them of the fig-leaf aprons that they had made in an attempt to cover their sin by their own efforts. He replaced this inadequate covering, this attempt at self-righteousness, with the skins of animals that had to be killed in order to clothe them. The message was clear: Sin really does bring death in spite of the Serpent's claim that death is unreal and his seductive promise that Adam and Eve could become like God.

In keeping with the rest of the Bible, Adam and Eve must have been instructed to sacrifice animals as sin offerings to God symbolizing the sacrifice upon the cross that Christ would make as the "Lamb of God who takes away the sin of the world."[6] We are told that Abel offered a lamb to God "by faith"[7]; and since "faith comes by... hearing the word of God,"[8] he must have offered this kind of a sacrifice in response to a command from God. Surely his parents, Adam and Eve, also followed the same instructions in the sacrifice they offered to God.

We are told that Cain refused to offer a lamb. Perhaps he believed in the sacredness of all life, like Hindus and today's animal rights extremists, and on the grounds of "nonviolence" refused to kill an animal. Instead, he offered the works of his hands in the form of the fruits and vegetables from the garden that he so industriously labored over. As Abel's sacrifice of the lamb symbolized the sacrifice of Christ, so Cain's offering symbolized the self-righteous insistence that good works can pay for sin. God rejected Cain's offering and told him that a "sin offering" crouched at his door.[9] Though he proudly refused to kill an animal as a sacrifice for his sins, Cain murdered his own brother Abel, because Abel did offer the lamb that God had commanded.

In view of the above, it is most interesting that the bronze statue in the North Visitor's Center portrayed Adam and Eve kneeling before an altar that contains fruits, vegetables, and a sheaf of wheat—the very offering of Cain that God rejected! The lamb that Abel offered and which was accepted of God is also shown in the statue. Significantly, however, it is not dead upon the altar as the symbol of Christ's sacrifice for sin, but is shown very much alive, posing contentedly and untethered in front of the altar, like the sin offering that God said was lying at Cain's door, but which he refused to sacrifice as commanded.

Not long after this book was first published exposing Mormonism's complete misunderstanding of God's reasons for His actions with Cain, Ed was in Salt Lake City and visited the statue. Ed describes the event: "I happened to be in the Visitor Center and fell into a group of tourists being guided through the center by a Mormon hostess. When we came up to the statue of Adam and Eve kneeling at the altar, I let out an audible gasp. Pointing my finger at the statue, I kept repeating in a shaky voice, 'Look! Look!' over and over again until the lady cried out, 'What?' in a loud wail. 'It's the offering of Cain!' I wailed back."

Two weeks later, without a word of explanation, the statuary was removed from the building and went into exile and obscurity somewhere out of sight and mind. Today, it has been replaced with a statue of Adam and Eve standing apart from each other, looking for all the world to be in a total state of confusion.

The Missing Cross

It is not only in that revealing piece of statuary in the North Visitor's Center that the Mormon Church has openly aligned itself with Cain's religion of self-effort. Mormonism teaches and practices the same thing: that Latter-day Saints must prove their worthiness and earn eternal life by obedience to thousands of laws and ordinances, and repetitive performances of secret Temple rituals. This is because Mormonism denies that Jesus Christ, the Lamb of God, died for our sins and thereby purchased eternal life to be given as a free gift of God's grace to all who receive Him by faith. Because they reject the full value of Christ's blood poured out in death for sin on the cross, Mormons take bread and *water* at their communion services instead of bread and *wine* (or grape juice) as Christ commanded; and they display no cross inside or outside their chapels and Temples, but do display many Masonic and other occult symbols. Mormons have an almost fanatical aversion to the cross and the shed blood of Jesus Christ.

In the official LDS booklet *Plan of Salvation*, there are detailed explanations of Mormonism's peculiar theories under such headings as "Premortal Life of Christ," "Why We are Here," "Faith and Signs," "Baptism," "The Laying On of Hands," "Christ Visits the Spirit World," and "Salvation for the Dead." Nowhere in the entire booklet, however, does it state that Christ died for our sins or that eternal life is offered as a free gift of God's grace to all who receive it by faith; none of the many Bible verses that state this is quoted;[10] and, in fact, exactly the opposite is taught in that booklet. Under the heading of "Faith," it is explained that "the commandments of God are obeyed only by those who have faith that blessings will follow their obedience."[11] In contrast, the Bible teaches that no one ever kept all the commandments,[12] but "that a man is justified by faith without the deeds of the law."[13] The Bible declares that "by him [Christ] all that believe are justified from all things, from which you could not be justified by the law of Moses."[14]

Also under the heading of "Faith," the LDS booklet emphasizes that those who don't have faith "in the divine calling of Joseph Smith, the Prophet and Seer... are depriving themselves of glorious blessings,"[15] but there isn't even a hint that "he that believeth on the Son [Christ] hath everlasting life."[16] Under the heading "Forgiveness of Sins," the booklet declares that "Paul knew... that obedience to Christ's law was necessary for salvation."[17] However, the Bible says that "the law was given by Moses, but grace and truth came by Jesus Christ,"[18] that "by the deeds of the law there shall no flesh be justified in his sight,"[19] and that we are "justified freely by his grace through the redemption that is in Christ Jesus."[20]

How then is Mormonism the "true Christianity" that Joseph Smith and the modern Prophets of Mormonism claim? This is explained by the astonishing proposal that true Christianity is actually the successor to its pagan rivals, the mystery religions. Therefore, to restore Christianity, Joseph Smith went back to the mystery religions as they had been imperfectly preserved in Masonry. Having allegedly by revelation from God recovered the original purity of the Luciferian religion in the form of the true Masonry, Joseph Smith introduced it into Mormonism as his final act in the mission that the gods from Kolob had chosen him to fulfill: the restoration of Christianity to earth. This is consistent with the mainstream of occult tradition, as expressed by one of the world's leading occultists, Manly P. Hall:

> The ideals of early Christianity were based upon the high moral standards of the pagan Mysteries, and the first Christians who met under the city of Rome used as their places of worship the subterranean temples of Mithras, from whose cult has been borrowed much of the sacerdotalism of the modern church.[21]

It was not to the words of Jesus or His apostles in the New Testament or the Hebrew prophets in the Old that Joseph Smith looked to find the truth, but to the mystery religions that have always been Christianity's pagan rivals. In the process of restoring the true Masonry and "true Christianity," Smith "restored" the Bible also, rewriting it in an attempt to bring it into agreement with Mormonism. Published today by the Reorganized Church of Latter-day Saints, even Smith's "inspired version" contradicts his "restoration" theories and doctrines. Debate continues among Mormons concerning the question of whether Smith actually finished this "God-given" monumental task. Many wonder why any one of the "living Prophets" have neither given a definite answer to that question nor finished the work himself.

We are not suggesting that the average Mormon knowingly follows Lucifer or would willingly worship him. Only Masons of the very highest degrees are aware of the true nature of their religion, and even they are convinced that Lucifer is God and not Satan, or they wouldn't follow him. Although it comes from Masonry, Mormonism is even less open about its Luciferian nature. Even the highest levels of Mormon initiates would sincerely deny that theirs is a Luciferian religion. However, they have no adequate explanation for the fact that Lucifer defies their "god" and dominates the Temple rituals, all the while giving true LDS doctrinal instructions.

The Great Difference

In the name of true Christianity, Joseph Smith restored the pagan mysteries in Masonic form. It was necessary for Satan to establish his rival religion under the guise of Christianity, thereby convincing millions that his lie is really the truth. Mormonism teaches that "the Devil told the truth,"[22] and denies that Adam and Eve sinned when they disobeyed God, proposing instead that "Adam fell in the right direction . . . toward Godhood."[23]

Lucifer's promise of godhood to Eve through the Serpent was to be realized by her initiation into secret knowledge of good and evil and by her demonstration of personal worthiness through the practice of good and rejection of evil. Masons embrace Lucifer's religion of doing good in order to reach the Celestial Lodge above. In like manner, Mormons accept Lucifer's religion of self-effort and personal worthiness. They are taught that the simple gospel in the New Testament (that "Christ died for our sins" and "whosoever believeth in him . . . hath everlasting life" as a free gift from God),[24] is a twisted perversion of what the Bible originally said.[25]

Mormons protest that they believe in salvation by grace, but in Mormonism "grace" is only for those who keep all the commandments and prove themselves worthy. In the Bible, however, grace is for the unworthy, for if we deserved salvation it wouldn't be grace. This concept of forgiveness of sin by grace is found only in biblical Christianity, and is opposed by all its pagan rivals.

The great difference between biblical Christianity and all rival religions is, of course, Jesus Christ. All of the world's great religious leaders, whether Buddha, Mohammed, Confucius, Zoroaster, or whoever, left codes of conduct that they themselves could not live up to, which only condemn both them and their followers, and for the violation of which there is no forgiveness. In contrast, the Bible asserts that Jesus Christ died for our sins and rose to life again, and on that basis God offers to pardon all who will receive Christ as their Lord and Savior. Because it provides forgiveness of sins, Christianity embraces the lowliest and even the most wicked, if they truly repent and receive Jesus Christ. We are forgiven and receive eternal life not by becoming "worthy," but by admitting that we are unworthy sinners and receiving everything solely by God's grace.

This free gift of eternal life by grace to those absolutely unworthy of it is precisely what distinguishes Christianity from all rival religions; and it is this that the mystery religions and their modern successors complain about. It is from them that Masonry and Mormonism inherited their emphasis upon personal worthiness. One had to be "worthy" to be initiated into the mysteries, just as one must be "worthy" to enter either the Mormon Temple or a Masonic Lodge. Occultists therefore complain bitterly that Christianity embraces the unworthy.

Initiates of the Mysteries

The close relationship that Masonry and Mormonism bear to the pagan mystery religions is more than clear. It would be absurd to write this off as coincidence. The following specific elements are held in common: 1) There are "mysteries" involved; 2) these are passed on to only a select few; 3) to receive these mysteries one must be personally worthy, as defined, determined, and solely judged by the leaders; 4) a process of initiation is required; 5) the initiation involves secret rituals; 6) this takes place only in certain sanctuaries closed to outsiders, which are usually called Temples; 7) in the process, the initiates are sworn to secrecy; and 8) the penalty for revealing this secret gnosis (knowledge) to the uninitiated is death. Manly P. Hall explains the ancient traditions:

> In all cities of the ancient world were temples... [and] seclusive philosophic and religious schools. The more important of these groups were known as the *Mysteries.*
>
> Many of the great minds of antiquity were initiated into these secret fraternities by strange and mysterious rites, some of which were extremely cruel....
>
> After being admitted, the initiates were instructed in the secret wisdom which had been preserved for ages....
>
> Much of the ritualism of Freemasonry is based on the trials to which candidates were subjected by the ancient hierophants before the keys of wisdom were entrusted to them....

The Mysteries were organized for the purpose of assisting the struggling human creature to reawaken the spiritual powers which . . . lay asleep within his soul. In other words, man was offered a way by which he could regain his lost estate.[26]

Anyone who has been initiated into the higher levels of Joseph Smith's "restored" gospel will immediately recognize that all eight elements outlined above are involved in the most sacred (secret) parts of Mormonism. That these were all introduced into the Mormon Church after Joseph Smith was initiated into the secrets of Masonry cannot be denied, and is prima facie evidence against Smith's claim of inspiration from God. True to the occult tradition behind these alleged revelations, Joseph Smith carried into Mormonism the unspeakably horrible death penalties that he had sworn in Masonry and which it had inherited from the pagan mysteries.

The cloak of secrecy and the pledge to forfeit one's life for revealing these mysteries can hardly be called Christian. This is paganism in its rawest and most gruesome form. Yet this is at the heart of the most sacred (secret) part of Mormonism which also shares the pagan goal of "recovering one's rightful place among the gods." Rather than admitting the truth, however, Mormons persist in denying that there is anything secret in their religion.

Sacred or Secret?

When asked what could be so secret that visitors aren't even allowed to look inside a Mormon Temple once it has been dedicated, the tour guides at Temple Square will reply sincerely that there is nothing secret about what goes on in the Temple, only sacred. Since the most essential elements of their religion are performed in a secrecy so dark that it is maintained by death oaths, Mormons are continually trying to excuse the secrecy as a necessity created by the sacredness of these rituals. The official LDS pamphlet *The Purpose of The Temple*, which is a reprint of remarks by President David O. McKay at the September 11, 1955, dedication of the Mormon Temple in Berne, Switzerland, explains defensively: "Temples are built for the performance of sacred ordinances—not secret, but sacred."

The implication that Mormons are always laboring to convey is that anything sacred must be kept secret. This would presumably excuse the death oath of secrecy imposed upon Temple Mormons as a legitimate necessity for preserving the sacredness of the ceremonies performed inside Mormon

Temples. However, there is neither biblical nor logical support for this. There is not one example in the Bible (or the Book of Mormon, for that matter) of any ritual, ceremony, or act of worship that was practiced in secret—much less an example of an oath forfeiting one's life for revealing something sacred.

It is true that only certain members of the Aaronic priesthood were allowed inside the Temple sanctuary, and that no one but the high priest himself could go into the Holy of Holies. However, the Bible explains that it was only because Christ had not yet died for our sins upon the cross that the High Priest had to enter alone behind the veil, symbolizing the entrance that Christ would make as our Forerunner into heaven itself.[27] None of the priests involved in the main sanctuary, nor the High Priest who went alone into the Holy of Holies, ever swore oaths promising not to reveal what went on inside the Temple. In all that was most sacred to Israel—and surely it was at least as sacred as what takes place in Mormon Temples today—there was *nothing* that was not to be known and discussed openly and freely for all. Yet those who participate in Mormonism's "sacred" Temple rituals must swear to have their throats slit from ear to ear, tongues torn out, and hearts and vitals ripped from their bodies should they tell anyone what goes on in these alleged houses of the Lord! At least they did that until recently when the Mormon "God" changed his mind again.

Did Jesus Found a Secret Society?

Secrecy is contrary to Christianity. Jesus did not found a secret society. When falsely accused of many things before the Sanhedrin, and when the high priest demanded to know His doctrine, Christ specifically stated: "I spoke openly to the world; I always taught in the synagogue and in the temple where the Jews always resort, and *in secret have I said nothing.*"[28] Moreover, He warned His disciples against secret doctrines and practices with these words: "For nothing is secret that shall not be made manifest.... Therefore whatever you have spoken in darkness shall be heard in the light, and that which you have spoken in the ear in closets shall be proclaimed upon the housetops."[29] The Bible declares that the "hidden things" are to be reproved and brought to light,[30] and that anything done in secret will receive special attention in the judgment.[31] As for secret revelations beyond those given in Scripture, the Bible clearly rejects this idea by repeated affirmations of its sufficiency and completeness. For example:

All Scripture is given by inspiration of God, and is profitable for doctrine, for reproof, for correction, for instruction in righteousness, that the man of God may be perfect [mature, complete, lacking nothing], thoroughly furnished unto all good works.[32]

According as his divine power hath given unto us all things that pertain unto life and godliness, through the knowledge of him that hath called us to glory and virtue. . . .[33]

If any man shall add unto these things, God shall add unto him the plagues that are written in this book.[34]

Secret Doctrines and Secret Societies

The idea of a secret doctrine known only to an enlightened elite and protected by death oaths of secrecy was always a key element in the pagan mysteries, and remains so among those secret societies descended from them. This is also an integral part of the occult, which means literally "hidden."

Mormonism is but another descendant or offshoot of the pagan mysteries in modern form that seeks to hide its true anti-Christian nature beneath the camouflage of professed Christianity and biblical terminology. We will see later that Mormonism has a secret ambition of taking over the world, which is also consistent with the role that secret societies have traditionally played. James H. Billington, who taught history for 17 years at Harvard and Princeton and has for the past ten years been director of the Woodrow Wilson International Center for Scholars in Washington, D.C., has pointed this out in his definitive study of the modern revolutionary movement from the late eighteenth to early twentieth centuries.

The plain fact is that by the mid-1810s there were not just one or two but scores of secret revolutionary organizations throughout Europe—extending even into Latin America and the Middle East. These groups, although largely unconnected, internationalized the modern revolutionary tradition. . . .

In what follows I shall attempt to show that the modern revolutionary tradition as it came to be internationalized under Napoleon and the Restoration grew out of occult Freemasonry. . . .

The [Masonic] rituals leading to each new level of membership were not, as is sometimes suggested, childish initiations. They were awesome rites of passage into new types of association, promising access to higher truths of Nature once the blindfold was removed in the inner room of the lodge.

In the Masonic milieu, normally conservative people could seriously entertain the possibility of Utopia. . . .

In the early days of the revolution, Masonry provided much of the key symbolism and ritual . . . [and] Masonry was deliberately used by revolutionaries in the early nineteenth century as a model and a recruiting ground for their first conspiratorial experiments in political organization.[35]

The Necessity and Tragedy of Secrecy

It will become increasingly clear how the revolutionary Mormon Church and its founder, Joseph Smith (who grew up in this "Masonic milieu" and period of awakening revolutionary consciousness), fit into this entire pattern which Billington rightly calls "romantic occultism,"[36] the common force shaping occult groups into secret societies determined to bring about a Utopian order upon earth. It is no coincidence that the most sacred and important doctrines and practices in Mormonism are cloaked in secrecy. They cannot be found in Mormon scriptures, much less in the Bible. There is nothing about the Mormon Priesthoods in the Book of Mormon, nor is there anything about the secret Mormon Temple ceremonies and death oaths in any of the standard works of the Church. Those who regularly participate in these secret ceremonies are forbidden to discuss them outside the Temple. Even husbands and wives, under penalty of death, cannot speak of these most "sacred" things together.

This extreme secrecy is required because pagan rituals are performed inside Mormon Temples that The Brethren desperately want to keep from the outside world, and even from those Mormons who haven't yet qualified to enter the Temple. The necessity for this becomes clear in talking with those who have undergone these shamanic initiations. Many express the shock and revulsion they experienced when suddenly faced with what actually transpires inside a Mormon Temple. Had they known what was involved ahead of time, most would never have entered the Temple to participate. The fact that they were not given the information in advance (which would have made it possible for them to exercise a free choice in the matter) creates resentment among many Mormons, who never return to the Temple for this reason.

The secrecy surrounding the very heart of Mormonism prevents the truth from being told by the missionaries to prospective converts. One is called upon to embrace Mormonism as the "true Christianity restored" without being told the most sacred (secret) parts of what he is being asked to commit himself to. Thus the very presentation of Mormonism by the missionaries is dishonest in the extreme. Converts are persuaded to join the Church of Jesus Christ of Latter-day Saints as the "only true Church" and to embrace Mormonism without knowing its darkest secrets. It is our conviction that these secrets ought to be exposed, so that those who truly want to be initiated into Mormonism will at least know what they are being led into, and that others who might unwittingly fall victim will be warned in advance.

Changes to the Pure and Unchangeable Rituals

To a true Mormon believer, there is no more sacred place on earth than an LDS Temple, and there is nothing in the world more sacred than the rituals performed within those Temples. A Mormon's eternal journey is tied to the Temple, for celestial exaltation and godhood can only be attained by the mysterious procedures, signs, tokens, and secret handshakes learned therein.

Since Mormonism is based on the premise that evil days and evil leaders fell upon the true church of Christ's time, its restoration of the alleged original truths and the purity of the restored gospel is the cornerstone of faith. Essential to this restoration were the precise Temple rituals Smith initiated. Imagine then that much of the ritual which had been restored as essential to Mormonism's eternal goals was abandoned or altered. Imagine further that the changes made—the parts of the ritual now expunged or modified—are the very same parts of the ritual that books like *The God Makers* and films like *The God Makers* and *The Temple of The God Makers* exposed as pagan and satanic. Impossible? That is exactly what has happened!

In the 1993 Harvest House book *The God Makers II*, by Caryl Matrisciana and Ed Decker (pages 80-83), the authors reported on these changes, using detailed information which Chuck Sackett revealed in his April 1990 report. The news received wide circulation when it was duplicated in full in the September 1990 edition of *The Evangel*, a monthly newspaper produced by the ministry of John L. Smith, Utah Missions, Inc., in Marlow, Oklahoma. (The report was later carried in the Saints Alive newsletter.)

The Sackett report detailed a number of significant changes, and with his permission we will quote his description of them at length:

1. The execution of the penalties have been removed from the Priesthood Signs. No longer will every initiate be required to perform the three morbid gestures associated with having their lives taken if they reveal any of the temple secrets. These gestures were:

   A. Running the right thumb across the throat from left ear to right ear, signifying having one's throat slit from ear to ear.

   B. Drawing the right hand across the chest from left breast to right breast, signifying having one's chest ripped open and one's heart torn out.

   C. Running the right thumb across the abdomen, signifying having one's body cut asunder and one's vitals and bowels gush out.

   What a relief this will be to thousands of civilized and sensitive Mormons who have been offended by this barbaric atrocity with each temple visit, and also to those who decline to attend the temple because of this highly offensive [symbology]!

2. The most awesome spectacle of the entire series of temple rituals is gone! *The Sign of the Second Token of the Melchizedek Priesthood, the Patriarchal Grip, or Sure Sign of the Nail* has been eliminated. No longer will temple initiates be required to chant in unison the infamous *"Pay Lay Ale, Pay Lay Ale, Pay Lay Ale"* as they raise and lower their arms three times in the universal gesture of obeisance. No longer will thinking Mormons travel home wondering, as we did so often, what does *"Pay Lay Ale"* really mean? A number of years ago the Sacketts showed that the words were a quick step-to-the-side from words in Hebrew that mimic, in its harshest translation, *"O Marvelous Lucifer."*

3. The Masonically inspired *Five Points of Fellowship* through the temple veil has been eliminated. No longer will temple initiates be required to embrace "the Lord" through the veil in this mystical, highly occult configuration while they whisper in his ear the *Name of the Second Token of the Melchizedek Priesthood, the Patriarchal Grip, or Sure Sign of the Nail.*

The embrace is out, but it is likely that the incantation associated with it is still in. Apparently initiates will still be required to repeat back to "the Lord" through the veil: *"Health in the navel, marrow in the bones, strength in the loins and in the sinews. Power in the Priesthood be upon me and upon all my posterity, through all generations of time and throughout all eternity."*

4. Lucifer's hireling lackey, the Christian minister, is out. No longer will initiates watch the devil hire a Christian pastor (representing all Christian clergymen) to teach his satanic doctrines to Adam. No longer will they watch him mock and ridicule the most basic doctrines of Christianity. No longer will they watch as this Christian hireling abandons his faith and teachings and changes altars to join Adam and Eve in the Mormon Priesthood program of works and rituals.

   The liturgical significance of this change is profound. It is through the initiates' personal identification with Adam or Eve, as they renounce and deny the basic tenets of Christianity, that the purging of all remnants of Christian commitment in the initiates is accomplished. This crucial act in the Mormon conversion process would seem to have been eliminated! What will be substituted to accomplish this vital function spiritually bonding the initiates to LDS Priesthood power?

5. Women will no longer be required to veil their faces during the prayer in the Endowment prayer circle. However, they will still wear the veil as their regular head covering. This was a vital symbol of the subservience of women in the Priesthood and the dominance of the man in all aspects of Mormonism. The veil is to be lifted only by her worthy resurrected husband in his process of resurrecting her.

6. Women (single and married) will no longer be required to swear an oath and covenant of obedience to their husband. This change may have the most radical effect on Mormonism of all! The oppressive stigma of female singleness will no longer be officially imposed by the Mormon god in the temple. Single women will be somewhat relieved of the extreme pressure to marry. The wife will no longer be reminded with each temple visit that her only channel to her god is through her husband and that his faithfulness determines her eternity. Each Mormon husband can no longer rely on his wife (or wives) to constantly prod and motivate him to do his duty to the church based upon her total dependence upon him for her eternal exaltation. What will become of the church as a result

of the change? How many worthy Priesthood leaders will become indifferent or lazy due to this major doctrinal change? We will have to watch and discern the inevitable decline in vigor taking place.

11

LYING PROPHETS
AND APOSTLES

The history of Mormonism is filled with plottings, intrigues, murders, robberies, and sex scandals involving its Prophets and Apostles. The early Mormons were urged by their founding Prophet to put everything down in daily journals or diaries; enough evidence was recorded to put Joseph Smith, Brigham Young, and many of the other Mormon Apostles and Prophets in prison. The Mormon Church has carefully locked the incriminating documents away in those secret files in Salt Lake City—but much of the scandal has leaked out.

Mormons are obsessed with secrecy, which plays a major part in their religion. They even wear secret underwear with occult Masonic markings that allegedly give it magic protective powers. The pathway to godhood involves secret occult practices that are performed in Mormon Temples. One Temple secret more than any other obsessed Mormon leaders for the first 70 years of the Church's history. The Brethren lied to deny it was practiced, then lied to establish it as the most sacred doctrine of the Church, then lied again to abandon it. The astonishing doctrine is part of a cover-up that has devastating consequences for every Mormon today.

Eternal Marriage in the Temple

To commemorate the twenty-fifth anniversary of the Los Angeles Temple (built in 1956) on March 21, 1981, "In 72 continuous sessions, stretching over 36 hours, more than 12,000 temple patrons completed 15,439 endowments [for the dead]. Approximately 1,000 patrons were in the temple each hour."[1] Temple president Elder Robert L. Simpson remarked, "It [the Los

Angeles Temple] is a holy temple wherein Church members are able to open the gates of life eternal for millions of their beloved forebears."[2]

Thus far in Mormon Temples around the world more than 100 million marriages and baptisms by proxy have been performed for dead ancestors. However, Thomas E. Daniels, public affairs director at the huge Mormon Genealogical Library in Salt Lake City, estimates that, with 52 million people dying annually, the Temple "ordinance work" is "falling behind by 95% each year."[3] That must be discouraging to sincere Mormons who really believe they are the saviors of the world. More discouraging is the belief that one's genealogy must be traced all the way back to Adam, and Temple ceremonies performed for all of these ancestors—an obviously hopeless task.

It all begins with the first step: husband and wife being married for eternity and their children "sealed" to them for eternity in the Temple. There is no doctrine more central to Mormonism today nor more firmly held than that of eternal or celestial marriage, which must be performed for the living and the dead. This doctrine is causing thousands of divorces among Mormons, as we have already explained. Milton R. Hunter has written: "Marriage [in the Temple] is not only a righteous institution, but obedience to this law is absolutely necessary in order to obtain the highest exaltation in the Kingdom of God."[4] Joseph Fielding Smith explained that "eternal life" means to produce life eternally by bearing children in the hereafter,[5] and that Celestial Marriage is a necessity if one is to become a "god":

> If you want salvation in the fullest, that is exaltation ... you have got to go into the Temple of the Lord and receive these holy ordinances, which belong to that house, which cannot be had elsewhere ... and thereafter keep all the commandments.[6]

> Civil marriage makes servants in eternity... Celestial Marriage makes Gods in eternity.[7]

There is not one verse in either the Bible or the Book of Mormon that teaches celestial marriage for eternity involving secret or even sacred rituals in a Temple, much less that says it is essential for eternal life. Nor was this teaching part of early Mormonism. In the first edition (1835) of *Doctrine and Covenants* (considered by Mormons to be inspired Scripture on an even higher level than the Bible), Section 101 honored "all legal contracts of marriage" and even stated that "all marriages in this Church ... should be solemnized in a public meeting. . . ." Marriages involving secret rituals in a Temple were not even dreamed of until Joseph Smith produced a startling "revelation" at Nauvoo, Illinois, on July 12, 1843, concerning a "new and everlasting covenant" that shook the Mormons and severely tested their loyalty to their leader. It became Section 132 in *Doctrine and Covenants*. Verifying the great importance of this particular "revelation," Joseph Fielding Smith declared:

> So if you want to enter into exaltation . . . then you have got to abide in his law. . . all that pertains to the new and everlasting covenant.[8]

The New and Everlasting Covenant

The "new and everlasting covenant" made polygamy an essential part of celestial marriage and a requirement for godhood. Canonized in 1876 and still applicable Mormon scripture today, Section 132 warns that all who refuse to practice polygamy are "damned" and will be physically "destroyed."

Most people have the vague notion that the early Mormons got involved in polygamy because there were not enough men to go around. In fact, there were more men than women. Joseph F. Smith, sixth Mormon President, stated: "Some people have supposed that the doctrine of plural marriage was a sort of superfluity, or non-essential to the salvation of mankind."[9] He went on to explain that the Mormon goal of godhood cannot be reached without the practice of polygamy. The *Latter-day Saints' Millennial Star* declared:

> And we . . . are believers in . . . plural marriage or polygamy. . . as a principle revealed by God, underlying our every hope of eternal salvation . . . a vital principle of our religion.[10]

Strangely enough, on October 1, 1842, the Mormon publication *Times and Seasons* (vol. 3, pp. 939-40) had stated just the opposite:

> We are charged with advocating a plurality of wives. . . . Now this is as false as the many other ridiculous charges which are brought against us. No sect has a greater reverence for the laws of matrimony. . . and we do what others do not, practice what we preach.

It was a blatant lie, but protested very self-righteously and repeatedly by Mormon leaders. The *Latter-day Saints' Millennial Star* was also promoting the same deliberate deception, including the assurance that polygamy would *never* be allowed among the Latter-day Saints. The contradictions would be amusing were they not so damning. What a contrast between the above statement from the *Millennial Star* calling polygamy "a vital principle of our religion" and the following cover-up from the *Star* that came earlier (vol. 3, p. 74):

> But, for the information of those who may be assailed by those foolish tales about two wives, we would say that no such principle ever existed among the Latter-day Saints, and *never will.*

> This is well known to all who are acquainted with our books and actions, the Book of Mormon, Doctrine and Covenants; and also all our periodicals are very strict on that subject, indeed far more so than the Bible.

It was true indeed that the early Mormon scriptures condemned polygamy in very clear terms, but equally true that it was being practiced secretly in violation of the scriptures. The consistent record of lies and deception leaves us with no choice but to conclude that leaders in the Mormon Church, then and now, have a contempt for truth and honesty when it comes to defending their "Prophet" and their religion.

Something Rotten in Mormondom

One of the best examples of typical Mormon deceit and intrigue is found in the background of Section 132 of *Doctrine and Covenants*. Reading this section, one would never suspect that this 1843 "revelation" wasn't included in *Doctrine and Covenants* for 33 years until 1876. Moreover, whereas editions through 1890 introduced this "revelation" as "*given* through Joseph the Seer July 12, 1843," subsequent editions were changed to read "*recorded* July 12, 1843." The intention is to imply that the actual receiving of the "revelation" by the "Prophet" came earlier. Mormon historian B.H. Roberts wrote that the "date in the heading of the Revelation on the Eternity of the Marriage Covenant, including Plurality of Wives, notes the time at which the Revelation was committed to writing, not the time at which the principles set forth in the revelation were first made known to the Prophet."[11]

We now know that this was an attempt to cover for Joseph Smith in case the suppressed truth was discovered that he had been practicing polygamy for years before 1843. Joseph Fielding Smith, who later became the tenth

Mormon President, made the following statement to J.W.A. Bailey while he was Church historian in a letter dated September 5, 1935:

> The exact date I cannot give you when this principle of plural marriage was first revealed to Joseph Smith, but I do know that there was a revelation given in July 1831, in the presence of Oliver Cowdery, W.W. Phelps and others in Missouri, in which the Lord made this principle known through the Prophet Joseph Smith.
>
> Whether the revelation as it appears in the Doctrine and Covenants was first given July 12, 1843, or earlier, I care not.
>
> It is a fact nevertheless, that this principle was revealed at an earlier date.[12]

The dishonest attempt to establish an earlier date for the polygamy "revelation" creates more problems than it solves, because of repeated denials by Joseph Smith and other Mormon leaders that the polygamy commanded by the 1843 "revelation" was practiced among the Mormons prior to or even after that time. Consider the following out of the many examples that could be given, published in the *Latter-day Saints' Millennial Star* of August 1, 1842. It was in response to the public accusations of one Martha Brotherton that Brigham Young had tried to seduce her to "marry" him secretly, with the assurance that Joseph Smith had a "revelation" from God authorizing polygamy:

> I do hereby testify that the affidavit of Miss Martha Brotherton that is going the rounds in the political and religious papers, is a base falsehood, with regard to any private intercourse or unlawful conduct or conversation with me.
>
> (signed) Brigham Young
Sworn to and subscribed before me
this 27th day of August, A.D. 1843.
(signed) E. Robinson, J.P.
(Justice of the Peace)

Either Brigham was solemnly swearing to a deliberate lie, or a host of Mormon leaders have lied in saying that their Prophet had received the polygamy "revelation" as early as 1831, 11 years before Miss Brotherton testified that Brigham Young had told her there was such a "revelation." In one of his sermons later from Salt Lake City, Brigham Young denounced

monogamy as "a source of prostitution and whoredom"[13] "commenced by
the founders of the Roman empire,"[14] praised polygamy as "the only popular
religion in heaven,"[15] and declared that "the Lord's servants have *always*
practiced" polygamy.[16] Yet he denounced Martha Brotherton for saying basically the same thing. In another sermon, this second President of the Mormon Church, its "Prophet, Seer and Revelator," declared bravely from the
safe haven of the Mormon-controlled Utah Territory:

> If I had forty wives in the United States, they did not know it, and
> could not substantiate it. . . .
>
> I live above the law, and so do this people.[17]

Brigham Young not only lived above the civil laws that declared polygamy to be a crime, but he lived above the laws of God that warn us, "Thou
shalt not bear false witness."[18] His comment that "they did not know it" only
verifies that he and the other Mormon leaders were practicing polygamy in
secret; and his boast that they "could not substantiate it" confirms the fact
that he and other Mormon leaders were lying in order to cover their crimes.
To cover his own deception, Brigham Young called Martha Brotherton a liar
and a mean harlot. If she was, one can only wonder why the Mormon Endowment House Records show that Brigham Young, after Martha Brotherton's
death, "sealed" her to himself "for eternity" in a "proxy marriage" on August
1, 1870.

There is more than ample evidence to prove that Joseph Smith, Brigham
Young, and many other early Mormon leaders were liars, cheats, adulterers,
and seducers—men without regard for the rights and interests of others,
claiming "divine revelation" to justify their crimes against humanity. The
secrecy itself speaks loudly. If Joseph Smith had a genuine revelation from
God, then why not stand up for it openly? Even a superficial inquiry into the
alleged 1843 "revelation" indicates that there was something very rotten in
Mormondom. Probing deeper, one finds a tangled web of intrigue and deception. In the process of unraveling that, the very fabric of Mormondom's
boasted foundation of "Prophets" and "Apostles" is pulled to pieces.

Lying Prophets and Apostles

The sad truth is that Mormon Church officials past and present have
known that Joseph Smith, Brigham Young, and other Mormon leaders of that

time were already deeply involved in polygamy long before 1843, and therefore by Mormon scriptures should have been excommunicated. The Church tried to establish an earlier date for the "revelation" to protect its founding "Prophets" and "Apostles." The Brethren today continue the cover-up.

What about the 1831 "revelation" that Joseph Fielding Smith referred to? Wouldn't that solve the problem? If so, the Mormon Church would produce it, not just hint at it. Dr. Hyrum Andrus of Brigham Young University let slip the fact that the 1831 "revelation" is safe and secure in the vault of the LDS Church Historical Department, and that in substance it said "that *in due time* the brethren would be required to take plural wives."[19] So the lies and cover-up persist.

Incredibly, right up to the time of his death in 1844, Joseph Smith made repeated public and private denials that he was a polygamist or had ever practiced the very polygamy which the 1843 "revelation" required and in fact declared that Smith had already been practicing for some time. The official Mormon *History of the Church* records that on May 26, 1844 (nearly one year after the polygamy "revelation"), Joseph Smith (who had scores of wives by that time) solemnly declared in response to a charge that he had "six or seven":

> What a thing it is for a man to be accused of committing adultery, and having seven wives, when I can only find one.
>
> I am the same man, and as innocent as I was fourteen years ago; and I can prove them all perjurers.[20]

In fact, Joseph Smith was the perjurer. Only false prophets lie. In his 1843 (or earlier?) "revelation," "the Lord" had said that Joseph had already received plural wives and commanded his first wife, Emma, to accept them or be "damned." There is no escaping the conclusion that Joseph Smith was a fraud.

A Pattern of Cold, Calculated Deceit

The indisputable fact is that, long before and long after the 1843 "revelation," polygamy was being practiced in secret by Mormon leaders, who compounded their sin by public denials that were just plain lies. At the time of his self-righteous denial and empty threat that he could "prove" his accusers "all perjurers," Joseph Smith had at least four and probably seven *times* the seven wives he was accused of having! If he lied about this issue, what else would he lie about? How could anyone accept anything he said?

Joseph F. Smith, sixth Mormon President, tried to call these lies "seeming denials." His statement betrays the mentality that persists among Mormons even today which allows them to deny the obvious with an apparently good conscience: "Joseph Smith . . . and his brother Hyrum did practice the doctrine [of polygamy] in their lifetime, and until their death, notwithstanding their seeming denials in the *Times and Seasons*."[21] The brazen hypocrisy and deceit of Mormon Presidents and Apostles can be seen in the following "seeming denial," published in *Times and Seasons*. We now know beyond the shadow of a doubt that they were lying, and in the process making a scapegoat out of an expendable Mormon Elder:

THURSDAY, FEBRUARY 1 1844

NOTICE

As we have lately been credibly informed, that an Elder of the Church of Jesus Christ of Latter-day Saints, by the name of Hiram Brown, has been preaching polygamy, and other false and corrupt doctrines, in the county of Lapeer, state of Michigan.

This is to notify him and the Church in general, that he has been cut off from the church, for his iniquity; and he is further notified to appear at the Special Conference on the 6th of April next, to make answer to these charges.

(signed) Joseph Smith
(signed) Hyrum Smith
Presidents of said Church

Joseph Smith's unconscionable contempt for truth is staggering. The polygamy that was commanded by "the Lord" in the 1843 "revelation" and which Joseph Smith and other Mormon leaders had been secretly practicing for years is denounced by the "Prophet" as a "false and corrupt" doctrine when spoken of in public! In a hypocritical refrain that is as common among Mormons today as it was then, Mormon Apostle John A. Widtsoe (apparently believing his own lie) has protested, "The Church ever operates in full light. There is no secrecy about its doctrine, aim or work."[22] In contrast, with refreshing honesty, Mormon writer William E. Berrett admits.

In 1840 the doctrine [of polygamy] was taught to a few leading brethren who, with the Prophet, secretly married additional wives in the following year. . . .

Only the secrecy surrounding its practice prevented a wholesale apostasy from the Church in 1844.[23]

The Plot Thickens

The 1843 "revelation" was intended to rescue Joseph Smith from a mounting wave of discontent caused by renewed charges of adultery. Too many people had heard about his secret and growing harem. Disillusionment and doubts that he was a Prophet were spreading. There was danger that the Church would rebel against its founder. Consequently, Joseph Smith came forth with a "revelation" that turned his vice into virtue. Predictably, "the Lord" from Kolob vindicated his "Prophet" by commanding everyone to practice polygamy, by damning those who refused, and by declaring that polygamy was absolutely essential for the coveted "godhood."

The situation had grown so serious that even some of the top leaders in the Church were becoming disillusioned and were defecting—among them men he couldn't afford to lose, such as Apostle Orson Pratt, a mathematics professor and one of the few educated men among the early Mormons. Joseph Smith had attempted to seduce Pratt's wife, Sarah, and when she had accused him in Pratt's presence Smith had lied, and Pratt was sure of it. This had shattered Pratt's world. Joseph Smith's diary of July 15, 1842, included: "It was reported early in the morning that Elder Orson Pratt was missing. I caused the Temple hands and the principal men of the city to make search for him."[24] So devastated that "his mind collapsed," and on the verge of suicide,[25] Pratt had been found "five miles below Nauvoo, in a state of frenzy, sitting on the bank of the Mississippi River."[26] Brigham Young's *Journal* for August 8, 1842, included this:

Assisted by Elders H.C. Kimball and Geo. A. Smith, I spent several days laboring with Elder Orson Pratt, whose mind became so darkened by the influence and statements of his wife, that he came out in rebellion against Joseph, refusing to believe his testimony or obey his counsel.

He said he would believe his wife in preference to the Prophet. Joseph told him if he did believe his wife and followed her suggestions, he would go to hell.[27]

The threats of damnation didn't convince Pratt, and he was "cut off from the Church" on August 20, 1842. The "revelation" of 1843 apparently restored his confidence in the "Prophet," and Pratt returned with his wife to the Mormon Church. Although Sarah stuck to her story to her dying day, Pratt became the "chief spokesman for the Church in defense of the principle of plural marriage."[28]

Some of the statements that Apostle Orson Pratt made on the subject of polygamy are very interesting indeed. If they were true when he made them, then they must still be true, which should give every Mormon today serious cause for concern:

> ... I have heard now and then ... a brother or sister say, "I am a Latter-day Saint, but I do not believe in polygamy." Oh, what an absurd expression! What an absurd idea!
>
> A person might as well say, "I am a follower of the Lord Jesus Christ, but I do not believe in him." One is as consistent as the other. ...
>
> I did hope there was more intelligence among the Latter-day Saints, and a greater understanding of principle than to suppose that anyone can be a member of the Church in good standing and yet reject polygamy.
>
> The Lord has said, that those who reject this principle reject their salvation, they shall be damned, saith the Lord. ...
>
> I want to prophecy that all men and women who oppose the revelation which God has given in relation to polygamy will find themselves in darkness; the Spirit of God will withdraw from them the very moment of their opposition to that principle, until they will finally go down to hell and be damned, if they do not repent. ...
>
> Oppose it ... and teach your children to do the same, and if you do not become as dark as midnight* there is no truth in Mormonism.[29]

---

* Joseph Smith taught that black or dark skin is a curse from God upon the descendants of Cain for not fighting valiantly against Satan in the preexistence. This is an apparent reference to a similar judgment upon those who don't fight valiantly for polygamy.

By Apostle Pratt's own words there must be "no truth in Mormonism," because no one yet who has opposed it has "become dark as midnight." This is typical of the most solemn pronouncements of Mormon Apostles and Prophets—time has proven them to be brash boasts and empty threats.

Secret Sin, Public Denial

When Pratt preached that sermon, polygamy was out in the open, which it never was during Joseph Smith's lifetime. There was in fact no public declaration of this "revelation" in 1843, and for *Doctrine and Covenants* to present it as such is quite typical for the Mormon Church, which suppresses and hides documents, lies, and distorts with no apparent conscience. The July 12, 1843, "revelation" was privately concocted by Joseph Smith at the suggestion of his brother Hyrum to be presented to Joseph's first wife, Emma, in order to justify to her the many additional wives he had taken. Emma wouldn't stand for it, and within two or three days she had persuaded Joseph to give her the "revelation" he had written, and she burned it.[30] That the alleged "revelation" was not pronounced publicly by Joseph Smith to the Mormon Church and accepted as scripture is confirmed by Joseph F. Smith:

> When the revelation was written, in 1843, it was for a special purpose, by the request of the Patriarch Hyrum Smith, and was not then designed to go forth to the Church or to the world.[31]

So polygamy was being practiced secretly and being lied about publicly. Unable to impress Emma with his alleged revelation from the Lord, Joseph tried to hint at it in a sermon to test the reaction of the Church. The members couldn't believe their ears. Was their Prophet admitting that the accusations of polygamy that had been made against him and which had been so often publicly denied were true after all? The official account states:

> . . . The Prophet goes up on the stand, and, after preaching about everything else he could think of in the world . . . makes a bare hint at the law of sealing [plural wives], and it produced such a tremendous excitement that, as soon as he had got his dinner half eaten, he had to go back to the stand and unpreach all that he had preached, and left the people to guess at the matter.[32]

Here then are the unpleasant facts. The divine and holy "revelation" set forth in Section 132 was suggested by Hyrum Smith as a way to persuade the

Prophet's wife, Emma, to go along with polygamy—not some grand announcement from heaven to the Church and the world. When it was presented to Emma, she rejected and burned it. Instead of being "destroyed," as the "revelation" warned would be her fate if she opposed it, she lived another 36 years—time enough to abandon her husband's Church and join the rival Reorganized Church of Jesus Christ of Latter-day Saints that repudiated polygamy and many other early Mormon doctrines. The "Prophet" who gave the "revelation" that promised great blessing to those who obeyed it was dead in less than a year, still never having openly presented this "most important and holy revelation" to his Church. Surely a genuine Prophet would have the courage to publicly proclaim a revelation from God.

Thirty-two years after Joseph Smith's death, Mormon leaders took Section 101 condemning polygamy out of *Doctrine and Covenants* and inserted Section 132 in its place, all without explanation and in a manner that would lead today's reader to assume this was the way it had been since the July 12, 1843, date of this "revelation." When questioned in court concerning the substitution of Section 132 for 101, Wilford Woodruff and Lorenzo Snow, fourth and fifth Presidents of the Mormon Church, testified on the witness stand that they did not know how or why or by whom it had been done.[33] Lorenzo Snow admitted that Joseph Smith had taken his sister as a "plural wife" before the July 12, 1843, revelation and that this had meant that he was guilty of adultery by the Mormon scriptures. Having admitted that, however, in response to the question, "What kind of a position did it put your sister and Joseph Smith in?" he defiantly said, "It put them in a first-rate, splendid condition for time and eternity!"

Mormon leaders considered the polygamy "revelation" to be "the most holy and important doctrine ever revealed to man upon earth."[34] It hardly builds confidence either in their morals or their judgment. The persistent duplicity of early Mormon Prophets and Apostles involved in the polygamy caper is almost beyond belief. Their conduct in this entire affair should give any reasonable person serious cause to question their sincerity and the truth of everything else they swear to, no matter how many "revelations" they claim in support of it.

12

ANOTHER
ANGEL STORY

If Joseph Smith were just an ordinary prophet, the question of whether he was an adulterer or a divinely inspired polygamist would not be so important. However, as the *founding* Prophet of Mormonism, *everything* rests upon him. He was the discoverer and "translator" of the Book of Mormon, which he declared to be "the keystone of our religion."[1] He also said, "Take away the Book of Mormon and the revelations, and where is our religion? We have none."[2] The credibility both of Joseph Smith as a Prophet and of the Book of Mormon itself depends upon the existence and identity of the "angel" (called both Moroni and Nephi) that led him to the gold plates, and of the "angel" (presumably the same one) that showed these plates to the Three Witnesses. If this was an "angel of God," then Mormonism ought to be believed. If it was an "angel of Satan" or Joseph's imagination or a deliberate lie, then it ought to be exposed as such and repudiated. For as Apostle Orson Pratt said:

> The Book of Mormon claims to be a divinely inspired record. . . . It professes to be revealed to the present generation for the salvation of all who will receive it, and for the overthrow and damnation of all nations who reject it.

> This book must be either true or false. If true, it is one of the most important messages ever sent from God. . . . If false, it is one of the most cunning, wicked, bold, deep-laid impositions ever palmed upon the world, calculated to deceive and ruin millions. . . .[3]

It is also claimed that the Mormon doctrine of plural wives is a divinely inspired revelation. Apostle Heber C. Kimball called it "one of the most holy principles that God ever revealed to man"[4]; the Mormon publication *Millennial Star* called it "a vital principle of our religion ... revealed by God underlying our every hope of eternal salvation ..."[5]; and Joseph F. Smith declared that "every man in this Church who has the ability to obey and practice it in righteousness and will not, shall be damned...."[6] The importance of polygamy can hardly be overstated. Apostle George Teasdale said, "I believe in plural marriage as a part of the gospel just as much as I believe in baptism by immersion for the remission of sins."[7] One would hardly think, then, that a revelation of such importance would have been given without the ministration of an "angel," as in the case of the Book of Mormon. This, in fact, is the claim. The polygamy "revelation" involves another angel story told by Joseph Smith, and one that for sheer drama exceeds the alleged angelic encounter that led him to the Book of Mormon. This was reported by Joseph F. Smith, sixth President of the Mormon Church, in a sermon:

> When this principle was revealed to the Prophet Joseph Smith, he very naturally shrank, in his feelings, from the responsibilities thereby imposed upon him....
>
> ... It was not until an angel of God, with a drawn sword, stood before him and commanded that he should enter into the practice of that principle, or he should be utterly destroyed [that he obeyed]....
>
> It need scarcely be said that the Prophet found no one any more willing to lead out in this matter in righteousness than he was himself.... None excelled or even matched the courage of the Prophet himself.[8]

A Two-Edged Sword

It was Joseph Smith's testimony that polygamy had been forced upon him by an angel at the point of a sword that convinced his followers to accept this "revelation" when nothing else would. The angel's sword, however, is a two-edged one. If the story is true, then no one dare reject polygamy any more than they dare reject the Book of Mormon. On the other hand, if polygamy is not a revelation from God, then the "angel" that forced it upon the "Prophet" was either from Satan, a hallucination, or the invention of a deliberate liar. Moreover, the true identity of the polygamy "angel" would say a great deal about the identity of the Book of Mormon "angel." It would not be likely that one could be from God and the other from Satan, for surely a man of God would know the difference.

This is clearly the logic behind the statement of Apostle George Teasdale: "I bear my solemn testimony that plural marriage is as true as any principle that has been revealed from the heavens [through Joseph Smith]...."[9] For if Joseph Smith lied or was deceived about this "revelation," then one could hardly have any confidence in his other "revelations." If polygamy is not from God, then neither is anything else in Mormonism, because it all rests upon the foundation of Joseph Smith. Recognizing this, Apostle Orson Pratt declared:

> If the doctrine of polygamy, as revealed to the Latter-day Saints, is not true, I would not give a fig for all your other revelations that came through Joseph Smith the Prophet; I would renounce the whole of them....[10]

The polygamy issue is extremely important in evaluating Mormonism, because we have so much information about it. No one else saw the angel Moroni when he allegedly met Joseph Smith annually for four years at the Hill Cumorah and finally gave him the gold plates. Three witnesses claimed that the "angel" showed the plates to them "in a vision," but we have already seen that this story and the witnesses themselves have some serious built-in problems. With polygamy, however, we have the record of *many* witnesses as well as far more written about it not only by Joseph Smith but by many others as well. Consequently this particular "revelation" is ideal for testing the credibility of the "Prophet" and the "restored gospel" of Mormonism that rests in its entirety upon him.

Modus Operandi of the Polygamist Prophet

We have seen that the evidence indicates that the polygamy "revelation" was not intended, at least when Joseph Smith first wrote it down on July 12, 1843, for either the Church or the world. Instead, it was designed for an individual: Joseph Smith's wife, Emma. That is not only the way it was reported in Joseph Smith's own official *History of the Church* and *Journal of Discourses*, but this is consistent with an established behavior pattern. Joseph Smith produced numerous "revelations" on this subject, but always in private and generally to convince some woman he coveted, whether single or married, that the Lord had given her to him. If she was convinced, then they were married in a secret ceremony, and thereafter clandestine trysts were arranged. Sarah Ann Whitney is one example of many. According to Orson F. Whitney, her nephew, she was married to Joseph Smith almost one year prior to the 1843 "revelation":

> This girl was but seventeen years of age, but she had implicit faith in the [secret] doctrine of plural marriage.... The revelation commanding and consecrating this union is in existence, though it has never been published.
>
> It bears the date of July 27, 1842, and was given through the Prophet to the writer's grandfather, Newel K. Whitney, whose daughter Sarah, on that day, became the wedded wife of Joseph Smith for time and eternity.[11]

Although several did resist Joseph Smith's amorous advances, it was not easy for any Mormon woman to turn down an affair with a handsome "Prophet" when it was not only sanctified by "revelation" and commanded by the Lord, but great glory in the hereafter was the promised bait on the hook, and destruction here and damnation hereafter the solemnly pronounced penalty for refusal. How could Joseph carry on so many affairs? We get some insight from the following excepts of a letter* to Sarah's father, Bishop Newel K. Whitney, signed by Joseph Smith:

> ... All three of you [mother, father, and Sarah] can come and see me in the fore part of the night.... The only thing to be careful of, is to find out when Emma comes then you cannot be safe, but when she is not here, there is the most perfect safety....
>
> I think Emma wont come tonight if she dont dont fail to come tonight, I subscribe myself your obedient and affectionate, companion, and friend.

(signed) Joseph Smith

It was not easy for a busy "Prophet" leading a public life to do the duties of a husband to his growing number of wives, but Joseph was very resourceful. To better conceal the truth about his relationship with Sarah, the

---

* A photograph of this letter was discovered by Michael Marquardt in the George Albert Smith Collection at the University of Utah Library.

"Prophet" arranged for and performed a sham "marriage" between her and a very pliable and obedient Mormon named Joseph C. Kingsbury. That the "Prophet" would sign this certificate—"I hereby certify that I have upon this the 29th day of April 1843, joined together in Marriage Joseph C. Kingsbury and Sarah Ann Whitney, in the city of Nauvoo, Illinois"—is further astonishing evidence of his utter disregard for truth and propriety. That he molded his pliable victims to his lustful will by "revelations" promising great reward in heaven is also evident from the following statement by the innocent dupe Kingsbury:

> ... On 29th of April 1843 I according to President Joseph Smith conseil & others agreed to Stand by Sarah Ann Whitney as supposed to be her husband & had a prete[n]ded marriage for the purpose of Bringing about the purposes of God in these last days as spoken by the mouth of the Prophets Isiah Jeremiah Ezekiel and also Joseph Smith, & Sarah Ann Should Recd a Great Glory Honor, & eternal lives and I also S[h]ould Recd a Great Glory, Honor & eternal lives to the full desire of my heart in having my Companion Caroline in the first Resurrection to claim her & no one have power to take her from me & we both shall be Crowned & enthroned together in the Celestial Kingdom of God....[12]

One has to give Joseph Smith the credit he deserves: He had come a long way from the young glass-looker who duped greedy men into paying him for telling them where "treasure" was buried on their land. Now he was a "Prophet" to thousands, who put him in the same class as Isaiah, Jeremiah, and Ezekiel and blindly believed almost anything he said. They would even commit adultery or make a mockery of marriage (Sarah and Kingsbury lived together for years as supposed husband and wife) so long as the "Prophet" assured them that it was "bringing about the purposes of God in these last days."

Reading the often-pitiful entries in the diaries of this period, one is stunned not only by Joseph Smith's apparently incurable passion for new sexual partners, but also by the astonishing charismatic power he wielded that allowed him to practice not only widespread and blatant adultery, but even to demand and receive the consent of the husbands whose wives he stole. Something of this incredible hypnotic influence is revealed in the following excerpt from a sermon delivered at the famous Mormon Tabernacle in Salt

Lake City on February 19, 1854, by Jedediah M. Grant, second counselor to Brigham Young:

> When the family organization was revealed from heaven—the patriarchal order of God—and Joseph began on the right and on the left to add to his family, what a quaking there was in Israel.

> Says one brother to another, "Joseph says all covenants are done away, and none are binding but the new covenants; now suppose Joseph should come and say he wanted your wife, what would you say to that? . . ."

> If such a man of God should come to me and say, "I want your gold and silver, or your wives," I should say, "Here they are, I wish I had more to give you, take all I have got!"[13]

Justifying the Prophet

Serious public accusations of adultery had first been leveled against Joseph Smith as far back as 1837 by Oliver Cowdery, one of the Three Witnesses to whom an angel had allegedly shown the "gold plates." Cowdery had accused Joseph of adultery with one Fannie Alger.[14] This charge had proved to be true. An unusually attractive young woman, Fannie had lived in Joseph Smith's home since 1835, and she and the Prophet had carried on a secret affair that Cowdery and Warren Parrish, Joseph Smith's private secretary, had tried in vain to persuade him to stop for the good of the Church. Fannie is included today in the official list of 27 of Joseph Smith's scores of wives in Church documents, and is described by Andrew Jensen, Assistant LDS Church Historian, as "one of the first plural wives sealed to the Prophet."[15] Justifying his beloved "Prophet's" adultery, John J. Stewart explains, apparently in all seriousness:

> Joseph as a servant of God was authorized to enter plural marriage, and it is not at all unlikely that he did so in the early or mid-1830s.

> Perhaps Nancy Johnson or Fanny Alger was his first "plural" wife, at Hiram or Kirtland, Ohio.[16]

Responding in character to Cowdery's charge, Joseph Smith brazenly lied. (Parrish lost his job for his trouble, and Cowdery was excommunicated.) Such would be the fate, or worse, of all who dared to accuse "the

Lord's anointed." In utter disregard for the laws of God and man (for he was, as Brigham Young said, "above the law"), Joseph continued his secret adulterous affairs with increasing numbers of Mormon women, justifying his apparently uncontrollable lust to the few insiders who discovered the truth (some of whom began to join him in practicing polygamy secretly) by stating that God had given him a "revelation" about polygamy, but it couldn't yet be revealed to the "Saints" for fear they would rebel. Nor did the "Prophet" ever openly reveal this most important of all doctrines during his entire lifetime.

The sordid truth has been fully documented and published by many researchers, including some Mormons. There is no doubt that for a number of years prior to presenting to Emma the alleged "revelation" of a "new and everlasting covenant" making polygamy mandatory for "exaltation," Joseph Smith had been engaging habitually in sexual intercourse with increasing numbers of women among his devoted followers. That number apparently grew to at least 84 or more "plural wives." During this time, both the Book of Mormon and *Doctrine and Covenants* (to say nothing of the Bible and civil laws of the land) clearly condemned what Joseph was doing as adultery. There were those close to him who pleaded with the "Prophet" to curb his insatiable appetite for women, but to no avail. As the "Prophet," he could do whatever he pleased, and call down the judgment of his "gods" from Kolob upon whoever stood in his way—and he often did.

The full story of Joseph Smith's scandalous depravity cannot be told here. It includes intrigue, deceit, hiding the shameful truth from his wife, Emma, for years, as well as seductions and attempted seductions. This involved not only single young women, but the wives of Church leaders, especially when the husbands were away on extended missions assigned to them by the "Prophet." Unbelievable but true, Joseph Smith finally demanded "by revelation" the wives of every one of the 12 Mormon Apostles.[17] That it was lust for one more body to add to his harem is clear from some of the accounts. For example, Vilate Kimball, first wife of Apostle Heber C. Kimball, pleaded to remain with her husband in spite of Joseph's demand that she be "consecrated" over to him according to a "revelation" he had received. Very apologetically, not wishing to go against the "counsel of the Lord," Apostle Kimball asked whether "his daughter wouldn't do as well as his wife." The "Prophet" replied that "she would do just as well, and the Lord would accept her instead."[18]

Loyal Mormons have tried to justify their "Prophet" by suggesting that the accusations of taking other men's wives were lies told by his enemies to discredit him. However, the stories were told by too many people, many of them loyal to Joseph Smith, and agree in too many details, to be explained away as lies. John D. Lee tells of being on a trip with one H.B. Jacobs, who was "bragging about his wife and two children, what a true, virtuous, lovely woman she was . . . but little did he think that in his absence she was sealed to the Prophet Joseph and was his wife."[19]

Stealing Wives for Eternity

William Hall reported that he had heard Brigham Young say to Jacobs after Joseph Smith's death, "The woman you claim for a wife does not belong to you. She is the spiritual wife of brother Joseph, sealed to him (October 27, 1841).[20] I am his proxy, and she, in this behalf, with her children, are my property. You can go where you please, and get another. . . ." Apparently accepting whatever Brigham Young said as Joseph Smith's successor, Jacobs "stood as witness in the Nauvoo temple in January 1846 when Zina was sealed to Brigham Young 'for time' and to Joseph Smith 'for eternity.'"[21] The comments of Ann Eliza Young, one of Brigham's many wives, give further insight:

> He taught them [married women] that all former marriages were null and void, and that they were at perfect liberty to make another choice of a husband. The marriage covenants were not binding, because they were ratified only by Gentile laws . . . [which] the Lord did not recognize, consequently all the women were free.

> One woman said to me . . . : "the greatest trial I ever endured in my life was living with my husband and deceiving him, by receiving Joseph's attentions whenever he chose to come to me." This woman, and others . . . were seduced under the guise of religion. . . .

> Some of these women have since said they did not know who was the father of their children; this is not to be wondered at, for after Joseph's declaration annulling all Gentile marriages, the greatest promiscuity was practiced. . . .[22]

Leading Mormons have tried to justify their "Prophet" by suggesting that he practiced a special kind of celestial marriage, whereby married women were "sealed" to him for eternity, but that he had no sexual relations with them on earth—that would only begin in heaven. This may have been true for some of his 84 or more wives, but certainly not for all of them. Typical of this attempt to justify the "Prophet" is the following from Apostle John A. Widtsoe:

> Zealous women, married or unmarried, loving the cause of the restored gospel . . . asked that they might be sealed to the Prophet for eternity. They were not to be his wives on earth, in mortality, but only after death in the eternities. . . . Such marriages led to misunderstandings by those not of the church . . . yet there may be women who prefer to spend eternity with another than their husband on earth."[23]

According to Jesus, there is no marriage relationship in heaven.[24] Even if there were, however, Widtsoe's argument is a strange one that assumes it is less of a crime to steal another man's wife for eternity than to steal her for a few years on earth. Wife-stealing among the Mormons was so common that many other examples could be given if we had space. The case of Mary Elizabeth Rollins Lightner, however, is of particular interest because she told her story in a public speech at Brigham Young University in 1905:

> . . . He not only preached [polygamy], but he practiced it. I am a living witness to it. It was given to him before he gave it to the Church.
>
> An angel came to him . . . with a drawn sword in his hand and told Joseph if he did not go into that principle he would slay him.
>
> I asked him if Emma knew about me and he said, "Emma thinks the world of you."
>
> I had been dreaming for a number of years I was his wife. I thought I was a great sinner . . . but when Joseph sent for me he told me all of these things.
>
> "Well," said I, "don't you think it was an angel of the Devil that told you these things?"
>
> Said he, "No, it was an angel of God. God almighty showed me the difference between an angel of Light and Satan's angels."[25]
>
> Joseph said I was his before I came here and he said all the Devils in Hell should never get me from him. I was sealed to him in the Masonic Hall . . . by Brigham Young in February 1842. . . .

Heber C. Kimball [gave] the blessing.... My husband was [traveling] far away from me at the time....[26]

What Mentality Is This?

No Mormon today has any excuse for being ignorant of the fact that in order to become a "god" he must practice polygamy, for it is the declared essence of God-making. Brigham Young put it bluntly: "The only men who become Gods, even the Sons of God, are those who enter into polygamy."[27] This "restored gospel" is absurd just on the basis of statistics: There aren't enough women for very many men to have even one extra wife, much less the scores and even hundreds promised by Joseph Smith! Apostle Heber C. Kimball boasted that in heaven Mormon men who wanted more wives could go to the Prophet Joseph Smith with their request and he would say, "Here are thousands, have all you want."[28]

Apparently there will be more wife-stealing in heaven, because according to the teaching on "exaltation," no woman can get there without a husband. Though not now practiced openly (there are thousands of Mormon fundamentalist polygamists in Utah) because of the insistence of the federal government, polygamy will be the rule in the kingdom, when the Mormon Church is expected to be in control of the world. Even now it remains a central doctrine of Mormonism. Those who deny it must deny their entire Mormon religion. John J. Stewart reminds fellow Mormons: "... Seven of our nine Church presidents have lived plural marriage, and ... this principle still is and always will be a doctrine of the Church."[29] Wilford Woodruff, fourth President of the Church of Jesus Christ of Latter-day Saints, who signed the 1890 Manifesto agreeing to cease the practice of polygamy but who perjured himself in court and continued to lead his Church in violation of his sworn promise, left this reminder for all Mormons today:

> If we were to do away with polygamy... then we must do away with prophets and Apostles, with revelation and the gifts and graces of the Gospel, and finally give up our religion altogether....[30]

President Woodruff left no middle ground. Either go along with Joseph Smith's polygamy or renounce Mormonism entirely. Any Latter-day Saint honestly facing the plain language of Section 132 in *Doctrine and Covenants* would have to do just that, denouncing Joseph Smith as a false prophet and worse. Verse 1 begins with the Lord saying that He is responding to Joseph's *inquiry* concerning polygamy. Forgetting the many contradictions (such as God approving polygamy in the Bible, which is false), in verses 51 and 52 Joseph's wife, Emma, is commanded of the Lord to "receive all those [plural wives] that have been given unto my servant Joseph." So the "revelation" itself confirms the fact that, in brazen disobedience to the Book of Mormon, Section 101 of *Doctrine and Covenants*, the Bible, and the laws of the land, Joseph had already taken plural wives before he checked it out with "the Lord." Even Mormon leaders have admitted that by all laws he was a wanton adulterer.

What kind of mentality would cause anyone, much less a "Prophet," to ask God, in view of all of the Scriptures against it, whether He approved adultery? This mentality was inherited by Joseph Smith's successors and is thoroughly embedded in Mormon thinking today: the belief that God contradicts Himself, so that "revelation is what President Joseph Smith said, unless the current President Gordon B. Hinckley says differently." The consequences of such amoral thinking are both ludicrous and destructive. This mentality causes Mormon missionaries to ask prospective converts to pray about whether Joseph Smith is a true Prophet and the Book of Mormon is true. Both Smith and the Book of Mormon contradict in many ways what God already has said through biblical prophets. It is just as perverse to ask for divine endorsement of obvious contradiction and falsehood as it is to ask God whether adultery is all right. When Joseph Smith did that, he received the "revelation" he desired. In similar manner, those who pray for a "burning in the bosom" to verify the divine call of Joseph Smith and his Book of Mormon will, if that is what they want, just as surely get it—and from the same source.

What mentality did the "Prophet" have? Contemptuous of truth, he changed or created Scripture to serve his own ends. "Sealing" in the Temple for eternity and celestial marriage were just devices to get what he wanted, including wealth, power, and sex. He deceived thousands in his day, and continues to deceive millions today. The following statement was sworn by Apostle Orson Pratt's first (and at that time only) wife, Sarah:

> You should bear in mind that Joseph did not think of marriage or sealing ceremony for many years. He used to state to his intended victims, as he did to me, "God does not care if we have a good time, if only other people do not know it."

He only introduced a marriage ceremony when he found out that he could not get certain women without it. . . .

If any woman, like me, opposed his wishes, he used to say: "Be silent, or I shall ruin your character. My character must be sustained in the interest of the Church."[31]

Facing the Consequences

Although the majority of the Mormon women were not happy with the new "revelation" (some complained bitterly against it and some committed suicide in despair), many of the men, especially the leaders, embraced it enthusiastically. Polygamy became one of the most dogmatically held doctrines in the Church. It was declared that Adam, God the Father, and Jesus Christ were all polygamists,[32] that being a polygamist was synonymous with being a Latter-day Saint,[33] that it was the cure of all social evils,[34] and that it was as much a part of the gospel as baptism for remission of sins.[35] In effect it became the cornerstone of the faith. Orson Pratt, who had been in despair upon learning that Joseph Smith had attempted to seduce his wife, returned to the Church after the "revelation" and became an Apostle and the outstanding apologist of Mormonism. Pratt said:

> . . . If plurality of marriage [polygamy] is not true . . . then marriage for eternity is not true, and your faith is all vain, and all the sealing ordinances and powers pertaining to marriages for eternity are vain, worthless, good for nothing; for as sure as one is true the other also must be true.[36]

The sad facts are clear. Unfortunately for the credibility of Mormonism, the entire structure is built upon Joseph Smith alone and either stands or falls with him. Moreover, the very Apostles and Presidents who rightly declared that anyone who renounced polygamy ought logically to renounce all of Joseph Smith's other "revelations" and Mormonism itself did themselves consent to the Manifesto of 1890 doing away with polygamy. Many of them admitted later in court that they had lied when making this pledge and had secretly continued to live in polygamy and even to "seal" plural marriages in the Temple.[37] In 1904, however, plural marriages were finally dissolved by the Church, and polygamy was equated with fornication and adultery. It was too late, however, to change the many inspired pronouncements by Mormon

Prophets and Apostles to the effect that giving up polygamy was the same as abandoning Mormonism altogether.

This leaves the sincere Mormon in a perplexing dilemma. The key to his "exaltation" (godhood), the "new and everlasting covenant," the most important "revelation" ever given to man, the very essence of Mormonism, and the religion of heaven that Mormon Prophets and Apostles swore would never be given up has now been declared by these same men to be a crime! The zealous Mormons who practice polygamy today in obedience to Joseph Smith's most important "revelation" are excommunicated from the Mormon Church. When will The Brethren change their minds again? The obvious answer to that question is *whenever they please*; for they, like Brigham Young, are above the law, and their god from Kolob frequently contradicts himself through his chosen "Prophets."

Where Is the Courage of Conviction?

Today's Mormons affirm that polygamy is still all that Joseph Smith claimed, but that the Church is temporarily excommunicating and branding as criminals any Mormons who practice it to prevent wholesale persecution and imprisonment of its members by the government and destruction of Mormondom.

Since when did real servants of God bow to godless government edicts and compromise their faith for expediency's sake or to save their own skins? Why was Joseph Smith's "unexcelled courage" so great in practicing polygamy in secret, but so pitifully weak when it came to proclaiming it to the world—so much so that he made repeated public denials that he even believed in this most holy doctrine? And why did his successors do the same, bowing to the United States government and making the cornerstone of their faith a crime punishable with imprisonment and excommunication? If polygamy is indeed the very heart of the "restored gospel of Jesus Christ," the key to salvation, then this good news of exaltation through polygamy ought to be preached to the whole world at all cost; and woe to those who shrink from doing so in order to stay out of prison.

Christ commanded His disciples and all who would be His true followers to go into all the world and preach the gospel to every person. He never said that we were free not to do so if it meant that we might suffer for it. Millions of Christians have died for their faith down through the centuries—from the

Roman coliseums to the gas chambers of Hitler's Germany and the gulags of Russia and China—and are still suffering imprisonment and death for their Lord and His gospel. There were and are almost no Mormons among these millions of faithful martyrs.

Mormons today complain that they are being persecuted whenever someone disagrees with them and tries to reasonably point out the fallacies in what they believe. But they know little of the torture and death that millions of Christians have endured. That is why Christians today find it more than a bit ironic that Mormons claim there was a total apostasy for 1800 years, and that they have "restored" true Christianity—yet Christians died for their faith all these centuries, but present-day Mormons won't stand up openly for what they believe because it would mean they might have to go to prison as polygamists.

Beginning of the End

Mormons claim that Joseph Smith did indeed go to prison for his beliefs, and that he died as a martyr. It would be stretching the facts beyond credibility to maintain that claim. The fact is that Smith went to prison for *denying* his beliefs, not for standing up for them. He was arrested and imprisoned for persecuting other people, and he died in a blazing gun battle in which he killed at least two men and wounded another. The mob that murdered him committed a heinous crime, but the fact is that he did *not* die quietly, like a lamb led to the slaughter, as did Jesus Christ. Joseph Smith answered back viciously against those who accused him, and they didn't accuse him wrongfully, as the Pharisees did Jesus. Joseph Smith was no martyr, but a fighter who in utter disregard for the freedom of the press and rights of others physically destroyed a newspaper that criticized him. This was the crime for which he was arrested and imprisoned.

Not all of the Mormon leaders went along with polygamy. Some tried to reason with Smith, but found it impossible. They were also concerned about his political ambitions. Joseph Smith had been crowned "king" over the Mormon kingdom, and was running for president of the United States in 1844. Distressed by the immorality among the leadership of the Church, these men decided to publish a newspaper that would tell the truth to Mormons and non-Mormons alike. Called the *Nauvoo Expositor*, it had only one edition. The following is a sample from that first and only edition:

It is notorious fact, that many females . . . are requested to meet Brother Joseph, or some of the Twelve [Apostles] at some insulated point, or at some particularly described place on the bank of the Mississippi, or at some room, which wears upon its front—POSITIVELY NO ADMITTANCE.

. . . After having been sworn in one of the most solemn manners, to never divulge what is revealed to them, with a penalty of death attached, that God Almighty has revealed it to him, that she should be his [Joseph's] spiritual wife, "for it was right anciently and God will tolerate it again: but we must keep those pleasures and blessings from the world, for until there is a change in government, we will endanger ourselves by practicing it. . . ."[38]

The *Expositor* was exposing the truth, and Joseph Smith knew it would bring down his empire. True to form, he moved quickly to silence his accusers. As mayor of Nauvoo, which was now the largest city in Illinois, Joseph Smith called the city council together, where he and his brother Hyrum perjured themselves once again by denying any involvement in polygamy or adultery. Having on the basis of his own false testimony gotten a vote declaring the *Expositor* a public nuisance, Joseph Smith "immediately ordered the marshal to destroy it without delay."[39] An armed mob of several hundred men converged on the newspaper. They dragged the press, equipment, and supplies (including almost all of the first edition) out into the streets, smashed the press, and burned everything. It was for that crime, and the crime of treason in calling out the Nauvoo Legion to prevent officials of the law from arresting him, that the governor of the State of Illinois arrested and imprisoned Joseph and Hyrum Smith.

From Criminal to Martyr Hero

Bigamy was a crime in the State of Illinois, and government officials had been investigating the Mormons not only for this but also for many other alleged crimes. At the time of his murder in the Carthage jail, Joseph Smith was under indictment by the Carthage grand jury for polygamy, and likely would have been sentenced to prison for that crime had he not been killed. If his murder saved him from imprisonment for polygamy, it probably also saved the Mormon Church from destruction by causing the "Saints" to rally around Joseph Smith as their martyr hero. As a result, the polygamy that he had loved so well became one of the most staunchly held doctrines by the leadership that succeeded him. Besides the sexual attraction of polygamy, it was in Joseph Smith's successors' own interest to build up the "Prophet" as perfect in everything he had done, in order to establish their power as the ones upon whom his mantle had fallen. Therefore, when they finally had the courage to bring polygamy out into the open, the "Prophets" and "Apostles" competed with each other to see who could most loudly and eloquently sound the praises of polygamy. If what Joseph Smith and dozens of other Mormon "Prophets" and "Apostles" said about polygamy was true, then no prohibition by the United States government can change its virtues. The consequences for every Mormon today could not be spelled out more clearly than by Apostle Orson Pratt:

> The Lord has said that those who reject this principle [polygamy] reject their salvation, they shall be damned.[40]

These men were either telling the truth or they were liars. If they told the truth, then the whole Mormon Church, from its President on down, is in a state of apostasy for rejecting polygamy even temporarily. If they along with Joseph Smith lied or even exaggerated about polygamy, then nothing else they said can be trusted. The foundation of Mormonism collapses either way.

Whether polygamy is accepted or rejected does not change the sordid facts surrounding this "revelation" that exposes Joseph Smith as an incurable womanizer, seducer, and liar who brought forth a "revelation" from "the Lord" to sanctify his lust. If such a man were really visited by angels, they wouldn't be angels of God. Nor would an angel of God force anyone into the secret practice of polygamy at the point of a sword. There is only one other possibility. This tells us all we need to know about the "angel" Moroni, who gave Joseph Smith the Book of Mormon and stands sentinel atop Mormon Temples.

13

SECRETS, SURPRISES, AND PERILS OF GOD-MAKING

It is an inescapable fact that Joseph Smith kept polygamy a secret teaching and practice, denying it publicly right to the time of this death on the night of June 27, 1844. Although he claimed to have had a "revelation" that polygamy was an essential step on the path to "godhood," Smith shared this secret only with an inner corps of the elite, which meant that most Mormons were deprived of this great "truth," and many died without ever having been told. It was eight years after Smith's death before this essential requirement was at long last published, and 32 years before it became scripture. Now it has been taken away by the Church authorities, depriving the average Mormon once again of an understanding of this essential "key" to "exaltation." In view of the many conclusive statements by Mormon "Prophets" and "Apostles," such as the following by President Joseph Fielding Smith, it is clear that the present Mormon Church leaders are holding back from their followers that "key" without which all their other attempts to reach "godhood" are doomed to fail.

> ... The doctrine of the eternal union of husband and wife and of plural marriage is one of the most important doctrines ever revealed to man in any age of the world.
>
> Without it we could never be exalted to associate with and become Gods. ...[1]

It is therefore only prudent to ask whether there are other essentials for godhood that are not being honestly explained to Mormon members by the leaders of the Church of Jesus Christ of Latter-day Saints. Are there perils and problems that are not being fully disclosed that could catch the average Mormon by surprise? From a careful study of the sermons and writings of Mormon General Authorities, it becomes clear that there is indeed much crucial information being held back, which, if it were generally understood, would cause many Church members to give up any hope of ever reaching Mormonism's ultimate goal. In a sermon that many Mormons consider to be Joseph Smith's most important (delivered just seven weeks before his death, at the conference held in Nauvoo, near the Temple), Joseph Smith declared:

> When you climb a ladder, you must begin at the bottom and ascend step by step until you arrive at the top; and so it is with the principles of the Gospel; you must begin with the first, and go on until you learn all the principles of exaltation.
>
> But it will be a great while after you have passed through the vail [of death] before you will have learned them all.
>
> It is not all to be comprehended in this world; it will be a great work to learn our salvation and exaltation even beyond the grave.[2]

The Unknown Path

So there is much more to the "restored gospel" than Joseph Smith knew himself. There could be, then, some shocking surprises along this path which continues into the hereafter. Neither the Bible nor the Book of Mormon speak of this path; indeed, they both condemn the very idea. We have only Joseph Smith's word for this, and even he wasn't fully informed. That puts the Mormon in an extremely uncomfortable and precarious position. Not even the "Prophets, Seers, and Revelators" of the Church know all that is involved or how long it will take to reach the coveted status of a "god" or "goddess."

The late Prophet Spencer W. Kimball wrote: "The Lord Jesus Christ ... has given us our map—a code of laws and commandments whereby we might attain perfection and, eventually, Godhood."[3] What does he mean by "eventually"? No details are given. It could be a very long and grueling climb up Joseph Smith's ladder to heaven.

The Bible offers eternal life as a free gift that can be received by simple faith here and now. The Christian "is [already] passed from death unto life."[4] The moment we open our hearts to Christ, He comes in according to His promise,[5] and by the witness of the Holy Spirit within we "*know* [present knowledge] that we *have* [present possession] eternal life."[6] In contrast, the Mormon "Christ" points the LDS toward a path that is so endless and so difficult that no one can be sure he will ever reach the hoped-for "eternal life" lying at the end of it. President Kimball said, "All transgressions must be cleansed [by Temple rituals and good deeds], all weaknesses must be overcome before a person can attain perfection and godhood."[7] He still hasn't told us how to do it or how long it will take. Kimball went on to say:

> After a period there would be a resurrection . . . which would render us immortal and make possible our further climb toward perfection and godhood.[8]

So even after the resurrection one must keep on striving *toward* the goal of eternal life. When will a Mormon reach this fabled state? That is a question to which Mormonism offers no answer. Those who accept the "new and everlasting covenant" of Temple marriage for eternity and polygamy have committed themselves to a perilous and uncertain path which Joseph Smith himself neither fully understood nor credibly explained. That it could be a very long and disappointing journey seems evident from this special message of the First Presidency under Joseph F. Smith (Joseph F. Smith, John R. Winder, and Anthon H. Lund):

> Man is the child of God, formed in the divine image and endowed with divine attributes, and even as the infant son of an earthly father and mother is capable in due time of becoming a man, so the undeveloped offspring of celestial parentage is capable, by experience through ages and aeons, of evolving into a God.[9]

The Masonic Parallels of the "Restored Gospel"

The relationship to Freemasonry's upward path is very clear. In the *Entered Apprentice's Handbook*, Masonic authority J.S.M. Ward explains that the secret Masonic Temple rites represent an upward path being climbed to perfection by the individual Mason, symbolized in the building of Solomon's Temple. High Masonic authority W.L. Wilmshurst writes: "A Master

Mason . . . is no longer an ordinary man, but a divinized man."[10] It was only after he became a Master Mason that Joseph Smith began to teach that "god" is a divinized man and that men can become "gods." The emphasis upon personal worthiness as the basis for exaltation is common to both Mormonism and Masonry. The Mason repeats at Lodge meetings, "The All-Seeing Eye will reward us according to our merits." The following Masonic Crafting Hymn could also be sung of the Mormon climb to "godhood" through Temple rituals and good deeds:

> Brothers faithful and deserving,
> Now the second rank you fill,
>
> Purchased by your faultless serving,
> Leading to a higher still.
>
> Thus from rank to rank ascending,
> Mounts the Mason's path of love;
>
> Bright its earthly course and ending,
> In the glorious lodge above.[11]

The pagan origins of Mormonism are very clearly seen in the explanations of how men become "gods." The Mormon "God" owes his status to two things: 1) the willing obedience of the trillions of "gods" under him, who could vote him out at any time;[12] and 2) his own obedience to mysterious universal "laws and forces" that have existed forever in "untold numbers"[13] in and of themselves (i.e., laws without a Lawgiver). These are thus greater than the "gods," for it is these "principles of exaltation" that have literally made the "gods," all of whom were once mortal men. These are ancient occult ideas that are being revived and gaining new respectability in today's New Age movement.

Initiates of the Secret (Occult) Path

The whole purpose of Mormonism as revealed through Joseph Smith is to initiate its members into this secret path to "godhood" and to provide them with occult "keys, secret signs, names, handshakes" and various passwords to gain access to unspecified "laws and forces." By obedience to these universal laws, mastery is to be gained over mysterious cosmic forces, thus enabling the worthy Mormon eventually to become a "god" or "goddess" like all the "gods" and "goddesses" who have climbed up before along this same path to "exaltation."

Prior to entering the LDS Temple, most initiates attend a "Temple preparation" class. The manual *Achieving a Celestial Marriage* (1976, Corp. of the President of the Church of Jesus Christ of Latter-day Saints) is singularly interesting in that there are no instructions about what to do once you are inside the temple—just how to be worthy for the endowment and celestial marriage.

Milton R. Hunter explained it in these words:

> Then how did he become glorified and exalted and attain his present status of Godhood? . . . [He] undoubtedly took advantage of every opportunity to learn the laws of truth and as he became acquainted with each new verity he righteously obeyed it.
>
> From day to day he exerted his will vigorously, and as a result became thoroughly acquainted with the forces lying about him. As he gained more knowledge through persistent effort and continuous industry, as well as through absolute obedience, his understanding of the universal laws continued to become more complete.
>
> Thus he grew in experience and continued to grow until he attained the status of Godhood.[14]

In essence, the "restored gospel of Jesus Christ" that was revealed through Joseph Smith offers the Mormon a chance to step onto this same endless and laborious path (that all the "Gods" have ascended in ages past) in quest of his own "Godhood." The "good news" proclaimed by Mormonism is that sinful, mortal humans have the wonderful opportunity to pull themselves up by their bootstraps and (by discovering all of these untold laws and forces and by perfectly living up to all they require of us) become "gods" and create their own universes. This same fantasy has been expressed in thousands of myths since the dawn of history.

All of the above is simply an introduction to an understanding of the secret rituals that take place in Mormon Temples. These eternal "laws and forces" are the mysterious power that the Mormon Melchizedek Priesthood is designed to tap into. That Priesthood enters the path to "exaltation" through secret pagan rituals performed in Mormon Temples. To the average Mormon, there is an overpowering mystique associated with these sanctuaries. And well there might be, for the secret Mormon path to "godhood" winds back and forth through the Temple in repetition of occult ceremonies, 98 percent of which are for the dead. The most important of these is celestial marriage (which includes polygamy) and "sealings" for eternity of family members to one another. According to Dr. Goodman:

> The goal of every Latter-day Saint is to be married as a family unit in the "House of the Lord," and there receive these sacred blessings that will allow us eventually, if we're worthy, to dwell and be in the presence of our heavenly Father.
>
> We need to receive certain instructions, certain information and certain ordinances. . . . That is the only way that we can be with Him to rule and reign with Him. Otherwise, we could not be in His presence.[15]

Becoming Worthy

There is that same word eventually again. How long will it take before Mormons can *eventually* gain access to the "presence of our heavenly Father"? Dr. Goodman doesn't explain, because not even Joseph Smith knew. That phrase "if we're worthy" represents a mammoth and undefined "if." Everything depends upon it; whereas, the Christian's salvation depends upon Christ's worthiness, and the admission on the individual's part that he is an unworthy sinner. According to the Bible, because Christ's sacrifice upon the cross has paid the full price for our sins that was demanded by infinite justice, every true Christian has instant access into the Father's presence through prayer; and upon death his soul and spirit go immediately to heaven.

Paul described this transition through death as "absent from the body and . . . present with the Lord."[16] When Christ returns, all those who have received Him as Savior and Lord will be "in a moment, in the twinkling of an eye . . . caught up together with them [the resurrected dead] in the clouds, to meet the Lord in the air; and so shall we ever be with the Lord."[17] Not so for the Mormon, who according to the "restored gospel" must struggle for "ages and aeons" to get *eventually* to heaven, if somehow he is able to become worthy enough to merit it.

To learn how to become "worthy" to do their Temple work, Latter-day Saints attend special "Temple Preparation Seminars." Eagerly beginning these classes and expecting to learn at last what really goes on inside

Mormondom's tightly guarded sanctuaries, the candidate is in for a perplexing disappointment. Instead of receiving specific instruction about Temple ceremonies, he finds that he is being prepared to face an unknown but crucial initiation ritual that he cannot be informed about in advance. Nor will he be informed, until he has been admitted inside the Temple. The Temple preparation manual, *Achieving Celestial Marriage* (ACMM), is just as evasive as everything else surrounding the mysteries of the Temple, but it does point each member to that path to exaltation.

> If God became God by obedience to all of the gospel law with the crowning point being the celestial law of marriage, then that's the only way I can become a god. [Answer:] Right! (ACMM, page 3).

> The endowment is the celestial course of instruction ... being enabled to give them the key words, the signs and tokens, pertaining to the priesthood and gain your eternal exaltation in spite of earth and hell (ACMM, page 203).

Emphasizing loyalty to Joseph Smith and the Church he founded, 11 of the 12 seminar lessons focus upon the personal worthiness required to become part of a secret circle of Mormon elite called "Temple Mormons." In the twelfth session the instructor finally discusses the actual Temple visit, but without revealing a single sacred secret. To the candidate's disappointment, his anxious questions continue to receive the by-now-monotonous response required in the instructor's manual: "You will learn the answer to *that* as you serve in the Temple." The closest the candidates come to learning that Temple work is really only the first step in a long and arduous journey is when they are given Brigham Young's instruction:

> Your endowment is to receive all those ordinances in the House of the Lord, which are necessary for you, after you have departed this life, to enable you to walk back to the presence of the Father, passing the angels who stand as sentinels, being enabled to give them the key words, the signs and tokens pertaining to the Holy Priesthood, and gain your eternal exaltation in spite of earth and hell.[18]

Tony and Debbie didn't get that far. While they were taking the Temple Preparation Seminars, so many serious questions were sidestepped by the instructor that this constant "You'll learn *that* in the Temple" began to sound evasive. Instead of answering questions, the seminars were raising more questions and creating doubts. Why all the secrecy? And why wasn't there something in the Bible or at least in the Book of Mormon about Temple work? There were a few references in *Journal of Discourses* and *Doctrine and Covenants*, but nothing very revealing about the ceremonies. How could the Church expect Tony and Debbie to commit themselves to Temple work, yet refuse answers to honest questions? Tony told us:

> My wife and I knew that we couldn't obtain our exaltation to "Godhood" without going through the Temple, so we enrolled in a Temple Preparation class.

> Although the instructor wouldn't answer our questions about the Temple, we were learning that everything depended upon our becoming "worthy."

> One evening after coming home, we decided to see what the Bible said about the Temple and its ceremonies. There was *nothing* in the Bible about "Christian" temples.

> However, in Romans 4 we read that a man is justified by faith and not by works, and even that good works were a stumbling stone to those who try to pursue their salvation that way.

> We really began to doubt that the Temple ceremony was biblical, even though the Church had told us it was. Studying more, we found that the Bible was in serious conflict with Mormon theology and doctrine.

> We went through a period where we were in a very depressed state. In order for us to accept what we were reading about the true and living Jesus Christ . . . we would be alienated from all of our friends and relatives.

> We went ahead and decided that Jesus was to be the way, the truth, and life for our family.

The Staggering Burden of Perfection

Having completed the seminar series, the candidate now vaguely realizes that inside the Temple he will be learning secrets and gaining mysterious Priesthood powers. If he learns and applies them *perfectly*, these will enable him to pass safely whatever fearsome tests await him in the spirit world and eventually to gain access to the heavenly Father's presence, perhaps in a few trillion years, when he has attained perfection. In spite of the joyful anticipation of entering the Temple, a disquieting feeling that will grow into a heavy burden is settling upon him. He now realizes that regardless of whatever lip service Mormonism may give to Jesus Christ as Savior, the awesome responsibility for his own salvation, in the final analysis, rests upon him.

The most sobering realization is that nothing less than 100 percent *perfection* will do.

In fact, during the actual Temple ritual (in a confrontation between the yet-to-be-born apostles Peter, James, and John), Lucifer, still teaching pure Mormon doctrines, has this to say to the Temple patrons:

> LUCIFER: Aah! You have looked over my kingdom, and my greatness and glory. Now you want to take possession of the whole of it. (Lucifer turns, and stares into the camera.) I have a word to say concerning these people. *If they do not walk up to every covenant they make at these altars in this temple this day, they will be in my power!* [emphasis added—temple script on file].

What a curse to lay upon the heads of the Mormon people!

The candidate now hopes fervently that the secrets he will learn in the Temple will give him the power to attain this perfection. The late Mormon "Prophet" and President, Spencer W. Kimball, wrote these words:

> This progress toward eternal life is a matter of achieving perfection.

> Living all the commandments [there are over 4300 in Mormonism] guarantees total forgiveness of sins and assures one of exaltation through that perfection which comes by complying with the formula the Lord gave us.[19]

In Mormonism, the blood of Christ atones for Adam's sin only, which brings resurrection to all, including animals and birds.[20] Christ's blood doesn't atone for a single individual sin,[21] which can be paid for only by 100 percent obedience to every command, or in some cases with one's own blood being shed, according to the "restored gospel."[22] Moreover, no one can be saved in ignorance.[23] Therefore, not only must the Mormon know every one of the more than 4300 Mormon laws, but after the resurrection he must somehow discover the other untold numbers of laws and *perfectly obey every one of them.* Joseph Smith's logic can't be faulted at this point, for if one is to become God, then surely nothing less than *100 percent perfection* will do.

When they understand what is really involved in achieving "exaltation," many Mormons begin to have serious doubts about whether they want to become "gods" and "goddesses" after all. It seems a very long path and too great a responsibility for humans. They wonder at this point whether the "restored gospel" of Joseph Smith is in fact the "good news" it seemed to be when they first heard it but didn't fully understand it. Unfortunately, for most Mormons it is too late to turn back at this point. They have committed themselves too deeply. The price would be too great in loss of friends, family, prestige, and self-esteem to back away from the Church. And what else is there, since all other churches are an "abomination"? They remain Mormons in name only, for social reasons. As for the coveted "godhood," they've got enough problems just being humans without aiming for that. Their conscience tells them that it just isn't possible.

Credit Card to Eternity

To be admitted to the Temple, every Mormon must obtain a "Temple Recommend" by satisfactorily passing an interview first with his local Ward Bishop (comparable to a pastor) and then with his Stake President (who presides over up to ten Wards). Among the 17 specific areas covered, the candidate must satisfy these Church officials that he abstains from the use of coffee, tea, alcohol, tobacco, and cola drinks; that he "sustains" the General Authorities and local authorities of the Church; and that he attends all meetings possible, deals honestly with everyone, is morally clean, and tithes ten percent of his income to the Church; that he doesn't associate with apostate groups (non-Mormons) and has no "anti-Mormon literature" (anything that questions Mormonism) in his home; and that he is fully obeying *all* of the "commandments of the Gospel." To think critically for oneself is not only discouraged by the Mormon hierarchy, but is also considered to be inspired by the Devil.[24]

Needless to say, no Latter-day Saint, no matter how "worthy" in his own or his Church's eyes, is perfectly obeying all of the laws included in Mormonism's "restored gospel." The Bible declares: "If we say that we have no sin, we deceive ourselves, and the truth is not in us. . . . If we say that we have not sinned, we make him a liar, and his word is not in us."[25] However, the desire for the annual "Temple Recommend" is so great that it bends the truth and dulls consciences. What indescribable joy for the Mormon who walks out of those interviews approved for another year! Possession of that small piece of paper certifying one's "worthiness" is like having a credit card to eternity and breeds a self-righteous pride that is almost immune to the normal pangs of conscience.

Point of No Return

Once inside the Temple, the candidate has just seconds to make decisions of eternal consequence. Like a blind person being led by the hand, he must now commit himself unreservedly to Joseph Smith and the Mormon hierarchy, or else abandon the Temple and all hope of "exaltation" in shame. This is when many Mormons want to cut and run, but few do. The candidate must commit himself to participate in still-unknown ceremonies, from which there will be no retreat. It is like being asked to jump over a cliff with the promise that there is a net to catch you at the bottom. For many a Mormon, fear and uncertainty replace eager anticipation at this point. Yet the programmed belief that the long-sought secrets of the Temple hold his only hope for gaining eternal life pushes him on despite unanswered questions and haunting doubts.

An inner conditioning process that has been going on for months or years is now reaching a climax beyond which there will be very little likelihood of ever consciously questioning The Brethren again, no matter how many red flags are waved by reason and conscience. There has been a blind commitment to Joseph Smith and the Church he founded ever since that "burning in the bosom," a willing surrender of one's mind to let the hierarchy do the thinking and dictate the demands. There have been moments of doubt, nagging questions that were put on the shelf. But once that step forward to participate in the Temple rituals has been taken, something clicks inside the soul, like a door being slammed shut, putting those questions forever out of reach. This is the final step, the full surrender to an endless path of self-righteous striving to be perfect that conscience has warned against again and again; but from now on conscience must remain silent.

"Temple Recommend" clutched in hand, and having swallowed hard with determination to go through with it, the nervous initiate is in for several quick shocks. Husbands and wives joyfully anticipating having their marriage "sealed" in the Temple for eternity are immediately parted and will only come together briefly after having endured two hours of rituals separate from each other. Led first to men's and women's dressing rooms, they are instructed to strip stark naked. Oddly enough, each person *locks* his clothes in an individual locker, though no one but worthy Temple Mormons has access to the carefully guarded premises.

"Garment (Underwear) of the Holy Priesthood"

After partially covering their nudity with a poncho-like piece of thin cotton completely open on both sides, to which the key to their locker is pinned, the "Temple patrons," as they are called, are led to the "washing and anointing" room. There Temple workers first ceremoniously "wash" the various parts of their nude bodies with water, reaching under the open "shield," as it is called, and then "anoint" the initiates with oil in a similar manner. During this startling process, a singsong formula is recited by the Temple worker bestowing a special blessing upon each body part being "washed" or "anointed." This is the preparation for being dressed in the "Garment of the Holy Priesthood" (a sort of "magic underwear," much like an old-fashioned set of long johns with those Masonic markings sewn into it). The Temple worker recites:

> ... Having authority, I place this garment upon you [for and in behalf of (patron, then worker, both speak the name of the deceased), who is dead], which you must wear throughout your life.
>
> It represents the garment given to Adam when he was found naked in the Garden of Eden, and is called the Garment of the Holy Priesthood.
>
> Inasmuch as you do not defile it, but are true and faithful to your covenants, it will be a shield and a protection to you against the power of the destroyer until you have finished your work here on earth.
>
> With this garment I give you a new name, which you should always remember, and which you must keep sacred, and never reveal except at a certain place that will be shown you hereafter.
>
> The name is _____.[26]

To remain in good standing as a Temple Mormon who continues to perform the rituals essential in getting off to a good start on the infinite journey to "godhood," both men and women must wear the magic underwear 24 hours each day for the rest of their mortal lives. Jim and Judy expressed their feelings after having worn these sacred long johns for years. "This garment is supposed to be all-magical and all-protective," said Jim, "keeping you from harm if you're living the gospel of the Latter-day Saints." This is one more example of what otherwise-intelligent people will do when they have surrendered the right to think for themselves.

His wife, Judy, added, "The garment is supposed to be worn next to your skin, and with your other underclothes on top of that to protect your body. It's really just like wearing a rabbit's foot. It's a superstition." Granny Geer explained how seriously this is taken by devout Mormons:

> After I had helped my grandmother to bathe and helped her out of the tub, we would dry the left leg and put the clean garment on it . . . and *only then* would she take the old garment off the right leg.

As late as 1916, Mormons were reminded by a message from the First Presidency that the magic underwear of the elite corps of Temple Mormons had to be "of the approved pattern" and must be "worn as intended down to the wrists and ankles, and around the neck."[27] But fashions change, and Mormon women especially found it embarrassing to be wearing underwear that was so incompatible with modern dress. There were exhortations from Church leaders not to succumb to worldly fashion, and solemn warnings that it would jeopardize one's "godhood" to deviate from the pattern that Prophet Joseph Smith had received from heaven.[28] Nevertheless, in 1923 the Mormon hierarchy finally capitulated to changing styles (the Mormon "God" apparently deciding that he could be somewhat flexible in his requirements about magic underwear). Now a two-piece garment cut off above elbow and knee is allowed to be worn. And when it is difficult to keep this sacred garment a secret, such as in the military or while participating in athletics, it may even be temporarily discarded. Fundamentalist Mormons are troubled by such deviations from "revelation" that seem to make a mockery of solemn pronouncements by past "Prophets," such as this from President Joseph F. Smith:

> The Lord has given unto us garments of the Holy Priesthood . . . which should be held by [Mormons] the most sacred of all things in the world next to their own virtue . . . [and kept] unchanged and unaltered from the very pattern in which God gave them.[29]

That Occult Connection Again

Dressed now in the secret and magic underwear, the Temple patrons go back to their lockers, where they put on white clothing, over which they will later wear the Robe of the Holy Priesthood. On a speaking tour in Brazil, Ed Decker dressed himself in the Mormon Temple costume to show his audience what it looked like, unaware of the effect it would have. When he came out on the stage of the large auditorium, the audience took one frightened look at him and panicked. There was a great commotion, as though someone had yelled "Fire!" That was how he learned that the high priests of the satanic Macumba cult wear white costumes almost identical to Mormon Temple clothing, including the peculiar white hat and unique robes of Joseph Smith's Melchizedek or High Priesthood.

The Temple rituals, with their secret signs and magic incantations, are pure occultism—pagan and not Christian. They violate the Bible, the Book of Mormon, and common sense. What kind of "God" honors secret handshakes and passwords, or needs them? This is the playacting of children's fantasies, the stuff of myths. Yet it is also how countless secret societies operate, for it encourages their delusion that they are superior to the uninitiated, that they have a special mission to "take over" the world, and that they are in touch with higher beings and mysterious powers known only to an inner circle of elite.

It is a double abomination for these occult rituals to go on in the name of Christ, for they deny His sacrifice upon the cross for our sins. The God of the Bible looks right into our hearts and is neither deceived nor impressed by secret signs and formulas. Indeed, He forbids this attempt to replace His grace and forgiveness with magic. Yet Adam and Eve, before being cast out of the Garden, are depicted in the Mormon Temple ceremony making "a secret covenant with Elohim ("The Father" in Mormonism) and receiving a secret token (handgrip), with its name, sign and penalty (blood/death oath)."[30] This is both nonsense and an abomination. The Bible says that we are known by our fruits (love, joy, peace, patience, etc.), not by magic signs. The blood of Christ shed for our sins—not secret handshakes—provides access to the presence of God.

In the dramatization they are watching, Temple patrons see Peter, James, and John sent by Elohim to rescue Adam and Eve, with no explanation how this could happen thousands of years before these apostles were born. These strange invaders from the future "prove" their identity by giving Adam and Eve the secret Masonic signs of the Mormon Priesthood. With Adam and Eve, the patrons advance to the Telestial Kingdom and the Terrestrial World, where they are put under covenant to obey more laws, and are taught their accompanying Priesthood tokens, names, signs, and penalties.[31] Here they are also clothed in the Robes of the Holy Priesthood and taught the "True Order of Prayer."

Now the patrons are given a "test" such as they will allegedly face in the hereafter. At an elaborate "Veil," they are challenged to give the secret signs and passwords which they have just learned, and only by doing so will they be allowed to pass through to the other side. The Jewish Temple at Jerusalem (after which Mormon Temples are supposedly fashioned) had a veil so heavy that it took many priests to raise it enough for the high priest to enter once each year. When Christ cried upon the cross, "It is finished!" this veil was torn by the hand of God from the top to the bottom showing that the way into the presence of God had been opened up through His sacrifice for our sins.[32] In Mormon Temples, however, this veil has been replaced by a flimsy, very thin, though beautiful curtain. Divided into sections with a men's and women's side, the "Veil" has numerous holes and Masonic markings corresponding to those on the magic underwear.

Behind each segment of this elaborate curtain, a Veil Worker representing "the Lord" challenges each patron being led up and assisted through the ritual by a Temple Worker. Patrons are told that they will someday have to meet the Mormon "God" in this exact manner; and if they cannot then remember all the tokens, signs, names, penalties, they will not be allowed to enter into His presence. Reaching their hands through holes in the flimsy Veil, each patron assumes with "the Lord" on the other side of the Veil the position of the "five points of fellowship" as in Masonry: inside of right foot to inside of right foot, knee to knee, breast to breast, hand to back and mouth to ear. In this "holy" position, the patron must perfectly repeat the following Mason's incantation: "Health in the navel, marrow in the bones, strength in the loins and in the sinews, power in the Priesthood be upon me and upon my posterity through all generations of time throughout all eternity."[33] While the recent changes in the rituals now leave out the breast-to-breast routine, the deeply occult incantation remains.

Since each patron is wearing the Luciferian fig-leaf apron which God rejected but Mormons have adopted, one need hardly wonder what power in what Priesthood the patrons are solemnly putting themselves under for eternity. In fact these oaths have put them in Lucifer's kingdom. Remember, just before they received the Robes of the Holy Priesthood, the patrons listened solemnly as Lucifer gave forth with Mormon doctrine, warning them that, "If they do not walk up to *every* covenant they make at these altars in this temple this day, they will be in my power!"[34] No one except Jesus has ever perfectly kept the Ten Commandments. Certainly no Mormon can do that, much less maintain 100 percent obedience to every one of the thousands of laws in the "restored gospel." Therefore, every Mormon going through the Temple and making these covenants has placed himself by solemn blood oaths completely under Satan's power and in full submission to The Brethren.

What Good Is a "Secret" That's No Longer Secret?

Mormons boast their Temples are guarded by God and angels, and that no one who is not "worthy" can enter without detection and expulsion. This has been proven to be a vain delusion on more than one occasion, when a "Gentile" or an "apostate" has gone through the entire Mormon Temple ceremony with a hidden tape recorder undetected by the Mormon "gods" and angels. The complete transcript with explanation has been published by former Veil Worker Chuck Sackett under the title *What's Going On in There?*

This was done to show the folly of "secrets" that can't be kept secret.

In the original edition of *The God Makers*, Dave and Ed asked these two questions:

> 1) Now that the Mormon Temple secrets are no longer secret, will The Brethren change the Temple rituals to establish new secrets?
> 2) By what authority and for what purpose?

The answer is that The Brethren have made significant changes, taking out things that books like *The God Makers* and Chuck Sackett's *What's Going On in There?* have exposed as right out of the occult. To The Brethren, it was easier to change it than explain it, since no active Mormon would ever dare question their authority.

In exposing these former secrets, we only wish to help Mormons by demonstrating the folly of imagining that "secret" grips and signs are of any value. The God of the Bible looks into each heart, into each thought, and neither needs nor honors the childish secret passwords that seem impressive to men. Jesus said:

> I am the good shepherd, and know my sheep, and am known of mine . . . and I lay down my life for the sheep. . . . My sheep hear my voice, and I know them, and they follow me: and I give unto them eternal life; and they shall never perish, neither shall any man pluck them out of my hand.[35]

The secret formulas and incantations learned in Mormon Temples are supposed to enable those initiated into them to pass through ever-higher levels of initiation and eventually to take their rightful place among the "gods." This is what Satan told Eve she could do if she only gained the knowledge to do so. Declaring that evil spirits (devils) regularly inspired him during his sermons, and the Mormons "could not get along without them," Brigham Young also said, "You cannot get your endowment without the devil's being present."[36] Lucifer plays a far more active role in the Temple than Christ. Could this be the Temple of the true God? Or is it the Temple of the original God-Maker from the Garden of Eden?

And now we have further and surprising uncertainty expressed at the highest levels of Mormonism on the key concept of men becoming gods. Was the Mormon "god of this world" whom the Mormons worship and serve really once a man whose ascent to godhood proves that male Mormons can follow the same path to "exaltation"? That question, which goes to the very heart of Mormonism, was recently presented to the current Mormon president, Gordon B. Hinckley, by two *Time* correspondents, who reported the following:

> On whether his church still holds that God the Father was once a man, he [Hinckley] sounded uncertain.
>
> "I don't know that we teach it. I don't know that we emphasize it . . . I understand the philosophical background behind it, but I don't know a lot about it, and I don't think others know a lot about it."[37]

"Philosophical background"? This doctrine was taught by Joseph Smith as a *revelation* from God, not a philosophical idea. Is the Mormon Church now preparing to abandon the major purpose for which it has built temples all over the world?

14

THE GREAT
TEMPLE / PRIESTHOOD SCAM

When plans were being laid for construction of the magnificent Salt Lake City Temple, Brigham Young had a brilliant idea for reducing labor and expense. Instead of cutting granite for the stone structure, he suggested that they use the much softer sandstone, which was cheaper and easier to work. Having taught for years that gold, silver, and stones "mature [grow] like hair,"[1] he was sure that sandstone, once in place, would grow into granite. Mormons were expected to take this seriously. Though it makes no sense, the "Prophet" must not be questioned, for "when our leaders speak, the thinking has been done."[2] Ezra Taft Benson, who was the next Mormon Prophet/President after Spencer W. Kimball, has said that the "Prophet" does not need to say "thus saith the Lord" to speak with authority, and that he can do so on any subject; and if science seems to be in conflict with what the "Prophet" has said, the voice of the "Prophet" must prevail.[3]

Latter-day Saints are taught that the multiplying Mormon Temples (soon to exceed 65) are being built around the world to implement the "restoration" begun by Joseph Smith of the "true Christianity" that was practiced in similar Temples since the days of Adam, and even in early America. There is no record, however, either in history or tradition to indicate that a "Christian temple" ever existed anywhere, much less that Christians ever practiced the pagan rituals now performed in Mormon Temples.

It is clear from the New Testament that the early Christians never participated in Temple ceremonies of any kind, much less secret ones. Mormon Apostle LeGrand Richards admitted that Mormon Temple doctrines "did not come to the Prophet Joseph Smith by reading the Bible...."[4] The very concept of Temples designed for sacred rituals contradicts biblical Christianity. The individual Christian's body is described as "the temple of the Holy Spirit,"[5] and the collective body of Christians throughout all ages is described by Paul as growing together into "a holy temple"[6] comprised of "living stones"[7] (i.e., the individual Christians). Joseph Fielding Smith admitted that "the saints of the primitive Christian Church did not have access to a temple. The [Jewish] temple in Jerusalem was the only temple...."[8] Of course, they could have had access to that temple, but that would have meant going back to the animal sacrifices offered by the Aaronic priests—a system which had been fulfilled and done away with by the once-for-all sacrifice of Christ upon the cross.[9]

Paganism Restored

Since they themselves were nearly all Jewish by birth, many of the early Christians living in Jerusalem continued for tradition's sake to frequent the Jewish temple until its destruction in 70 A.D. that Christ had predicted.[10] This had nothing to do, however, with Christianity, but with their Jewish heritage. The tabernacle that Moses built in the wilderness, followed by Solomon's temple (which stood in Jerusalem in the days of Jesus), were the only structures of their kind ever ordained by God in the history of the world. The ceremonies and animal sacrifices offered by Aaronic priests in the tabernacle and temple were "a figure [symbol] for the time then present,"[11] which was fulfilled and done away with when Jesus Christ upon the cross "offered himself without spot to God"[12] as the perfect and complete sacrifice once and for all for our sins.[13] This ended any further divinely sanctioned use of the temple in Jerusalem, which was destroyed by the Roman armies under Titus 40 years later and has not been rebuilt to this day.

Nevertheless, sincere Mormons are taught to believe Joseph Smith's fantasy that "true Christianity" (Mormonism) was being practiced in temples throughout the New World 2000 years ago by Jews called "Nephites." So says the Book of Mormon. Today's Mormon Temples have supposedly "restored" this "true Christianity" once again to America and the world. Unfortunately, not a trace has been found of the 38 major cities with their huge "Christian temples" mentioned in the Book of Mormon. (Christianity was first introduced by European settlers long after the Book-of-Mormon period had ended.) The many temples that archaeologists have uncovered in Central and South America involved the worship of pagan deities on altars that ran red with the blood of hundreds of thousands of human sacrifices. This is the real temple religion practiced in the Americas. If the Mormons want to claim a relationship to *this* religion, they are welcome to it.

The Serpent and the Mormon Christ

Incredibly, one of the most popular Visitor's Information Center pictures represents Christ's alleged visit to America as recorded in the Book of Mormon. It shows Jesus standing in the Yucatan in front of two well-known ancient temples, El Castillo and El Caracol. These were pagan, not Christian temples. Moreover, they were not built until about 1000 A.D., six centuries after the alleged Book-of-Mormon period ended and more than 900 years too late for Christ to have stood in front of either of them during his alleged visit to the Nephites. This type of deliberate misrepresentation is commonly used in the Church's attempts to give the Book of Mormon credibility, apparently without a twinge of conscience on the part of the Mormon hierarchy.

In trying to find historical support for the Book-of-Mormon visit of Christ to America just after His resurrection, Mormons have grasped at the legends of Quetzalcoatl. Milton R. Hunter states: "Quetzalcoatl could have been none other than Jesus the Christ, the Lord and God of this earth, and the Savior of the human family. Thus Jesus Christ and Quetzalcoatl are identical."[14] The tradition of Quetzalcoatl dates from about 2000 B.C., when this mythical pagan deity, to whom human sacrifices were offered, began to be represented as a feathered serpent. The Feathered Serpent Cult was rampant throughout the Americas during the alleged Book-of-Mormon period. The only benign figure associated with the myth was a Toltec king who took the name of Quetzalcoatl between 950 and 1000 A.D. and was banished by the bloodthirsty priests—a bit late to be confused with an alleged visit of Christ to America. The Mormon leaders' persistence in this fantasy says as much about their "Jesus Christ" as it does about their honesty. Milton R. Hunter's attitude is typical Mormonism. In his book about Christ's alleged visit to America, after expounding upon the relationship of the "feathered serpent" of the Americas to the "plumed serpent" of Egypt and the Serpent in the Garden of Eden, Hunter goes on to say:

In this chapter and throughout the book, the serpent will be presented as a symbol of Quetzalcoatl or Jesus, and no further reference will be made to its identification with the Prince of Darkness
or Lucifer.[15]

Having called the Serpent's lie to Eve "the truth," and having made his
seductive promise of "godhood" their ultimate goal, and having accepted his
offer of the fig-leaf apron patterned after his own Masonic apron, and having
adopted this emblem of Satan's "power and priesthoods" as the most prominent part of their Priesthood Temple clothing to be worn in life and in
death—it is not surprising that Mormons also identify their "Christ" with
the plumed serpent deity Quetzalcoatl. The comments in the Masonic
Entered Apprentice's Handbook concerning the serpent depicted on the
Masonic apron provide further evidence of the occult roots and meaning
behind the all-seeing eye, apron, beehive, square and compass, grips (special
handshakes), moon, star, sun, and other secret signs and symbols pertaining
to Mormonism's Aaronic and Melchizedek Priesthoods (all of which Joseph
Smith borrowed from Masonry):

> ... The Serpent is regarded as "the Shining One"—the Holy Wis-
> dom itself. Thus we see that the Serpent on our apron denotes that
> we are encircled by the Holy Wisdom....

> The snake is peculiarly associated with [the Hindu god] Shiva, the
> Destroyer, whose close symbolic association with the third
> [Masonic] degree is obvious.... He is depicted making
> the ... [sign] of a Master Mason.[16]

The Strange Paradox of Unworthy Saints

Prior to its dedication and sealing off to the "unworthy" in November
1980, the newly constructed Mormon Temple in Seattle was opened to visitors for guided tours of its 110,000-square-foot interior of opulent symbolism set on a beautiful 23.5-acre site. Thousands of Mormons and
non-Mormons came from near and far to stand even in the rain in long,
snail-paced lines for up to two hours to take the tour. Strangely enough, even
for most of the Mormons this would probably be their only opportunity ever
to enter one of the Temples built by their beloved Church—a Church that
boasts of its perfection and the family togetherness and high morals of its

members, yet excludes the vast majority of them from its most important functions on the ground that they are not worthy.

Almost 75 percent of Mormons have never even taken the steps required to become worthy enough to be initiated into Mormonism's inner secrets, so they don't know what takes place inside their own Temples. However, the very aura of mystery surrounding these forbidden-to-be-talked-about rituals gives the Temples a mystique that convinces the average Latter-day Saint that his Church must be the only true Church on earth. Having been told so often in such a tantalizing way about the "too-sacred-to-be-revealed" nature of Temple work, Mormons look forward to someday becoming worthy enough to enter these sacred sanctuaries and faithfully participate in the secret ceremonies—yet somehow most of them never make it.

President Joseph Fielding Smith declared: ". . . No person can receive an exaltation in the Celestial Kingdom without the ordinances of the Temple."[17] Consequently, the small percentage (probably about ten percent) of Mormons regularly involved in Temple work is just one more of the many strange contradictions in Mormonism. It doesn't seem to occur to most Mormons that this represents a 90 percent failure rate for their Church, nor to question how they can be "Saints" and yet not be "worthy"; or to ask themselves what kind of Church would deny the vast majority of its "Saints" participation in the most important part of the religion it represents. Whether "worthy" or not, however, Mormons stand in awe of their Temples.

Three Confusing Gods of This World

During the Seattle Temple open house, Saints Alive had volunteers distributing about 50,000 informative booklets, and a camera crew filming interviews with "Saints" who were eagerly lined up to get their first (and probably last) glimpse inside a Mormon Temple. One of the standard questions the volunteers asked many of the Mormons was, "Do you consider Mormonism to be Christianity?"

"Yes, I do," was the typical confident Mormon response. "We believe in God the Eternal Father and in His Son, Jesus Christ, and in the Holy Ghost." Dr. Goodman had told us in England, "Anyone who believes in Jesus Christ is a Christian." The June 5, 1983, Salt Lake City *Church News* declared that the Church of Jesus Christ of Latter-day Saints is Christian because *Jesus Christ* is in its name.

As recently as April 1997, the present Prophet of the Church, Gordon B. Hinckley, reiterated this inclusion of Christ's name as justification and evidence that Mormonism is truly Christian. When asked by Don Lattin, the reporter for the *San Francisco Examiner and Chronicle*, on April 13, 1997, about misconceptions regarding the Church, Hinckley laughed and said, "Well, the greatest misconception is that we are not Christians. That's the dominant misconception. And, of course, there isn't a bit of truth to it. If there's anybody who believes in Jesus Christ, we do. His name is a part of the name of the church."

In the January 1984 LDS Church magazine *The Ensign* (pages 17-19), Elder Robert E. Wells of the First Quorum of the Seventy wrote a 20-point article titled "We Are Christians Because..." and described the 20 key reasons Mormons consider themselves truly Christians. While he came close to the real reason most people are Christians in reason No. 12 (with the mention of Christ's Atonement), he negated the truth by adding that one must obey the law to receive the benefits of Calvary:

> We are Christians because "we believe that through the atonement of Christ, all mankind may be saved, by obedience to the laws and ordinances of the Gospel" (Articles of Faith 1:3). There is no other way to salvation.

Like every other cult, Mormonism is a works religion which denies both the full payment of sin's penalty by Christ on the cross and that salvation must be received as a gift of God's grace (Ephesians 2:8-10). The Mormon is saved only by total obedience to all those laws and ordinances of the Mormon gospel. Yet the Bible clearly tells us that Jesus Himself blotted out the writing of the ordinances that were against us, moving them out of our way by nailing them to His cross (Colossians 2:14,15). The Mormon Church has brought the curse of the impossible law back upon the shoulders of its own people.

For 140 years Mormons tried to emphasize that as the "only true Church" they were different from Christians. That approach changed a few years ago, and now there is a big push by the Mormon hierarchy to become accepted as "Christians." This deceptive campaign has been very successful. Today the Church's television and radio ads talk about calling a toll-free number to get a free copy of the Holy Bible, and the response is greater than ever before.

However, the Mormon Jesus is not the Jesus of the Bible and of Christians, but the literal brother of Lucifer in the "pre-mortal existence," who was conceived in mortality *not* by "a virgin . . . with child of the Holy Ghost,"[18] but through Elohim coming from Kolob to have sex with Mary (she is one of Elohim's many wives for eternity). The Mormon Jesus was not God who became a man, but he was a man who had to prove himself in a mortal body in order to become a "god." Mormons have a different heavenly Father, a different Jesus, and a different Holy Spirit from Christians.

Yet there seemed to be not the slightest suspicion by the average Mormon we interviewed in Seattle that his "man-become-God" the Father, his "spirit-brother-of-Lucifer" Jesus Christ, and his "couldn't-possibly-be-God" Holy Ghost were any different from the Father, Son, and Holy Spirit in the Bible, who are three Persons comprising one triune God. By Mormon theology, which ridicules the Trinity, their Father, Son, and Holy Ghost are declared to be "three separate Gods."[19] Yet over and over, God in the Bible is declared to be unchangeable, God from all eternity to all eternity, the one and only God.[20]

The Mormon Holy Ghost couldn't possibly be God, because he lacks both the physical body and eternal marriage that Mormonism claims are absolutely essential for godhood. To be bodiless and marriageless is the judgment meted out to the Devil, according to Mormonism.[21] There is much confusion about the Mormon Holy Ghost, who, for unknown reasons, has never come to earth to get a physical body and "prove" himself in a mortal state, which is the only way to become a Mormon "god." Yet in apparent contradiction to Joseph Smith's "revelation," by the latest calculation the Holy Ghost is still recognized as a "god" in Mormonism. In "Lectures on Faith," which was part of Mormon scripture in the *Doctrine and Covenants* from its first edition in 1835 until suddenly being deleted without notice in 1921, the Holy Ghost was not even acknowledged to exist. The Godhead was described as consisting of the Father, "a personage of Spirit," and the Son. Joseph Smith originally taught that the Holy Ghost was the common mind possessed by Father and Son;[22] Orson Pratt was not sure whether the Holy Ghost existed,[23] but if so, then "it" was probably "a living, all-pervading and most wonderful fluid."[24] President Joseph Fielding Smith wrote:

> I have never troubled myself about the Holy Ghost whether he will sometime have a body or not. . . .

In this dispensation, at least, nothing has been revealed as to his
origin or destiny; expressions on these matters are both speculative
and fruitless.[25]

When asked, "Who is God to you?" those Mormons standing in that long
line outside the Seattle Temple were quite confident in their response, which
usually approximated: "He is like you and me and every other human being
on the face of the earth."

"You mean that he's a man?" we asked.

"Yes, he is."

"How did he become God?"

This question was usually answered with less dogmatism and a good
deal of uncertainty. The general idea proposed was that God had moved from
manhood to "godhood" by somehow becoming perfect, and that Mormons
could become "gods" in the same way, following the same path. This uncertainty only reflects the fact that no Mormon really knows how or when "godhood" can be reached for sure. All of the Mormons, however, seemed to have
a vague idea that becoming a "god" very much involved and hinged upon
certain secret ceremonies that take place in the Temple—and, of course,
upon the Priesthood, which functions there and is of paramount importance
in Mormonism.

A Tale of Two Priesthoods

In Masonry there are two priesthoods: the Aaronic and the Melchizedek.
It is therefore not surprising that Mormonism has the same two priesthoods.
Some Mormons would insist this is just one more in an astonishing number
of "coincidences," as is the fact that in the LDS Temple ceremony Lucifer
states that the markings on his apron (which are the same as those on the
undergarment and the Veil) are the emblems of his power and priesthoods
[plural].

The Melchizedek, or "High" Priesthood, derives its name from the most
mysterious figure in the Bible, who appears suddenly and briefly in Abraham's day. With no information about his ancestors or descendants, birth or
death, he is simply identified as "Melchizedek king of Salem . . . the priest of
the most high God."[26] So intriguing has the Melchizedek Priesthood always
been that numerous occult groups and secret societies, including modern
UFO cults, have laid claim to it. During the ritual for the Masonic 19th degree

of Grand Pontiff, the initiate swears oaths of secrecy and total obedience, and is anointed with oil. Then these words are spoken to him: "Be thou a Priest forever after the order of Melchizedek." Likewise, Mormon members of their "Melchizedek Priesthood" are anointed with oil in Mormon Temples, where they swear similar oaths of secrecy and unquestioning obedience. One of the foundational doctrines of the Mormon Church that is earnestly believed by millions of sincere Mormons is that—

> ... no one may officiate in any ordinance of the Church of Jesus Christ of Latter-day Saints unless he has been ordained to the particular order or office of Priesthood by those possessing the requisite authority.

> Thus no man receives the Priesthood except under the hands of one who holds that Priesthood himself; that one must have obtained it from others previously commissioned; and so every bearer of the priesthood today can trace his authority to the hands of Joseph Smith the Prophet, who received his ordination under the hands of the Apostles Peter, James and John; and they had been ordained by the Lord Jesus Christ.[27]

Unfortunately, there is no historical evidence whatsoever that Joseph Smith was ever so ordained. In a letter dated September 26, 1960, Apostle LeGrand Richards admitted: "While we are a record-keeping people, as the Lord commanded, nevertheless our records are not complete.... We do not have the date that Peter, James and John conferred the Melchizedek Priesthood upon them [Joseph Smith and Oliver Cowdery]."[28] Mormon historian B.H. Roberts likewise admitted that "there is no definite account of the event [the conferring of the Melchizedek Priesthood] in the history of the prophet Joseph, or, for that matter, in any of our annals...."[29] That may come as a shock to most Mormons, but the convincing fact is that there were many journals kept and even histories published during the early years of the Church, but *none* of them contains so much as a passing mention of this most important event until many years after the alleged occurrence.

Beginning with its October 1834 issue, the official Church publication *Messenger and Advocate* carried a series of eight articles written by Oliver Cowdery with the close collaboration of Joseph Smith that should have mentioned this tremendously significant event, yet it was conspicuously absent. Entitled "Early Scenes and Incidents in the Church," the series was represented to be "founded upon facts . . . a full history of the rise of the church . . . [containing] the most interesting parts of its progress . . . a correct statement of events as they have transpired. . . . " This history related that an angel appeared to Joseph and Oliver and declared, "Upon you my fellow servants, in the name of Messiah, I confer this priesthood and this authority. . . . " There was only this one visit, by an unnamed angel, conferring one unspecified Priesthood. However, eight years later, when *Times and Seasons* published the serialized "History of Joseph Smith" in a number of installments in 1842, the story had changed remarkably: There were *two* visits, *two* Priesthoods, and *four* heavenly messengers. The Aaronic Priesthood had allegedly been conferred upon Joseph and Oliver by John the Baptist, followed some months later by Peter, James, and John conferring the Melchizedek Priesthood.

The facts are clear that: 1) there is absolutely no record in Mormon history of the alleged Melchizedek Priesthood ordination as an actual event; 2) Mormon authorities themselves admit that there is no evidence to substantiate this claim about the "restoration" of the Melchizedek Priesthood by Peter, James, and John, which forms the very foundation of Mormonism; and 3) there is much evidence that documents were later altered and scriptures falsified with the deliberate intent of making it appear that this ordination had occurred as claimed. We can only conclude that all of the evidence gives the ring of truth to David Whitmer's sad accusation:

> You have changed the revelations from the way they were first given . . . to support the error of Brother Joseph in taking upon himself the office of Seer to the Church. You have changed the revelations to support the error of high [Melchizedek] priests. . . .
>
> The office of high priests was never spoken of and never thought of being established in the Church until Rigdon came in. Remember that we had been preaching from August, 1829 until June 1831— almost two years—and had baptized about 2,000 members into the Church of Christ, and had not one high priest.
>
> During 1829 several times we were told by Brother Joseph that an elder was the highest office in the Church. . . .[30]

A Cut-and-Paste History

To any unbiased investigator, all of the evidence points to the conclusion that the 1842 account was fabricated in order to enhance the image of the Mormon Church in the eyes of its critics and to shore up the "Prophet's" sagging authority in the face of mounting rebellion, much of it due to growing rumors concerning his adulterous affairs. How else can anyone explain rationally why the 1834 official "full history" of events that claimed to be "particular [and] . . . minute" failed to mention these most important events that represent the entire basis for the Priesthood power and authority that the Mormon Church boasts is its exclusive right and possession under the so-called "restoration"? How else can we account for the undeniable fact that journals, letters, diaries, and printed matter written during this crucial time in Mormon history, as LeGrand Richards and B.H. Roberts admit, make absolutely no mention of these remarkable events that are so essential to the support of the entire structure of Mormonism? To explain this as an "oversight" by so many writers is simply not credible. Had these events actually occurred, they would undoubtedly have been among the first "proofs" mentioned to prospective converts then as now; and had they been known, it is unthinkable that they wouldn't have been mentioned by *anyone*. One can only conclude that these crucial events for the establishment of the Mormon Church did not in fact ever happen. This is further evidenced by what LaMar Petersen so clearly points out:

> The important details that are missing from the "full history" of 1834 are likewise missing from the *Book of Commandments** in 1833. The student would expect to find all the particulars of the Restoration in this first treasured set of 65 revelations, the dates of which encompassed the bestowals of the two Priesthoods, but they are conspicuously absent.
>
> The only reference to an angelic visitation is in Chapter 24, paragraph 7: "But after truly repenting, God ministered unto him by an holy angel . . . that he should translate a book."

---

* Most of the original printing was destroyed by a mob and fire, and it was later republished and added to as *Doctrine and Covenants.*

The notable revelations on Priesthood in the *Doctrine and Covenants* . . . are missing, and Chapter 28 gives no hint of the Restoration which, if actual, had been known for four years.

More than four hundred words were added to this revelation of August 1829 in Section 27 of the *Doctrine and Covenants*, the additions made to include the names of heavenly visitors and two separate ordinations.

The *Book of Commandments* gives the duties of Elders, Priests, Teachers, and Deacons and refers to Joseph's apostolic calling, but there is no menton of Melchizedek Priesthood, High Priesthood, Seventies, High Priests, nor High Councilors. These words were later inserted into the revelation on Church organization and government of April 1830, making it appear that they were known at that date, but they do not appear in the original Chapter 24 of the *Book of Commandments*. . . .

Similar interpolations were made in the revelations now known as Sections 42 and 68.[31]

That we are dealing with a cut-and-paste job is evidenced by the numerous contradictions that remain in the record, which it was impossible to eliminate after the fact. For example, we have Joseph Smith's own recorded statement that "the authority of the Melchizedek Priesthood was manifested and conferred for the first time upon several of the elders" at the fourth conference of the Church at Kirtland during June 3-6, 1831. This agrees with David Whitmer's statement that the Melchizedek Priesthood was first introduced in June 1831. No one remembered to rewrite this telltale statement when the later (and now official) claim was made that Peter, James, and John had already conferred this Priesthood two years earlier, in 1829. It is clear that, just as Whitmer charged, the "revelations" were changed. The cut-and-paste-job made it progressively more difficult to cover the fraud as the evolution of the "restored Priesthoods" continued to necessitate changes in prior "revelations" and "history."

In 1835, for example, Joseph Smith pronounced by "revelation" (now known as *Doctrine and Covenants* 107) that "the office of an elder comes under the priesthood of Melchizedek." Unfortunately, this "revelation" created further contradiction vis-à-vis Smith's earlier statement that elders had already existed prior to conferment of the Melchizedek Priesthood. We might generously put this down to a slip of the pen—except this would mean that William Smith made the *same* slip by coincidence when he reported that *elders* were instructed concerning "the priesthood of Melchisedec, to which they had not as yet been ordained."[32] Furthermore, the 1835 "revelation" declared that "the second priesthood is called the Priesthood of Aaron. . . . It is called the lesser priesthood, because it is an appendage to the greater, or the Melchizedek Priesthood."[33] How the "appendage" could exist [by earlier ordination] independent of and prior to conferment of the Priesthood to which it is appended has never been explained.

The Baptism/Ordination Charade

The strange manner in which, according to Joseph Smith's testimony, this "appendage" was "restored" raises further questions. In LDS doctrine, only a baptized person can baptize others, and only one who has the "Priesthood" can confer it. Because of the alleged total apostasy, the "authority" to baptize and ordain no longer existed on earth and had to be "restored" from heaven.* Yet under the alleged direction of an "angel" (who became John the Baptist years later), unbaptized Smith baptized Cowdery; then Cowdery, whose baptism was invalid, baptized Smith. Next, improperly baptized Smith conferred upon also improperly baptized Cowdery the Aaronic Priesthood, which Smith himself didn't have to confer; after this, improperly ordained Cowdery conferred upon Smith the Aaronic Priesthood by virtue of having supposedly received it from Smith, which clearly wasn't possible, since Smith hadn't yet received it, and never did.

The whole thing sounds like a farce, yet this is the foundation upon which the Mormon Church stands today. It would have been far more believable if John the Baptist, who certainly was competent, had simply baptized Smith and Cowdery. Why didn't he? No explanation is given. That question is answered by the evidence. By the time the angel had been turned into John the Baptist, it was too late to rewrite the entire story. So the absurdity of two unqualified men baptizing and ordaining each other, while John the Baptist watches, had to remain as the basis for Mormon Priesthood authority being "restored" from heaven after a total apostasy.

---

* Further contradictions arise here. Mormons believe that John the Apostle as well as three Nephite disciples of Jesus in America (3 Nephi 28:4-12) never died, but remain to the present on earth. Where they have been hiding all these centuries, what value that is, and why with four Apostles on earth a total apostasy could have occurred requiring "restoration" from heaven is not explained.

In 1839, after his excommunication for rightly accusing Joseph Smith of adultery with Fannie Alger, Oliver Cowdery had written in disillusionment that when the Church had first been organized, Joseph had been "First Elder, and I was called to be the Second Elder, and whatever he had of Priesthood (about which I am beginning to doubt) also had I."[34] No one could argue with that, for even by Joseph Smith's own testimony both had played at the charade together. Neither could claim to have received any more authority than the other, since they had mutually and equally conferred it upon themselves. After rejoining the Church in 1848, however, Cowdery declared: "I was also present when the higher or Melchizedek Priesthood (the second ordination) was conferred by the holy angel from on high."[35] It was a worthy attempt at getting back in good graces; however, someone had unfortunately failed to inform Cowdery that the "angel" had become "Peter, James, and John" during his absence from the Church. The mistake might have been worse, because some "angels" had even metamorphosed into God the Father and Jesus Christ while Cowdery had been in apostasy.

It must be shocking if not devastating to any Mormon today to realize that whatever Priesthood authority Joseph Smith ever had was received from Oliver Cowdery. It may be equally disconcerting to be reminded that, as the *Deseret News Church Almanac* faithfully makes unobtrusive notice of each year, it was those three "counterfeiters"—Cowdery, Whitmer, and Harris—who ordained all of the first 12 Apostles of the Church. In a letter dated December 16, 1838, Joseph Smith called these Three Witnesses to the Book of Mormon "too mean to mention; and we had liked to have forgotten them."[36] Unfortunately, there is no way they can be forgotten, because of their crucial role in the foundation of Mormonism. So the Church plays a deceitful, hypocritical game. When it comes to their excommunication, they are called "liars, cheats and blacklegs."[37] As for their renunciation of Mormonism,[38] the Church distorts facts, suppresses documents, and rewrites history.

Yet when mentioned in connection with their alleged "witness" of the gold plates, these apostates are described as "competent men, of independent minds and spotless reputations... [and] unchallenged honesty... [who] remained true to their testimonies throughout their lives without deviation or variation."[39] The Church has even built a monument to its own astonishing hypocrisy in the form of the Martin Harris Memorial Amphitheater, located near Harris's grave in Clarkston, Utah. In this monument the Church honors a man whom its own scriptures describe as that "wicked man"[40] and whom the *Millennial Star* said was "partially deranged, [subject to] fits of monomania... filled with the rage and madness of a demon... [and] a lying, deceptive spirit from the beginning."[41]

Such were the founders of the Mormon Church. Nor will it help to argue that their subsequent apostasy doesn't affect their earlier ordination of the original 12 Apostles. The problem is worse than that. Joseph Smith himself claimed he "saw the 12 in the celestial Kingdom of God." In fact at least half of the original 12 Apostles were excommunicated; and two of them in particular, William E. McLellin (of whom the Prophet had a most marvelous but false vision of him performing miracles "in the South") and Joseph Smith's own brother, William Smith, did their best to expose the lies, frauds, and rewritten "revelations" of the Mormon Church.[42]

If You're Going to Tell a Lie

Long before Hitler and Stalin used the technique so effectively, Joseph Smith had already learned by trial and error that if you tell a big enough lie often enough, many people will eventually believe it. Every Mormon Temple stands as an astonishing monument to a lie so huge and so bold that it becomes convincing. These Temples are supposed to be like the ones Enoch, Noah, and Abraham worshiped in, yet there were no such temples.

Only a "Prophet" who said the moon was inhabited and the Holy Ghost turned Gentile blood into Jewish blood could think up a lie so preposterous: Jewish-Gentile-Christian-Mormon Temples that prominently display the upside-down, five-pointed star (Goat of Mendes) that symbolizes Satan; blond, blue-eyed, pseudo-Aaronic Priests posing as both the true Israel and true Christians while performing secret pagan rituals and openly wearing a fig-leaf apron that symbolizes Lucifer's "power and priesthoods."

In the everlasting kingdom in the new universe after earth's final rebellion[43] at the end of the millennium, there will be *no temple* in the "new Jerusalem."[44] Nor is there so much as a hint in all the Bible that temples of any kind, except the one temple for Israel in Jerusalem, are or ever were authorized of God to be built anywhere or at any time. Yet the great dream of Mormons today and of the various "restoration" groups that have splintered off from the main Utah Church is to erect that fabled Temple that Joseph

Smith prophesied would be located in his lifetime on the sacred site he designated in Independence, Missouri, "Zion." Though that prophecy, as so many of the others, proved false, nevertheless, it is still believed that this must occur to prepare the way for Christ to return with Joseph Smith to rule the world.

The Secret Ambition

It is only when we see Mormonism as a revolutionary secret society determined to take over the world that we begin to understand the real purpose behind its Priesthoods. Apostle Parley P. Pratt wrote: "This Priesthood ... holds the keys of revelation of the oracles of God to man upon the earth; the power and right to give laws and commandments to individuals, churches, rulers, nations and the world; to appoint, ordain, and establish constitutions and kingdoms; to appoint kings, presidents, governors or judges...."[45] Just six weeks before his death, Joseph Smith boldly declared: "I intend to lay a foundation that will revolutionize the whole world."[46] Apostle Orson Hyde boasted: "What the world calls 'Mormonism' will rule every nation."[47] Third President of the Church, John Taylor, stated: "... That kingdom which the Lord has commenced to establish upon the earth ... will not only govern all people in a religious capacity, but also in a political capacity."[48] That this determined goal was adopted early in Joseph Smith's career is evident from the following excerpt of an affidavit sworn to in 1838 by Thomas B. Marsh, disillusioned former President of the Council of the Twelve Apostles:

> The plan of said Smith, the Prophet, is to take this State, and he professes to his people to intend taking the United States and ultimately the whole world.[49]

The Temple ceremonies performed by the Mormon Priesthoods, as the considerable evidence indicates, have nothing to do with the grace of God or the sacrifice of Christ for our sins. They involve secret names, signs, symbols, handshakes, and formulas of classic occultism and ritual magic which the initiate must use to ascend the ladder of hierarchy and thereby gain access to the coveted powers of the "gods." This was Satan's promise and this was Joseph Smith's dream. Gaining this power is the aim of the Melchizedek Priesthood. To achieve it in the afterlife, one must first grasp all the power available in this world here and now. That was the secret kingdom over which Joseph Smith was crowned as king and which he expected to expand to control the entire world. That is still the secret ambition of the Mormon hierarchy, though the average Mormon may be ignorant of it. Brigham Young alluded to this when he explained the occult power and real purpose behind the Melchizedek Priesthood in an important talk delivered in the Bowery, Salt Lake City, July 31, 1864:

> Our religion is founded upon the Priesthood of the Son of God—it is incorporated within this Priesthood.
>
> We frequently hear people inquire what the Priesthood is; it is a pure and holy system of government.
>
> It is the law that governs and controls all things, and will eventually govern and control the earth and the inhabitants that dwell upon it and all things pertaining to it.[50]

15

A Non-Prophet Organization

If Mormonism is really what it claims to be, then the entire human race ought to submit to the authoritarian claims of The Brethren and thereby hasten the return of the Mormon "Messiah" and Joseph Smith to rule the world. It is one thing, however, to submit to the real Lord and Savior, Jesus Christ, when He returns from heaven to reign upon earth, and it is quite another to give unquestioning obedience to Mormon "Prophets," who claim to speak and act for their "Christ" who is the spirit-brother of Lucifer. The absolutely authoritarian position of the Mormon "Prophet, Seer and Revelator" who fronts for The Brethren is evident from Brigham Young's description of himself on more than one occasion as "dictator."[1] Today The Brethren still follow in the footsteps of their founding "Prophet," whom they honor and from whom they have received their authority. Indicating how absolute that authority is and how submissive and compliant all Mormons are required to be, Joseph Smith declared:

> God . . . will make me to be god to you in His stead, and the Elders
> to be mouth to me; and if you don't like it, you must lump it![2]

Before submitting to such totalitarianism, it is only prudent to ask what it is based upon. Mormon doctrine claims that the true Church cannot exist without a "living Prophet" to head it, that there is only *one* true Prophet on earth at a time, and that the head of the Mormon Church is that one and only "living Prophet." How is this justified? Strangely enough, this belief has nothing to do with the actual performance of any Mormon "Prophet," past or present, none of whom has a record of prophecies that would inspire any confidence in anyone. In fact, the list of proven false prophecies beginning with Joseph Smith on down is so staggering that it ought to frighten away any prospective convert who takes the time to investigate.[3]

If the Mormon Church were truly led by actual prophets, one would think the missionaries would be actively handing out authorized books of those prophecies. But the reality is that there are none, because there are no prophecies beyond those uttered in futility by Joseph Smith.

Prophets Who Don't Prophesy

Joseph Smith used his "seer stone" to prophesy, but it has never been used by any Mormon "Prophet" since then, and is in fact locked away in the vault of the First Presidency. How then do Mormon "Prophets" prophesy? The astonishing answer to that question is that they don't! This is all the more startling because Mormons boast that they alone have a "living Prophet," and assert that Catholics (and Protestants by implication) are proven to be in apostasy because they have not added one single book to their canon since they first formed it.[4] They triumphantly declare: "The presence of revelation in the [Mormon] Church is positive proof that it is the kingdom of God on earth."[5] This is the blindest hypocrisy. As the Tanners point out:

> Excluding the Manifesto and the statement (*not* a revelation) on blacks, only three [Mormon] Presidents received revelations which were added to the "standard works."
>
> None of the [other] presidents has given revelations that have been canonized.[6]

Ask any Mormon to name the three most important prophecies uttered by the current "Prophet, Seer and Revelator," Gordon B. Hinckley, and he won't be able to mention one, because there have been none. Even the great Mormon "Prophet" Brigham Young admitted: "I am not a visionary man, neither am I given to prophesying. When I want any of that done I call on brother Heber [C. Kimball]—he is my prophet...." Yet there is no evidence that Heber C. Kimball or any other Mormon leader made any prophecies that came true.

Yes, the Mormon Church does claim that it is daily receiving heavenly guidance through its "living Prophet." However, its criticism against Catholics and Protestants for not adding to the canon of Scripture applies equally to itself, and by its own doctrines condemns it as apostate. The following excerpt of testimony given by Joseph F. Smith (sixth President of the Mormon Church) before a U.S. Senate hearing is significant:

> **SENATOR DUBOIS**— Have you received any revelations from God, which have been submitted by you and the apostles to the body of the church in their semi-annual conference ... [and] sustained by that conference, through the upholding of their hands?
>
> **MR. SMITH**—Since when?
>
> **SENATOR DUBOIS**— Since you became President of the Church?
>
> **MR. SMITH**—No, sir, none whatever. ... I have never pretended to nor do I profess to have received revelations.[7]

All of the evidence indicates that in spite of its proud boast that it is led by a "living Prophet" and on this basis is proven to be the only "true Church" on earth, in actual fact the Mormon Church is a non-prophet organization. Its "Prophets"—at least those in the past 100 years—don't prophesy. And, as we have shown, its earlier "Prophets" were dismal failures when they attempted to do this, for their "prophecies" were mostly wrong. Therefore, any justification for accepting the Mormon "Prophet" as king or dictator and giving him unquestioning obedience does not rest upon qualifications as a genuine "Prophet" that he himself has demonstrated. The fact is that all subsequent Mormon "Prophets" have relied upon the credentials of Joseph Smith, from whom they received their "authority."

If Joseph Smith were a true Prophet, it would be expected that the Mormon Church would have widely published his prophecies and gained many converts thereby. Yet even the most ardent student must labor endlessly to search out the many prophecies of the founding Mormon "Prophet." Why this strange paradox? Simply because his prophecies, with rare exceptions, were false and often ludicrous.

We have already seen that "Prophet" Smith's claim that he was ordained by John the Baptist and Peter, James, and John cannot be substantiated historically as an actual event, but that the evidence all supports the conclusion that this claim was pure fabrication. There is, however, one alleged justification for this claimed "authority" that we haven't yet examined. It is called the

"First Vision," and is in fact the real foundation of every Mormon pretense to authority and "restoration."

The First Vision

Any sincere attempt to get at the true facts and form a rational understanding of the actual history of Mormonism eventually involves the dizzying unraveling of contradictory accounts of fantastic events in a mind-numbing, frustrating journey through what Walter Martin has called *The Maze of Mormonism*.[8] This effort to sift fact from fancy is made all the more difficult, as we have already seen, by the countless changes in "revelations" and personal accounts, effected by the Mormon hierarchy without notice. The saga of the "First Vision" is a prime example.

The official account now published by the Church alleges that in 1820, when he was 14 years old, Joseph Smith "saw two Personages whose brightness and glory defy all description, standing above me in the air. One of them spake unto me, calling me by name, and said—pointing to the other—*This is My beloved Son. Hear Him!*"[9] Seizing this unusual opportunity to ask which church he should join, young Joseph was told that he "must join none of them for they were all wrong, and . . . all their creeds were an abomination in His sight. . . ."[10] This "vision" is crucial to all of Mormonism's claims. It is in the first lesson the Mormon missionaries teach to prospective converts, and a "testimony" of its authenticity is a prerequisite for baptism. The following foundational Mormon doctrines are implicit in this vision: 1) that God is a man with a physical body; 2) that the Father and Son are two separate Gods each with His own body; 3) that there had been a total apostasy, leaving all churches in hopeless heresy; and 4) that Father and Son had put in their first and only appearance on earth together in the history of mankind for the specific purpose of calling this young boy to "restore" the truth by founding the true Church.

There are a number of glaring contradictions in this story. The official account that the Church relies upon today was not published until 1842, some 22 years after it was alleged to have occurred. It is difficult to believe that the most important event in thousands of years—and in fact in all of human history—would have been kept secret for so long. Great importance is put upon this momentous happening by Mormons today; all the missionaries point to it as evidence that theirs is the only true Church—and yet the

First Vision was unknown during those early years when the Church was struggling for recognition and needed something like this story to help give it credibility. Surely no Mormons should complain if this fact causes a great deal of skepticism. Assistant Mormon Church Historian James B. Allen admits that during the 1830s "the general membership of the Church knew little, if anything, about it [the First Vision]."[11] Dr. Allen states that:

> ... None of the available contemporary writings about Joseph Smith in the 1830s, none of the publications of the Church in that decade, and no contemporary journal or correspondence yet discovered mentions the story of the first vision. ...[12]

In view of the above, any prudent person would be compelled to strongly suspect that the alleged "First Vision" is pure fiction concocted many years after it was supposed to have happened. Many other facts point in this same direction. In 1832 the by-then "Prophet" Joseph Smith claimed a "revelation" that without the Priesthood "no man can see the face of God, even the Father, and live."[13] This is still Mormon scripture. How then could Joseph Smith have "seen God" in 1820, nine years before he allegedly received the "Priesthood"? And if he had in fact "seen God" in 1820, wouldn't he have immediately recognized the 1832 "revelation" as spurious, or at least have commented upon how his case was an exception? Moreover, if he had seen God the Father in a physical body as a glorified man in 1820, why would Joseph Smith have approved the "Lectures on Faith" that declared the Father to be "a personage of Spirit"?[14] The "Lectures" were incorporated into Mormon scripture in 1835 and remained there until 1921, when they were quietly removed without explanation. And if Smith had seen Father and Son in two separate bodies in 1820, why would the "Prophet" in the mid-1830s (in the course of rewriting the entire Bible to correct alleged errors in translation) change Luke 10:22 to read (as it still does in the Mormon "inspired version"), "that the Son is the Father, and the Father is the Son"?

The statement by the "Personages" in this vision that all of the Christian creeds on earth "were an abomination" also doesn't ring true. The Apostles' and Nicene Creeds that were accepted by most Christian churches in 1820 simply state such basics as belief "in God the Father Almighty, Maker of Heaven and earth ... in Jesus Christ, His only Son, our Lord, who was conceived by the Holy Ghost, born of the Virgin Mary, suffered under Pontius Pilate, was crucified, dead, and buried, and resurrected," etc. One wonders what could be an "abomination" in creeds that are so biblical and even in agreement with what Joseph Smith himself believed for at least another ten years after this alleged vision. Stranger still is the fact that Joseph Smith and his family at that time were heavily involved in necromancy and divination, communicating with spirits of the dead and divining the location of buried treasure, which the Bible declares to be an abomination to God in no uncertain terms. What "God" could this be who has no word of reproof for Joseph's necromancy and divination, yet abominates all biblical creeds? Could that be why the "truth" that he calls Joseph Smith to "restore" turns out to be identical to the *lie* that Satan used to deceive Eve?

Joseph the Methodist

One of the strangest contradictions in the entire episode of the alleged First Vision is the fact that, having been twice forbidden in this same vision by the Father to join a church, the young "Prophet," who by this time has had many angelic visits, has been led to the gold plates and is translating the Book of Mormon, proceeds in 1828 to join the Methodist Church in Harmony, Pennsylvania. There is more than enough evidence to establish this as historical fact, and it is admitted even by Mormon writers.[15] Joseph's wife, Emma, had been a Methodist since the age of seven, so Joseph may have joined the Methodists to please her—but join he did. There are only two possibilities: 1) Joseph Smith was an incredibly disobedient and irresponsible "Prophet" and his "God" extremely forgetful in not reproving him for joining the Methodist "abomination," or 2) the First Vision didn't really happen, but was invented later. If Joseph Smith's "God" thought all Christians were an abomination, the Methodists had the same opinion about His "Prophet." The account given by two of Emma's cousins, Joseph and Hiel Lewis, of this incident in their local newspaper when questioned about it later is most interesting:

> I, with Joshua McKune, a local preacher at the time, I think in June, 1828, heard on Saturday that Joe Smith had joined the church on Wednesday afternoon....
>
> We thought it was a disgrace to the church to have a practicing necromancer, a dealer in enchantments and bleeding ghosts in it. So on Sunday we went to father's, the place of meeting that day, and got

there in season to see Smith and talked to him some time in father's shop before the meeting.

Told him that his occupation, habits and moral character were at variance with the discipline, that his name would be a disgrace to the church, that there should have been recantation, confession and at least promised reformation—that he could that day publicly ask that his name be stricken from the class book, or stand investigation.

He chose the former, and did that very day make request that his name be taken off the class book.[16]

The mention above of "bleeding ghosts" refers to the manner in which Joseph claimed he had found the gold plates. The Lewis brothers recalled hearing Joseph tell that he had learned "by a dream" the location of the buried gold plates, and having gone to dig them up had been confronted by a ghost that looked "like a Spaniard having a long beard ... with his throat cut from ear to ear, and the blood streaming down," who told him how to obtain the release of the plates from the enchantment that held them.[17] This is most interesting in view of an authenticated letter in the handwriting of Joseph's mother, Lucy Mack Smith, dated January 23, 1829, and written to her sister-in-law, Mary Pierce, of Royalton, Vermont. The letter was purchased in July, 1982, by Provo, Utah, lawyer Brent F. Ashworth and is an enthusiastic account by Mrs. Smith of the finding and translating (and contents in summary) of the marvelous gold plates. There is not a word of heavenly visitors, whether angels or "Gods," but Mrs. Smith relates to her sister-in-law that the Lord "has made his paths known to Joseph in dreams ... and he is able to translate [the gold plates] and he is able to recover these things also in dreams therefore beware that you do not mock."[18]

Dreams and Angels

The mention of a dream is the way that the story of finding the gold plates was at first told. From its absence for 20 years from diaries, letters, and Church publications, it is also quite clear that the "First Vision" was a later concoction. Interestingly enough, Lucy Smith ends the letter with "adieu" just before signing her name. This probably explains the origin of this French word for "goodbye" that appears in the Book of Mormon, supposedly from the lips of Jewish Indians living in America who allegedly communicate in "reformed Egyptian." In the confused and contradictory roots of Mormonism, the brazenness of the "First Vision" concoction is hard to top. There are nine different accounts, each of which contradicts the others on major points. As Sandra Tanner remarked when we interviewed her for the film:

> He changes the date, he changes how old he is, he changes the motivation, why he went into the woods to pray. He changes who was there and he changes what the message was that they gave him.

> If he were giving us an actual account of a real experience, we would assume he would have known the first time around whether it was God or Jesus, if it was both of them, what their message was, and when it happened.

> Yet we find him re-drafting this story. Well, if you were a witness of an accident and someone asked you to tell about it and you gave accounts as divergent as those, people would say you couldn't have witnessed the event.

The one thing that all the nine accounts (except the revised 1842 version) agree upon is that Joseph Smith in none of them claims to have seen God the Father, much less in a physical body. Yet this is the major point now made by the Mormon Church in what has to be a classic case of deception. For 130 years they kept hidden the one and only account written in Joseph Smith's own hand. Copies finally leaked out, and it proves the blatant and deliberate deceit behind this whole scam. Apparently written about 1833, in this account Joseph tells of a *heavenly vision* of the Lord (Jesus), *not an earthly visit* of Father and Son; and it is the Lord in heaven who says, "Joseph my son, thy sins are forgiven thee," *not* the Father who says, pointing to Jesus, "This is my Beloved Son."

Until the days of Joseph Fielding Smith, Mormon "Prophets" and "Apostles" testified that the "Personages" that Joseph saw in his "First Vision" were *not* the Father and Jesus, but one or more angels. Orson Pratt said that "God sent his angel to the 14-year-old Joseph."[19] Orson Hyde made it even clearer: "Why did not the Savior come himself—because to the angels was committed the power of reaping the earth. . . ."[20] From 1851 to August 1877, Brigham Young delivered 363 sermons, but in *none* of them does he assert that the Father and Jesus appeared to Joseph. He does say, however, that "the Lord sent his messengers to Joseph."[21] President Wilford Woodruff said "an angel."[22] John Taylor said, "The Prophet Joseph asked the angel which of the sects was right."[23] Heber C. Kimball said "an holy angel," and George A. Smith spoke of "the ministration of angels."[24] A hymn that Joseph Smith approved, loved, and sang—"An angel from on high the Long, Long Silence broke"—refers to the "First Vision." Still sung today, its very presence in the Mormon hymnal is an indictment of the blatant dishonesty of a Church that builds its claim to world domination on a lie so gross that the contradictions are still there to haunt believers after decades of suppression, revision, and deception.[25]

The Prophet with the World's Greatest Ego

Next to polygamy, there were two subjects that obsessed the founding "Prophet" of the Mormon Church more than any other. One was the destruction of the United States for failing to embrace Mormonism's "restored gospel," and the other was the establishment of "Zion" in Independence, Missouri. In the course of prophesying the destruction of his enemies, Joseph Smith pronounced his own greatness and triumph with such bursts of blind pride that the language is embarrassing to read even today. He continued these pronouncements right up to the time of his assassination, which dramatically proved all such prophecies false. Typical was the defiantly egotistical boast in the form of a "prophecy" at the semiannual General Conference a few months before his death, to the effect:

> . . . that he could not be killed within five years from that time; that they could not kill him till the Temple [in "Zion"] would be completed, for that he had received an unconditional promise from the Almighty concerning his days, and he set Earth and Hell at defiance. . . .[26]

Considering himself to be greater than any person who ever lived, including Jesus Christ ("I have more to boast of than ever any man had"[27]), Joseph Smith was dominated by a giant ego that was inflated to the point of mania. Although he hadn't even finished elementary school, much less law school, the "Prophet" declared: "I am a lawyer; I am a big lawyer and comprehend heaven, earth and hell, to bring forth knowledge that shall cover up all lawyers, doctors and other big bodies."[28] ". . . I know more than they all."[29] In one of the most astonishing flights of braggadocio in recorded history, the

"Prophet" was so carried away with presenting his own importance that his "God" came off as little more than a junior partner or assistant to Joseph Smith in his mythical heroic accomplishments:

> The whole earth shall bear me witness that I, like the towering rock in the midst of the ocean, which has withstood the mighty surges of the warring waves for centuries, am impregnable....

> I combat the errors of ages; I meet the violence of mobs; I cope with illegal proceedings from executive authority: I cut the gordian knot of powers, and I solve mathematical problems of universities, with truth—diamond truth; and God is my "right hand man."[30]

Spoiler of the Gentiles

The obsession with his own greatness was closely intertwined with the twin obsessions of the destruction of the United States and the establishment of "Zion." No egomaniac can endure rejection. It was an unbearable affront not only to his "God" but also to Joseph Smith that the "Gentiles" had not admitted that he was wiser than Solomon and submitted to his benevolent kingship. Mormon writer Hyrum L. Andrus explains that the "Gentiles" apparently understood well enough that the Mormon "Kingdom of God" would "require a major concession on the part of non-Latter-day-Saints: that of granting the appropriate Priesthood Councils in Zion the power to name men to governmental office...."[31] Quite naturally the "Gentiles" were not enthusiastic in leaping at the opportunity to surrender themselves to The Brethren. This unwillingness to join the "restoration" movement was taken by Joseph Smith and the Mormon Apostles to be an unreasonable and blasphemous rejection of the "restored" gospel, and it required sterner methods of persuasion. The *St. Clair Banner* of September 17, 1844, carried this sworn testimony of G.T.M. Davis:

> The great aim of Joseph Smith was evidently to clothe himself with the most unlimited power; civil, military and ecclesiastical, over all who became members of his society....

> ... [and] to satisfy his people ... that the authority with which God had clothed him ... extended over all mankind ... [and that] the Latter-day Saints, under Joe as their King and Ruler, were to

conquer the Gentiles, and that their subjection to this authority was to be obtained by the sword.[32]

Although Mormon apologists have tried to deny the facts, the evidence now seems overwhelming that Joseph Smith taught, organized, and encouraged his followers to rob, murder, and plunder those who opposed them. This was called "spoiling the Gentiles," and the plunder was "consecrated" to the "treasury" to be communistically shared among the poor "Saints" under the direction of a Bishop.[33] Several Mormon writers, such as Leland Gentry, have been honest enough to admit the truth, or at least part of it. Gentry says, "It was frequently observed among the [Mormon] troops . . . that the time had come when the riches of the Gentiles should be consecrated to the Saints."[34] Of course the "Gentiles" fought back, and the isolated skirmishes grew into what became known as the "Mormon War" in 1838. Mormon George M. Hinkle later testified in a Senate hearing:

> I spoke to Mr. Smith, Jr., in the house, and told him that this course of burning houses and plundering, by the Mormon troops, would ruin us; that it could not be kept hid, and would bring the force of the State upon us; that houses would be searched and the stolen property found.
>
> Smith replied to me, in a pretty rough manner, to keep still . . . that it would discourage the men; and he would not suffer me to say anything about it. . . .
>
> I saw a great deal of plunder . . . brought into camp; and . . . I understood this property and plunder were placed into the hands of the bishop at Diahmon. . . .
>
> Until lately, the teachings of the church appeared to be peaceable . . . but lately a different idea has been advanced—that the time had come when this kingdom was to be set up by forcible means, if necessary. It was taught that the time had come when the riches of the Gentiles were to be consecrated to the true Israel. . . .
>
> While the last expedition was in progress . . . Rigdon held in his hand a letter from Joseph Smith . . . in which, he said, there was a profound secret. . . . The letter as near as I recollect it, was as follows:
>
> That our enemies were now delivered into our hands, and that we should have victory over them in every instance.

The letter stated that, in the name of Jesus Christ, he knew this by the spirit of prophecy....[35]

Like almost every other "prophecy" that Joseph Smith uttered, this one also turned out to be false, in spite of the bluster and determination of the false "Prophet" and his army. Determined to fight to the bitter end, the Mormons called it a "war of extermination." In one famous sermon to the Church, President Sidney Rigdon said, "... It shall be between us and them a war of extermination; for we will follow them until the last drop of their blood is spilled; or else they will have to exterminate us."[36] Proving again the falseness of Mormon "prophecies," the "Mormon War" ended with the ignominious surrender of the warring "Prophet" and his rebels to the Missouri state militia at the end of October 1838. John Corrill related that, when the showdown came, "Smith appeared to be much alarmed, and told me to beg like a dog for peace.... [He] had rather die himself than have the people exterminated."[37] Indeed, the militia almost shot the "Prophet" on the spot. Imprisoned in Liberty Jail, Smith and his men were charged with "treason, murder, arson, burglary, robbery, larceny and perjury."[38] Sampson Avard, leader of the secret Mormon extermination squad called the Danites, testified in the trial that:

> I consider Joseph Smith, Jr., as the prime mover and organizer of this Danite Band. The officers of the band, according to their grades, were brought before him, at a schoolhouse, together with Hiram Smith and Sidney Rigdon: the three composing the First Presidency of the whole Church.
>
> Joseph Smith, Jr., blessed them, and prophesied over them: declaring that they should be the means in the hands of God of bringing forth the Millennial Kingdom. It was stated by Joseph Smith, Jr., that it was necessary this band be bound together by a covenant, that those who revealed the secrets of the society should be put to death.
>
> The covenant taken by all the Danite band was as follows, to wit: They declared, holding up their right hands, "In the name of Jesus Christ, the Son of God, I do solemnly obligate myself ever to conceal, and never to reveal, the secret purposes of this society... [or] I hold my life as the forfeiture."

Lyman Wight observed that before the winter was over he [Joseph Smith] thought we would be in St. Louis and take it.... Smith said...that one should chase a thousand, and two put ten thousand to flight; that he considered the United States rotten.

He compared the Mormon Church to the little stone spoken of by the Prophet Daniel; and the dissenters first, and the State next, was part of the image that should be destroyed by this little stone....

Smith, after erecting his bulwarks [the night after General Lucas with his militia arrived], asked me if I did not think him [Smith] pretty much of a general; and I answered in the affirmative.

We were advised, all the time, to fight valiantly, and that the angels of the Lord would appear in our defense and fight our battles.[39]

Destruction of the U.S.A.

In spite of the fact that every time he opened his mouth to "prophesy" he only further confirmed that he was a false "Prophet," Joseph Smith's giant ego wouldn't allow him to quit. Revenge upon the "Gentiles" became his obsessive madness. That revenge was to work itself out in two ways: the destruction of all of his enemies throughout the entire United States, and the establishment of his Independence, Missouri, "Zion," which was the key to reigning over the entire world. Mormons sometimes refer to Joseph Smith's so-called "Civil War Prophecy" as proof that he did indeed foretell the future. Of course, they cover up the fact that the "prophecy" was made in the midst of an earlier rebellion in December 1832. That rebellion ended quietly a few months later. It was years later, after Joseph Smith's death, that the Civil War (which had been generally considered inevitable) did break out and the earlier prophecy published. Even beyond its obvious reference to the earlier rebellion that never materialized, the "prophecy" was clearly false, for it never developed the international proportions he predicted:

> Verily, thus saith the Lord...behold, the Southern States shall be divided against the Northern States...and the war shall be poured out upon all nations.[40]

Mormon writer William E. Berrett admits that a secret society called "the Danites," "as historians agree," was organized within the Mormon Church "for the purpose of plundering and murdering the enemies of the

Saints."[41] Leland Gentry, also a Mormon, adds that the "Danites were apparently taught to obey the commands of their superiors without question or hesitation."[42] Joseph Smith, however, was above the law and would admit to having done no wrong. The "Gentiles" had rejected the "restored" gospel given to him by extraterrestrials from Kolob, so they had to be destroyed as apostates. What Mormons had failed to do by force of arms and subterfuge they called upon their "God" to do. "Revelations" that confirmed their desires began to come through the "Prophet." Illinois Governor Thomas Ford, who later had Joseph and Hyrum jailed in Carthage for inciting to riot and treason, thereafter reported:

> The Mormons openly denounced the government of the United States as utterly corrupt, and as being about to pass away, and to be replaced by the government of God, to be administered by his servant Joseph."[43]

After the "Prophet's" death, the obsessive desire to see the destruction of the United States took on the added dimension of a means to avenge Smith's death. As Brigham Young later declared:

> God Almighty will give the United States a pill that will put them to death, and that is worse than lobelia.

> I am prophet enough to prophesy the downfall of the government that has driven us out. . . . Wo [sic] to the United States: I see them going to Death and destruction.[44]

It was Joseph Smith who began this series of false "prophecies." In May 1843 he said:

> . . . And I prophesy in the name of the Lord God of Israel, unless the United States redress the wrongs committed upon the Saints in the state of Missouri and punish the crimes committed by her officers that in a few years the government will be utterly overthrown and wasted, and there will not be so much as a potsherd left.[45]

This is an obviously false prophecy again, identifying Joseph Smith as one of the false prophets that the Bible warns about. In 1833 Joseph Smith declared:

> And now I am prepared to say by the authority of Jesus Christ, that not many years shall pass away before the United States shall

present such a scene of bloodshed as has not a parallel in the history of our nation; pestilence, hail, famine, and earthquake will sweep the wicked of this generation from off the face of the land, to open and prepare the way for the return of the [ten] lost tribes of Israel from the north country.

The people of the Lord ... have already commenced gathering together to Zion, which is in the state of Missouri. ...

... Flee to Zion, before the overflowing scourge overtake you, for there are those now living upon the earth whose eyes shall not be closed in death until they see all these things, which I have spoken, fulfilled.[46]

Instead of the wicked of that generation being swept off the land and the Mormons finding refuge in "Zion," it was the "Saints" who were swept off the land, while the "wicked" remained. Driven from Missouri, they established themselves in Illinois, until they had to flee for Utah. The dream of Zion never left them, however, and down through the years the hope inspired by the many "prophecies" concerning the return of the "Saints" to "Zion" has never died. This is the heart of "restoration" groups today.

The Restoration of Zion

False prophecies, broken promises, lies, deception, egomania, and an incurable lust for power and sex were not enough to make the early "Saints" admit the awful truth about their "Prophet" and his Mormon religion. He had told them something that they desperately wanted to believe: that they were somebodies, the best people on earth, the real Israel, the only true Church, potential "gods"; that the "keys" to the promised "exaltation" were secret grips, names, signs, and occult incantations that could only be learned and practiced in the Temple. Nothing was going to shake the early "Saints" loose from that fantastic hope. At the heart of this delusion was the belief that the ultimate Temple must yet be built in "Zion" on the very "Temple lot" in Independence, Missouri, that the "Prophet" had pointed out. Of course, he had prophesied that he would live to see it built; and even after that was proven false, they still believed.

There was even a definite time limit set by Joseph Smith that held out a false hope for sincere but deceived Mormons for decades; and in spite of the overwhelming evidence that he was a false prophet, millions of Mormons today still base their hope for eternity upon the alleged "revelations" of Joseph Smith. On February 14, 1835, Oliver B. Huntington recorded in his diary that Joseph Smith had said that "God had revealed to him that the coming of Christ would be within 56 years."[47] The official *History of the Church* records the same false prophecy.[48] From that point on, the "Saints" fell back upon the vain hope that if not before then, at least no later than February 14, 1891, all would be well in "Zion." In 1886, the *Millennial Star* quoted Apostle Moses Thatcher's statement: "The time of our deliverance will be within five years; the time indicated [by Joseph Smith's "prophecy"] will be February 14, 1891."[49] Mormon writer Klaus J. Hansen makes this staggering admission:

> ... In 1890 there was a widespread belief among Church members that Joseph Smith's prediction of 1835, that fifty-six years would "wind up the scene," would be fulfilled.

> But such enthusiasm was short-lived. In 1903, Patriarch Benjamin F. Johnson ... could not conceal his disappointment when he remarked that "we were over seventy years ago taught by our leaders to believe that the coming of Christ and the millennial reign was much nearer than we believe it to be now."[50]

It is heart-wrenching to read the continual and blustering assurances that "Zion" would be built "in this generation" which were repeatedly trotted out and paraded before the Church long after the hopelessness should have been obvious to everyone. The "Apostles" and "Prophets" who followed Joseph Smith had to close their eyes to facts and common sense and uphold him as a "Prophet" of God or else renounce their own claims to the authority they had inherited from him. The price was too high then, as it is now. So they continued to insist that what was and is so obviously false was really true. In a sermon in 1845, Brigham Young bravely declared, to the accompaniment of loud "Amens," that "... as the Lord lives we will build up Jackson county in this generation."[51]

Apostle Heber C. Kimball stoutly affirmed:

> ... We are as sure to go back there as we exist.... Joseph the Prophet dedicated that land.... I shall yet see the day that I will go back there with brother Brigham and with thousands and millions of others, and we will go precisely according to the dedication of the Prophet of the living God."[52]

They believed it would happen because they believed Joseph Smith was "the Prophet of the living God." It was a false prophecy, proving that he was a false prophet—yet millions of Mormons today still believe him. Apostle George A. Smith exhorted the faithful, "Let me remind you that it is predicted that this generation shall not pass away till the temple shall be built. . . ."[53] It is astonishing that as late as 1900, nine years after the time limit Joseph Smith had set, President Lorenzo Snow "affirmed at a special priesthood meeting in the Salt Lake Temple that 'there are many here now under the sound of my voice, probably a majority, who will live to go back to Jackson County and assist in building that temple.'"[54] In spite of their "testimony" that Joseph Smith was a true Prophet, and the repeated affirmation that they believed the "promise of God" given through him, it never happened.

Millions of Mormons bear their "testimony" today in spite of the evidence to the contrary; but their repeated affirmations that Mormonism is true won't make it so. No one could have a stronger or more completely misplaced faith than that expressed by Apostle Orson Pratt:

> We believe in these promises as much as we believe in any promise ever uttered by the mouth of Jehovah.
>
> The Latter-day Saints just as much expect to receive a fulfillment of that promise during the generation that was in existence in 1832 as they expect the sun will rise and set tomorrow.
>
> Why? Because God cannot lie. He will fulfill all His promises. He has spoken. It must come to pass. This is our faith.[55]

Yet it didn't come to pass. Therefore, by the criterion established by God Himself, the Lord had not spoken through Joseph Smith. Speaking through the great prophet Moses, God warned of false prophets with these words:

> When a prophet speaketh in the name of the Lord, if the thing follow not, nor come to pass, that is the thing which the Lord hath not spoken, but the prophet hath spoken it presumptuously; thou shalt not be afraid of him."[56]

It would take an entire book to deal adequately with all that Joseph Smith solemnly prophesied in the name of his "God" from Kolob that never came to pass, and thus proved him again and again to be a false prophet.

The Coming Kingdom

After being put out of his own house, and heartbroken by words from Mormon family members saying that they wanted nothing further to do with him, Dick Baer wrote a letter begging his family to face the facts for their own sakes. In that letter Dick spelled out in detail dozens of inescapably false prophecies by Joseph Smith.[57] To his disappointment, he has found few Mormons inside or outside his family who are willing even to consider the evidence. Such is the astonishing power that Joseph Smith still wields through appealing lies which millions wish to believe.

Ed Decker and Bill Schnoebelen did a further study and came up with even more documented and absolutely false prophecies. To be fair, they also found five true ones, none of which had dealt with a single "kingdom" issue.[58]

It is tragic that so many Mormons are still clinging to the impossible dream of "exaltation" to a mythical "godhood" based upon their misplaced confidence in "prophecies" so fraudulent that it would seem impossible for anyone who openly and honestly examined the facts to continue to be deceived by Joseph Smith's false claims. The "prophecies" concerning "Zion" have obviously all failed.

Yet 10 million Mormons today, many of them sincerely deceived, are still entranced by the "restoration-of-Zion" theory. The rest of the package, which must be accepted in toto, includes the belief that The Brethren, by virtue of authority inherited from Joseph Smith, must be blindly obeyed because they hold the keys to exaltation and godhood.

The Mormon "Zion" fits into an emerging pattern of increasing occult activity leading to a one-world government that could well prepare for the fulfillment of biblical prophecies concerning Antichrist. To understand it properly, the "Zion" kingdom must be viewed in the broader context of the planned Mormon takeover of the world. This is the real "key," the secret hope Mormons cling to, and the basis for storing one year's supply of food, guns, and ammunition.

If you were to go through the avalanche of correspondence we have gathered over the years, you would see that while the individual stories are vastly divergent, one central question leaps from the pages: *"How could anyone in his right mind believe such teachings?"*

This is not meant to be some railing complaint against the mind-set of the Mormon people. Whenever Dave or Ed ask this kind of question, we are severely chastised for being unkind to the very people to whom we claim a ministry calling. But this kind of response has held back serious analysis of the problems and absurdities of the LDS gospel. How in fact do intelligent, well-educated, normal people end up with a complicated belief system that is more in line with Star Wars than with biblical and historical evidences of faith?

Simply, it comes down to the unshakable Mormon testimony: Everything The Brethren utter is God-breathed, and anything said otherwise is a lie. There is no moving off this line drawn in the sand of the Mormons' minds, because without this subjective testimony, based on feelings instead of facts, there would be no Mormonism at all.

Several years ago, Ed slipped quietly into an LDS Fast and Testimony Meeting. He went to just sit and listen. "I was transfixed by the testimonies I heard there. They were the *exact* wording of so many of those I had heard and shared myself while an active Mormon years before."

> I bear you my testimony that I know the Book of Mormon is true (or the Word of God), I know that Joseph Smith is a true Prophet of God (and that Gordon B. Hinckley is the true Prophet of God today), and I know that the Church is the only true church on the face of the earth today, and I know that Heavenly Father's Priesthood is on the earth today and I thank my Heavenly Father that I am a member of this Church (and/or Priesthood) and for the Bishop and for family home evening (or the Temple, Relief Society, genealogy), and I am so grateful for my home teachers (or visiting teachers, Priesthood leaders, the Stake Presidency) because [short faith-promoting story], and I say these things in the name of Thy Son, Jesus Christ, Amen.

While Ed sat and listened, he realized that there was a subtle mind-warp taking place in that meeting. Only two testimonies contained more than a few words out of sync. One lady who was obviously not a member of the fully approved group apologized in tears for not being worthy enough as the rest of the Ward sat nodding their heads in agreement. A little girl stood on the pew and gave a very sweet and halting rendition of the above, and everyone sighed happily with her beaming, teary-eyed parents.

Ed explains what was happening:

> My mind went back to an encounter I had some years earlier. I was
> asked by a local pastor to go with him to a Mormon Bishop's office.
> It seems that the pastor had led a young neighborhood girl to the
> Lord. The girl had been coming to his church with a few of her
> friends. The girl was an inactive member of the LDS Church, and
> when she had shared the joy of her new-found faith with her family,
> they were frightened and immediately called in the Bishop. The
> Bishop demanded that the errant pastor come to his office and get
> straightened out.
>
> When we arrived, the Bishop was there with the girl and her par-
> ents, but when he recognized me, he phoned someone and left his
> office until two other men arrived, apparently skilled in running off
> infidels. The meeting was difficult at best, but what made it so
> unique was that during their defense of the only true faith, one of
> the men backed himself into an indefensible corner from which
> there was no possible escape.
>
> He then did what every single Mormon will do in a similar situa-
> tion: He started to "bear his testimony." But this time I was sitting at
> a desk with my face just 15 inches from his. As he began his recita-
> tion, I noticed that his eyes had dilated just as though he were hyp-
> notized. He was at the part where . . . "I know the Book of Mormon
> is the Word of God . . ." and I slapped my hands together right in
> front of his nose and loudly asked, "What proof do you have that it is
> the word of God?" The man bounced back, his eyes slowly returning
> to normal, and he sat there confused and stuttering. He had no
> answer.
>
> I had broken through what I call the mind-warp of the LDS testi-
> mony, and this man was through for the rest of the meeting. The
> pastor was able to reinforce that special experience for the young
> girl, and with love and true spiritual authority he brought Christ's
> words home to those in the meeting.
>
> I had learned a valuable lesson that night and have used that knowl-
> edge during literally scores of similar encounters since then. What
> actually happens at every LDS Fast and Testimony meeting is a
> form of group hypnosis, and is a key part of the answer to this mys-
> terious question of how so many people could be so misled.

I know some will say I am being sensational, but the fact is that it is true! Every single member of the LDS Church listens to the same words being repeated over and over again with almost no variation. After years of doing this during a time of sacred fasting and avowing one's reason for faith in the supposed presence of one's god, the chant becomes bedrock truth.

It often seems that only when a Mormon is confronted or shocked with the *real truth* that we are able to get past the powerful control of his or her testimony and get down into the level of reason and analysis. Perhaps that is why *The God Makers* book and film have been so effective, and why so many active Mormons hate *even the name* of the book/film/authors.

Look at the words of the Mormon testimony. They testify of the Church, its authority, its scripture, its true Prophet leader. Not one word *talks of a relationship with God through Christ,* as Jesus Himself states in Scripture. The only Mormon connection to God (and godhood itself) is through the LDS system. The testimony will override every bit of logic, evidence, or scriptural truth that would challenge the faith of someone who has been brought through the mind-warp techniques described above. It is the same kind of system used on POWs, the same kind used by the hard cults, the same techniques used by the New Age mind-development programs. *These groups all use it because it works effectively upon every surrendered mind it touches.*

Look at the subjects of the LDS testimony. How can anyone irrefutably *know* that the Book of Mormon is true when it defies every historic and anthropological kind of evidence? Not only does scientific evidence refute any kind of Book of Mormon civilization, but there is concrete evidence of a totally different civilization in its place. *Yet any faithful Mormon KNOWS it is true.*

16

THE SECRET
KINGDOM

Investigative reporter Jeffrey Kaye concluded, "The Mormon Church, this American Zion, wields more economic power more effectively than the state of Israel or the Pope in Rome."[1] Actually, the word *church* is misleading when applied to Mormondom, for the power structure controlling its staggering resources is organized for the kind of absolute authoritarianism that one usually associates with a cult and not with a responsible church. Nor are the ultimate goals of The Brethren compatible with the normal aims of Christian leaders. They are essentially the same as those of cults in general and especially those of secret revolutionary groups working toward a takeover of the world. As one former teacher at Brigham Young University has said:

> The Mormons do intend to take over the world.... There is no secret about that—it's in the writings of Joseph Smith right on down.
>
> The Constitution of the United States will "hang by a thread" and the Church will save it by establishing a theocracy.[2]

Any who think the Mormon kingdom is a democracy are under a delusion. In fact it is a dictatorship ruled by its inner elite circle. As the front page of *The Wall Street Journal* recently said, "Today, from their 28-story marble-and-glass Church headquarters building in Salt Lake City, Mormon Church leaders oversee a vast and growing world-wide financial empire."[3] From these offices, their dictatorial control reaches out to every Church level and into every facet of Mormon life. Whatever "vote" there seems to be at the

Ward, Stake, and individual levels is part of a cleverly contrived illusion that continues to deceive millions of Mormons into imagining that they actually have some say in Church affairs. Although they do have the "freedom" to disagree with their leaders, to do so means excommunication and damnation. Excommunicated for openly disagreeing with The Brethren's position on ERA, Sonia Johnson has said:

> The Mormon church has become more powerful than we dare believe. It's downright terrifying, especially when you see how rich and influential it is. . . .

> I really think if we could ever get an investigation, it would uncover something so like Watergate, it would blow everything wide open.[4]

Totalitarian Theocratic Communism

Saints Alive was once involved in some litigation arising out of a physical attack upon one of its missionaries by an LDS tour guide on the street just outside Salt Lake City's Temple Square. In an interrogatory exchange, the surprising response by the Mormon Church revealed that it was an unincorporated association *without assets!* All wealth and power is owned and controlled by the closely held *Corporation of the President of the Church of Jesus Christ of Latter-day Saints, Inc.* Church members who have faithfully and sacrificially contributed their tithes, time, and energy are powerless to demand an accounting or to change a single action by the First Presidency, even if all ten million of them stood up in unison and "voted" unanimously for it.

The startling fact is that Mormon Church members have no vote or participation of any kind in the corporate entity that controls Mormondom. They can sincerely perform their functions as Bishops, Elders, High Priests, and Sunday school superintendents all they wish, but in the real world of legal ownership and raw power they are only pawns subject to manipulation from the top. All of this is part of a secret kingdom that Jeffrey Kaye has called the "Invisible Empire" and about which most Mormons have only the vaguest notions. This theocracy was alluded to by late Apostle Bruce R. McConkie: "Through this church and kingdom a framework has been built through which the full government of God will eventually operate."[5]

That "full government of God" involves what is known as the "United Order." "Revelations" that came through Joseph Smith described it as a theocratic communistic society. All property and income were to be given over to the control of the Church and then distributed to everyone according to his need as The Brethren defined it, so that "the poor shall be exalted, in that the rich are made low."[6] Those who transgressed were to be put out of the Church, in which case the property they had given into the "treasury" would not be returned to them.

Serious problems prevented full implementation of the "United Order." It never really worked. However, the Mormon Church still looks forward to the day when these "revelations" of God through the "Prophet" will be fulfilled and Mormon theocratic communism firmly established worldwide. That can only happen when the Church has taken full political power. When that time comes, woe to all who transgress the "laws" of the Mormon gospel. Excommunication with loss of earthly property will be supplemented with the death penalty.

The Doctrine of Blood Atonement

Since the early days of the Church it has always been Mormon doctrine that "... under certain circumstances there are some serious sins for which the cleansing of Christ does not operate, and the law of God is that men must then have their own blood shed to atone for their sins."[7] It is generally thought that these "serious sins" are in the category of murder and adultery. However, this is not clearly defined in Mormonism. Brigham Young said that "any man or woman, who violates the covenants made with their God will be required to pay the debt. The blood of Christ will never wipe that out, your own blood must atone for it."[8] In the same general vein, President J.M. Grant declared: "... If they are covenant breakers we need a place designated where we can shed their blood."[9] Besides murder and adultery, blood atonement was also advocated for stealing[10] and taking the name of the Lord in vain.[11] Likewise, the penalty for marrying an African "under the law of God is death on the spot. This will always be so."[12] (The 1978 decision opening the Priesthood to blacks didn't change that law.) Blood atonement was also required for lying[13] or "damn[ing] old Joe Smith or his religion...."[14] That most serious of all crimes, apostasy, bears the death penalty, and those who kill an apostate are saving his soul. This is a real concern of ex-Mormons. Many have received death threats and some have even been shot at. Brigham Young was very firm on this subject, as the following excerpt from one of his sermons as reported in *Journal of Discourses* indicates:

> I say, rather than that apostates should flourish here, I will unsheath my Bowie knife and conquer or die. (Great commotion in the congregation, and a simultaneous burst of feeling, assenting to the declaration.)

> Now, you nasty apostates, clear out, or judgment will be put to the line, and righteousness to the plummet. (Voices, generally, "go it, go it.")

> If you say it is right, raise your hands. (All hands up.)

> Let us call upon the Lord to assist us in this, and every good work.[15]

The doctrine of "blood atonement" was practiced in Utah prior to statehood, until the Mormon leadership realized that they must obey federal laws or have them enforced by the United States Army. There are rumors that this doctrine is still practiced secretly in Utah today. It would be strange if it were not, for Mormons boast that they of all people "practice what they believe"; and as Joseph Fielding Smith said, blood atonement "is scriptural doctrine, and is taught in all the standard works of the Church."[16] Certainly, Church leaders would openly carry this out today if they could. In fact, the Utah State Legislature with its Mormon majority has succeeded in legalizing one method of practicing blood atonement. Utah is the only state where the condemned may elect to be executed by a firing squad, which causes his own blood to be shed and thus by Mormon belief atones for his sins. The execution some years ago by a firing squad of condemned murderer Gary Gilmore, who was a Mormon, is an example. Brigham Young made blood atonement sound like a generous provision that the guilty would willingly embrace and the executioners gladly perform "in love":

> Now take a person . . . [who] knows that by having his blood shed he will atone for that sin. . . . is there a man or woman in this house but what would say, "shed my blood that I may be saved and exalted with the Gods"? . . . He would be glad to have his blood shed. . . .

> I could refer to plenty of instances where men have been righteously slain, in order to atone for their sins. . . .

This is loving our neighbor as ourselves.... If he wants salvation and it is necessary to spill his blood on the earth in order that he may be saved, spill it.... That is the way to love mankind.[17]

Regardless of the understanding of the average Mormon, The Brethren look forward to the day when they will once again be able to practice openly not only polygamy but blood atonement. When will that day come? In answer to that question, Bruce R. McConkie has written: "This doctrine can only be practiced in its fullness in a day when the civil and ecclesiastical laws are administered in the same hands."[18] If the Mormon Church should ever succeed in taking over the world, Mormonism in its most fanatical and bizarre practices will become the rule enforced unbendingly upon everyone. Dare anyone call this a conspiracy? Thinking he was denying it, one Mormon recently told us, "This isn't a *conspiracy*, it's our *destiny!*" As with polygamy in the past, the obsessive ambition of world domination is openly denied today but secretly plotted. Though less blatantly proclaimed, that ultimate goal hasn't changed since the early days when Mormon leaders brazenly boasted, as First Presidency member Heber C. Kimball declared in 1859: ". . . The nations will bow to this kingdom, sooner or later, and all hell cannot help it."[19]

Global Goal: A One-World Government

Of course, Mormon leaders call their empire the "kingdom of God." However, their "God" is an extraterrestrial from Kolob, definitely *not* the God of the Bible; and the "Zion" to which their spirit-brother-of-Lucifer Jesus Christ will return to reign is Independence, Missouri. Most Christians believe, as the Bible declares, that Christ will return to Jerusalem, Israel, to establish His millennial kingdom, whereas Mormons believe that *they* must establish a worldwide Mormon kingdom dictated from their Missouri base in order to make it possible for Christ to return. Therein lies a great difference, which is why the Mormon hierarchy, beginning with Joseph Smith himself, has always had worldwide and absolute *political power* as its goal. Mormon historian Klaus J. Hansen has written, "The idea of a political kingdom of God, promulgated by a secret Council of Fifty, is by far the most important key to an understanding of the Mormon past."[20] Mormon writer John J. Stewart has said:

The Prophet established a confidential Council of Fifty, or "Ytfif," (Fifty spelled backwards), comprised of both Mormons and non-Mormons, to help attend to temporal matters, including the eventual development of a one-world government, in harmony with preparatory plans for the second advent of the Saviour.[21]

The close relationship between Masonry, the Mormon Priesthood, and Joseph Smith's growing ambition to rule the world (in order to bring Christ back) has been pointed out by a number of Mormon writers. Like the Temple ceremonies, the secret Council of Fifty grew out of Masonry. The Prophet's divine "revelation about the political kingdom of God" came just three weeks after the Nauvoo Masonic Lodge was installed and Smith became a Master Mason.[22] These men were all members of the Priesthood, they all wore special robes, and the records of their meetings were often burned (those that remain in the possession of the Church today are not available even for Church historians to peruse). In 1884 Mormon spokesman Elder Lunt said, "We look forward with perfect confidence to the day when we will hold the reins of the U.S. government. . . . After that we expect to control the continent."[23] This secret organization was referred to in a "writ issued for the arrest of prominent citizens of Nauvoo for 'treasonable designs against the state.'"[24]

Numerous sources report that shortly before his death Joseph Smith was crowned by this secret council as king over the Mormon kingdom that he believed was destined to control the world. Not only was Joseph Smith crowned "king on the earth,"[25] but so were Brigham Young[26] and John Taylor.[27] The authority claimed even today for Mormondom's "living Prophet" is still that of an absolute monarch or dictator. One of the greatest authorities on Mormon doctrine, the late Apostle Bruce R. McConkie has said:

> The Church of Jesus Christ of Latter-day Saints as it is now constituted is the kingdom of God on earth. . . .
>
> The Church is not a democracy. . . [but] a kingdom . . . and the President of the Church, the mouthpiece of God on earth, is the earthly king.[28]

The "Secret Government"

The current importance of this ambition to rule the world is evident in the secret oaths still taken by each Mormon going through the Temple ceremonies. In one such oath, the patron "consecrates" all he owns, earns, and is "to the Church of Jesus Christ of Latter-day Saints for the building up of the Kingdom of God on the earth and for the establishment of Zion."[29] In the "Law of Sacrifice," Temple patrons swear even to sacrifice their lives to this cause.[30] This is not what Christians think of as the kingdom of God to be established by Christ Himself, but, as Mormon writer J.D. Williams has pointed out, it involves "a secret government, responsible not to the governed but to ecclesiastical authority, which will provide benign rule for all people, without election."[31] That most Mormons are not aware of the real purpose behind Mormonism doesn't change the facts. Mormon researcher Klaus Hansen's comments are of interest:

> Even among the Mormons, few were themselves aware of the revolutionary implications inherent in the concept of the political kingdom of God as taught by their prophet Joseph Smith to a small group of faithful followers, after he had initiated them into a secret Council of Fifty in the spring of 1844....
>
> Indeed, if few Mormons, in 1844, knew what kind of kingdom their prophet had organized that year, fewer know today.[32]

The fact that so few Mormons themselves, to say nothing of non-Mormons, know the truth about Mormonism today reflects the secrecy involved and the apparent intention of its leaders. Is so much of Mormonism plotted and practiced in secret because The Brethren know it can only be "sold" under false labels? Can Mormons reasonably expect the world to convert to a religion that is so dishonestly and secretly presented and much of it held back in secret because it is so "sacred"? If Mormons are indeed "the only true Christians," then let them emulate the founder of Christianity, who said, "I spake openly to the world ... and in secret have I said nothing."[33]

Corruption Rooted in Power

History confirms common sense in bearing witness that whenever the absolute control which The Brethren wield has rested for very long in human hands, the results have been tragic. The Bible declares that the heart of every human is "deceitful above all things, and desperately wicked...."[34] This applies to The Brethren as well as to everyone else. The worst despots in history have been those who claimed to be divine. This is because humans were never intended to exercise godlike power and control either over themselves or over others. When they attempt it, disaster results as surely as night follows day.

Much of the dishonest unwillingness to face facts unfavorable to their religion and the gullible willingness to believe the most outrageous lies that Mormons themselves admit is endemic among them can be traced to their belief that they are in the process of becoming "gods." How can a "god" ever be wrong? Surely the temptation to live by the adage "The end justifies the means" would be overpowering for anyone who really believes that his "end" will be "exaltation" to "godhood."

Under the grandiose dream that they are the God Makers, Mormonism's leaders have developed an utter contempt for truth when it conflicts with their goal of extending the Mormon kingdom, in the name of Jesus Christ, to encompass the entire world. As the absolute leaders of Mormonism, The Brethren have rewritten "revelations," suppressed facts, promoted fraud, honored false prophets, misrepresented their true beliefs and practices, and pretended to possess a divine authority which they obviously don't have, in order to control those under them and ensnare fresh millions in Mormonism. Though their religious zeal may be genuine, they have divorced their faith from truth and built an earthly empire upon the insistence that their followers dare not think for themselves or examine facts, but must blindly obey whatever The Brethren decree.

Some Extremely Grave Questions

Mormonism seems as American as apple pie, and Mormons seem to be the perfect citizens with their close families, high morals, patriotism, Boy Scout programs, Tabernacle Choir, and conservative politics. A *Los Angeles Times* article implied that Mormons have recently gained the image of "super-Americans ... [who] appear to many to be 'more American than the average American.'"[35] This may explain why such a high proportion of Mormons find their way into government. Returned LDS missionaries have "the three qualities the CIA wants: foreign language ability, training in a foreign country, and former residence in a foreign country."[36] Utah (and particularly BYU) is one of the prime recruiting areas for the CIA. According to BYU spokesman Dr. Gary Williams, "We've never had any trouble placing anyone who has applied to the CIA. Every year they take almost anybody who applies."[37] He also admitted that this has created problems with a number of foreign countries, who have complained about the "pretty good dose of [Mormon] missionaries who've gone back to the countries they were in as Central Intelligence agents."[38]

This may at least partially explain the reported close tie between the Mormon Church and the CIA.[39] A disproportionate number of Mormons arrive at the higher levels of the CIA, FBI, military intelligence, armed forces, and all levels of city, state, and federal governments, including the Senate, Congress, Cabinet, and White House Staff. Sincere and loyal citizens, most of them may be unaware of the secret ambition of The Brethren. What could be better than having such patriots as these serving in strategic areas of government and national security? Unfortunately, as we have noticed in every other area of Mormonism, the real truth lies hidden beneath the seemingly ideal image of patriotism presented by Mormons in public service. In fact their very presence in responsible government positions, particularly in agencies dealing with national security, raises some extremely grave questions that were expressed by Ed Decker in the following letter mailed to the addressees:

An open letter to:

The President, First Presidency and members of the General Authorities of the Church of Jesus Christ of Latter-day Saints

August 21, 1980

Gentlemen:

I was recently reflecting that although the actual blood oath and the oath of vengeance were removed from the Temple ceremonies sometime after 1930, you gentlemen [listing ten of the above] are of an age to have received your own endowments prior to their removal, and therefore, are still under these oaths.

I am particularly interested in your personal position on your oath of vengeance against the United States of America. As you recall, the oath was basically as follows:

> You and each of you do solemnly promise and vow that you will pray and never cease to importune high heaven to AVENGE THE BLOOD OF THE PROPHETS (Joseph and Hiram Smith) ON THIS NATION, and that you will teach this to your children and your children's children unto the third and fourth generation.

Have you officially renounced this oath? Or are you still bound by it?

If you have not renounced it, how can you presume to lead four-and-one-half million people under item 12 of your Articles of Faith and still be bound to call upon heaven to heap curses upon our nation? ("We believe in being subject to Kings, Presidents, Rulers and Magistrates, in obeying, honoring, and sustaining the law.")

If you have renounced it, how can you justify having sworn such an oath in the most holy of holy places on this earth, before the sacred altar of your omnipotent God, and then renounce it? Gentlemen, I call upon you to repent of this abomination and proclaim to both the Mormon people and to the people of the United States of America that you renounce that oath and all it represents.

I also call upon all members of the Mormon Church who hold office in our government, serve in the Armed Services, work for the FBI and CIA who have gone through the Mormon Temple and sworn oaths of obedience and sacrifice to the Church and its leaders (above), to repent of these oaths in the light of the obvious conflict of interest between their pledge of allegiance to the USA and their higher loyalty to a group of men who are sworn to seek vengeance against this great nation.

Sincerely,

(signed) J. Edward Decker

cc: President J. Carter
    Mr. Ronald Reagan

No response was received to this letter. The Brethren are so powerful that they are immune to criticism and feel no need to explain themselves or account to anyone for their actions. The Mormon Church already packs a political punch far out of proportion to its size. *The Wall Street Journal* explained how, in spite of the Constitutional separation between Church and State, public schools in Utah are used to instill Mormonism in young minds. It mentioned political reapportionment, airline deregulation, the basing of the MX missile, and the ERA as political issues affected by the power of the Church. For example, when the Church opposed the MX for Utah, those plans were immediately dropped by the federal government. The same *Wall Street*

Journal article quoted the following statement from J.D. Williams, a University of Utah political science professor:

> There is a disquieting statement in Mormonism: "When the leaders have spoken, the thinking has been done." To me, democracy can't thrive in that climate.
>
> They [Mormon politicians] don't have to be called to Church headquarters for political instruction. They know what they're supposed to do.
>
> That's why non-Mormons can only look toward the Mormon Church and wonder: "What is Big Brother doing to me today?"[40]

A Disturbing Possibility

While the election of a Mormon U.S. President seems unlikely, it is highly probable under the present swing toward conventional morality and conservatism that a Mormon could one day become a Republican Vice-Presidential nominee. With the power, wealth, wide influence, numerous highly placed Mormons, and large voting block under their virtual control, The Brethren have a great deal to offer a Republican Presidential candidate. Let's assume that a Mormon Vice-Presidential candidate is on the winning ticket, and thereafter the President dies in office or is assassinated, causing the Mormon to succeed him as President of the United States.

There is every reason to believe that the new President would immediately begin to gather around him increasing numbers of zealous Temple Mormons in strategic places at the highest levels of government. A crisis similar to the one which Mormon prophecies "foretold" occurs, in which millions of Mormons with their year's supply of food, guns, and ammunition play a key role. It would be a time of excitement and zealous effort by the "Saints" to fulfill Joseph Smith's and Brigham Young's "prophecy":

> The time will come when the destiny of the nation will hang upon a single thread.
>
> At that critical juncture, this people will step forth and save it from the threatened destruction.[41]

Not only does Mormonism predict the "saving" of America, but the precedent for an attempted takeover by force or subterfuge through political means has been set by the founding "Prophet" himself. In 1834 Joseph Smith organized an army and marched toward Independence, Missouri, to "redeem Zion." In spite of a humiliating surrender to the Missouri militia that proved his bold "prophecies" false, the "Prophet" later formed the "Nauvoo Legion" and commissioned himself a lieutenant-general to command it. Lyman L. Woods stated:

> I have seen him on a white horse wearing the uniform of a general....
>
> He was leading a parade of the Legion and looked like a god.[42]

Joseph Smith was not only ordained king on earth, but he ran for President of the United States just before his death, at which time Mormon missionaries across the country became "a vast force of political [power]."[43] Today's Church leaders are urging Mormons to prepare themselves for the coming crisis in order to succeed where past "Saints" have failed. A recent major article in *Ensign* about being prepared included this oft-repeated warning reminder:

> The commandment to reestablish Zion became for the Saints of Joseph Smith's day the central goal of the Church.
>
> But it was a goal the Church did not realize because its people were not fully prepared.[44]

Going back to our hypothetical crisis, what Mormons unsuccessfully attempted against impossible odds in the past they might very well accomplish with much better odds in this future scenario. Under cover of the national and international crisis, the Mormon President of the United States acts boldly and decisively to assume dictatorial powers. With the help of The Brethren and Mormons everywhere, he appears to save America and becomes a national hero. At this time he is made Prophet and President of the Church of Jesus Christ of Latter-day Saints and the Mormon kingdom of God, while still President of the United States. There is no provision in the Constitution to prevent this.

With the government largely in the hands of increasing numbers of Mormon appointees at all levels throughout the United States, the Constitutional prohibition against the establishment of a state church would no longer be enforceable. Mormon prophecies and the curse upon the United

States government in revenge for the blood of Joseph and Hyrum Smith would seemingly have been fulfilled. In effect, the United States would have become a theocracy exactly as planned by The Brethren, completing the first step in the Mormon takeover of the world. President John Taylor boasted of it 100 years ago:

> Let us now notice our political position in the world. What are we going to do? We are going to possess the earth ... and reign over it for ever and ever.
>
> Now, ye Kings and Emperors help yourselves if you can. This is the truth and it may as well be told at this time as at any other.
>
> There's a good time coming, Saints, a good time coming![45]

A More Likely Scenario

While the above presents an extremely disturbing possibility, it may seem highly speculative and improbable. There is another scenario, however, which is equally disturbing and much more likely. It arises from the fact that Mormonism is actually part of something much larger. We have already noted that the "revelations" that Joseph Smith received, far from being unique, were in fact very similar to the basic philosophy underlying many occult groups and secret revolutionary societies. Thus far in history, these numerous occult/revolutionary organizations have remained largely separate and in competition with one another.

If something should happen to unite them, and at the same time their beliefs should gain worldwide acceptance, a new and unimaginably powerful force for world revolution would have come into existence. There is increasing evidence of a new and growing secular/religious ecumenism persuasive enough to accomplish this unprecedented and incalculably powerful coalition. It could be the means of creating the one-world government that has not only been the long-standing hope and plan of The Brethren and many other occult/revolutionary leaders, but is increasingly gaining a wide acceptance through New Age networks as the only viable option to a nuclear holocaust and/or ecological collapse.

Improbable? Perhaps. But certainly it can no longer be summarily dismissed as impossible.

17

A TIME
TO CHOOSE

Out of genuine concern for those who are committed to or are seriously considering Mormonism, we have attempted to present carefully and factually the truth about what the Mormon Church really believes and practices. Any mistakes that can be pointed out to us will be quickly acknowledged and corrected. Likewise we would hope that our Mormon readers would be willing to admit and face the consequences of whatever we have said that is factual. It has not been our desire to attack Mormons, but only to help them by documenting the truth about Mormonism that many Latter-day Saints themselves do not understand.

Cindy discovered the truth for herself, but not until Mormonism had destroyed her marriage. With ancestors who had crossed the plains to Utah in handcarts, Cindy had been born into an LDS pioneer family and was an active Mormon for 30 years. Her husband, however, lost interest in the Church and wasn't living up to its standards. "He had no desire to be active in the Priesthood," Cindy told us, "so the Mormon leaders encouraged me to divorce him." It was in the midst of that trauma that Cindy began seeking some answers. Her story gives hope to others:

> As far as I was concerned, the Mormon Church was totally the right thing, and I would do whatever they said. I spent my entire life working in it and doing everything I could to promote it. I started teaching when I was 17 and was teaching seminary and genealogy when I finally left the Church.

What happened was that I began to study the Bible and became aware that the god of Mormonism was not the real God of the Bible. He was a counterfeit, probably one of the best counterfeits that Satan has come up with to keep people away from knowing the real and living Jesus Christ.

I had to make a choice, and I chose Jesus over Joseph, and being a Christian instead of becoming a goddess wife to some Mormon man/god.

Mormonism's Long-Standing Controversy with Christianity

Cindy's opinion that the Mormon "god" is a satanic counterfeit designed to keep Mormons from knowing the true God may seem harsh. However, we have given more than enough documentation—not only from former Mormons but also from Mormon Prophets and Apostles—to show that Mormonism (like Masonry, from which its secret Temple rituals came) is a Luciferian religion within the mainstream of anti-Christian pagan tradition. It is not even based upon the Book of Mormon, and is certainly not based upon the Bible. Brigham Young made the astonishing admission that he had "not read the Bible for years" and that when he had attempted to study it, he "did not understand the spirit and meaning of it...."[1] He further admitted that in his day the 12 Apostles of the Mormon Church included men who believed in reincarnation, rejected the existence of God, and denied that there was any value in the death of Christ for salvation.[2] One would think that such admissions as these and the many others equally damaging that we have quoted would cause every Mormon to seriously reevaluate his religion.

Sadly, however, from The Brethren on down, Mormons generally have not responded well to constructive criticism. They are afraid even to consider momentarily the possibility that there might be any error at all in their Church or its Prophets or doctrines. Any attempt to point out even the most obvious fallacies is met by the standard Mormon response: a wounded complaint that they are being attacked, along with the seemingly sincere protest that they attack no one. Mormons seem to forget that Joseph Smith declared all Christian creeds to be an abomination. Brigham Young said that all Christians were "groveling in darkness,"[3] and that the Christian God is "the 'Mormon's' Devil...."[4] John Taylor, third Mormon President, said that Christianity was "hatched in hell,"[5] and "a perfect pack of nonsense... The

Devil could not invent a better engine to spread his work. . . ."[6] Continuously around the world, for over a hundred years (until the publication of this book and film and others like it forced the ritual to be changed), hundreds of times each day in secret ceremonies before thousands of Mormon Temple patrons, all Christian ministers were ridiculed and slandered as absolute fools hired by Satan to deceive their congregations.[7]

Clearly, Mormonism from its very beginning has had a deep controversy with Christianity and has aggressively pressed its attack. The differences between the two are very real and need to be understood rather than denied. We have attempted to contribute to that understanding. If Christianity were indeed "hatched in hell" and the Christian God is "the 'Mormon's' Devil," then the change in tactics that now has Mormon missionaries protesting to Christians, "Our God is the same as your God," is extremely dishonest. Nor does it contribute to a mutual understanding or serve the cause of truth for well-meaning Christians to accept this misrepresentation in the name of broad-mindedness. If Christianity were not "hatched in hell," then Mormonism was. All sincere Christians and Mormons must decide for themselves. We have tried to provide a factual basis for choosing between these two diametrically opposed beliefs.

Perpetuating the Myth

Those Mormons who, after examining the evidence for themselves, choose "Jesus instead of Joseph" as Cindy did and become Christians, learn very quickly and often to their great surprise just how antagonistic Mormonism really is toward Christianity. They discover that it is impossible to be both a Mormon and a Christian. Any Mormon for whom Jesus Christ becomes more important than Joseph Smith and the Church he founded is in for serious trouble. The Brethren won't tolerate this for a moment, because it challenges their entire authority structure that is built upon Joseph Smith and the belief that membership in the Mormon Church is essential for eternal life. All those who meet the real Jesus of the Bible immediately learn that Christianity is based upon a relationship with Him and not with any organization. Such a person is a threat to Mormonism, and therefore friends and even family members will be warned not to have anything to do with him or her.

Even after leaving the Church, however, one's name will still be kept on the Church rolls. It will only be removed after a formal excommunication trial, which is a process the Mormon Church generally pursues only if it is insisted upon by the person who has left. Thereafter, false charges will very often be circulated in order to make it appear that the Church initiated the excommunication for some moral reasons. It would look bad to admit that an "apostate" insisted upon having his name removed because he had met the real Jesus and had discovered that Mormonism is anti-Christian.

Recently a young single woman who had become a Christian and was trying to have her name removed from Church rolls was told that her records would read, "Excommunicated for fornication." This was absolutely false, but the Bishop was firm. He claimed that with his "spiritual discernment" he "knew" that a single young woman living alone and outside the only true Church would inevitably be guilty of this sin. It was a brazenly dishonest yet common way of applying pressure to remain in the Church. Not until he received a stern call from her attorney did the Bishop decide to stop playing that game.

Tony told us, "After we left the Church, our friends were told to have nothing to do with us. My wife was very uncomfortable at the grocery store—people stared and then turned their backs without saying anything." When Janet became a Christian, her daughter Brenda, a student at BYU at the time, was warned not to talk to her own mother. After the entire family became Christians and left the Mormon Church, the rumor persisted that they had been excommunicated because the parents were guilty of adultery. It was another blatant lie, but apparently Mormon leaders consider such fabrications to be necessary in order to perpetuate the myth of Mormonism.

Passing On Occult Power and Bondage

Only after breaking away completely do former Mormons begin to realize that it wasn't just pressure from family and friends that held them, but that they were under heavy occult bondage that made it extremely difficult to escape. The spiritual power within Mormonism is very real and very strong. As with all occult groups, this power is passed on through special rituals, especially those imitating the biblical "laying on of hands." Temple Mormons are especially firmly bound by this occult bondage, for they wear the magic underwear as well as the apron emblem of Lucifer's "power and priesthoods" in life and in death; and at the Temple Veil they call down the "power in the priesthoods" upon themselves and their posterity. As we have documented, the entire Temple ceremony involves occult chants and rituals that bind participants under heavy spiritual control.

One of the most telling evidences of this occult demonic control within Mormonism came out recently when Bishop Glenn L. Pace of the Presiding Bishop's Office dropped a bombshell on the Church. In a special report to the Church's Strengthening Church Members committee dated July 19, 1990, and titled *Ritualistic Child Abuse,* Pace reported the activities of satanic ritual abuse taking place within the LDS Church. In part, he said:

> "Pursuant to the committee's request, I am writing this memorandum to pass along what I have learned about ritualistic child abuse. Hopefully it will be of some value to you as you continue to monitor the problem. You have already received the LDS Social Services report on Satanism dated May 24, 1989, a report from Brent Ward, and a memorandum from myself dated October 20, 1989, in response to Brother Ward's report. Therefore, I will limit this writing to information not contained in those papers.
>
> I have met with 60 victims. That number could be twice or three times as many if I did not discipline myself to only one meeting per week. I have not wanted my involvement with this issue to become a handicap in fulfilling my assigned responsibilities. On the other hand, I felt someone needed to pay the price to obtain an intellectual and spiritual conviction as to the seriousness of this problem within the Church.
>
> Of the 60 victims with whom I have met, 53 are female and seven are male. Eight are children. The abuse occurred in the following places: Utah (37), Idaho (3), California (4), Mexico (2), and other places (14). Fifty-three victims are currently living in the state of Utah. All 60 individuals are members of the Church. Forty-five victims allege witnessing and/or participating in human sacrifice. The majority were abused by relatives, often their parents. All have developed psychological problems and most have been diagnosed as having multiple-personality disorder or some other form of dissociative disorder.
>
> I'm sorry to say that many of the victims have had their first flashbacks while attending the temple for the first time. The occult along the Wasatch Front uses the doctrine of the Church to their advantage. For example, the verbiage and gestures are used in a ritualistic

> ceremony in a very debased and often bloody manner. When the victim goes to the temple and hears the exact words, horrible memories are triggered. We have recently been disturbed with members of the Church who have talked about the temple ceremony. Compared to what is happening in the occult along the Wasatch Front, these are very minor infractions. The perpetrators are also living a dual life. Many are temple recommend holders. This leads to another reason why the Church needs to consider the seriousness of these problems. In effect, the Church is being used.

> I go out of my way to not let the victims give me the names of the perpetrators. I have told them that my responsibility is to help them with spiritual healing and that the names of perpetrators should be given to therapists and law enforcement officers. However, they have told me the positions in the Church of members who are perpetrators. Among others, there are Young Women leaders, Young Men leaders, bishops, a patriarch, a stake president, temple workers, and members of the Tabernacle Choir. These accusations are not coming from individuals who think they recognized someone, but from those who have been abused by people they know, in many cases their own family members.

Frightening, yes. Unexpected, no. For a Church which was founded on the principles of the occult and witchcraft (folk magic, to use a kinder word), it is only to be expected. You don't get rid of these kinds of demonic powers and influences by hiding them from view. You can only get rid of them by repenting and confessing them as sin. It gets worse without repentance. Not better—just worse.

The greater sin (of which the above are merely offshoots) is the refusal to face the overwhelming evidence that Joseph Smith was a false prophet and the persistence in embracing the anti-Christian false gospel he taught. It is that sin which binds Mormons to Satan's lies and for which repentance is required of every Mormon.

It is not only Temple Mormons who are in occult bondage. Repeatedly throughout their lives the power of Lucifer's Priesthoods is given dominion even over Mormons who never go through the Temple. This begins shortly after birth, with the dedication ceremony, when the new infant is "blessed" by his father in front of the congregation at the Sunday morning Sacrament Service. Priesthood members gather around, support the babe on their hands, and bind it spiritually through Priesthood power to perpetual membership in the Mormon Church. The babe is named and pronouncements made over it by the power of the name of the "Holy Melchizedek Priesthood," such as that it will go on a mission, be married in the Temple, and never leave the Mormon Church.

Periodically thereafter, as a growing child, teenager, and adult, the active Mormon will be "called" to perform various jobs and offices in the Church. At such times, usually the hands of a Priesthood member will be laid on the head of the one "called" to the task, and once more the Luciferian claim upon this life is renewed by the power of the Mormon Priesthoods. Mormons are well aware of the power of this "laying on of hands" and consider jobs where this is not involved to be of lesser importance. In this way the occult bond is strengthened continuously. At confirmation as a member of the Church, hands are again laid on in the name of the Priesthood, and the person is *commanded* to receive the Holy Ghost. As we have already noted, the Mormon Holy Ghost is definitely not the Holy Spirit described in the Bible.

The Patriarchal Blessing

Each Mormon "Stake" has at least one and sometimes two or three "Patriarchs," of which there are several thousand. These men exert a spiritual influence upon active Mormons that is comparable to anything in the Temple, and is often even more powerful. Mormons eagerly look forward to the day when one of these "High Priests" will lay hands on their heads and bestow the "Patriarchal Blessing" upon them. It is like a "life reading" from Edgar Cayce or having one's fortune told. The Patriarch comes forth with an inspired utterance, often quite lengthy and specific about future events in the person's life and sometimes amazingly accurate. This is taken down by a tape recorder and a signed typed copy is presented. Most Mormons implicitly believe in the accuracy of and highly prize the official copy of their own personal "Patriarchal Blessing."

This can be one of the most powerful spiritual experiences in a Mormon's life. Devout Mormons will often fast for several days in preparation for it. Sometimes when the Patriarch's hands are laid upon the head, the recipient of the blessing begins to vibrate under a mysterious force and experiences a strange ascension into a "higher consciousness," where there is an extreme openness to occult power and bondage. Former Mormons testify that in such a state it is no longer necessary to listen to the words being spoken. Even before the Patriarch's thoughts are audibly expressed, the one being "blessed" is already hearing the words—and sometimes is even seeing everything in a fantastic moving vision. Similar experiences are common among numerous occultists; and the power over one's life that is produced thereby can only be broken by a complete renunciation of these forces in the name of Jesus Christ and receiving Him into one's heart and life as Savior and Lord. This personal relationship with Jesus Christ is the key in breaking occult bondage.

It is therefore no coincidence that The Brethren discourage their followers from having a personal relationship with Jesus Christ. They know that those who receive Christ as Savior and Lord will no longer be in their power. Apostle Bruce R. McConkie warned that those who seek "a personal relationship with Christ" and take this relationship with Him as "a goal in life and focus on it . . . become unbalanced."[8] McConkie also suggested that each Mormon have his "own personal plan of salvation."[9] He claimed that "no two persons should have the same Plan" and that those who do "the best they can are charting a course to Eternal Life."[10]

In contrast, the Bible teaches that there is only one plan of salvation, and Jesus carried it out when He died for our sins, paying a debt we could never pay. On that basis, God is able to forgive those who will receive Christ, and eternal life is offered as a free gift to anyone willing to receive it on God's terms.[11]

Preparation for Delusion

Jesus warned that the last days prior to His return would be characterized by religious deception involving false prophets, false Messiahs, and false miracles so convincing that they would deceive if possible the very elect.[12] The apostle Paul explained that this deception would sweep the world under the leadership of a man who would claim to be God and seemingly prove it by performing miracles through the power of Satan,[13] thus demonstrating that the Serpent's promise of "godhood" was genuine. Under the influence of a "strong delusion," this powerful lie would be believed by the world.[14] As we have thoroughly documented, this belief is the common foundation of Mormonism and paganism (occultism). Its ultimate goal is a one-world government under a false Messiah, as the apostle John prophesied.[15] From this perspective Mormonism takes on its real significance.

Far from being unique (as claimed), and in spite of Christian terminology, Joseph Smith's "revelations" were simply variations on timeworn occult themes common to numerous secret societies for centuries. Although these groups have been widely scattered and many of them have had no contact with similar groups, they all share the same basic Hindu concepts that also lie at the heart of Mormonism. This presents compelling evidence that Joseph Smith's inspirations came from the same nonhuman source that has been communicating with occultists worldwide as far back as history records. That these "revelations" consistently promise godhood and immortality on the same terms that the Serpent offered these to Eve conclusively identifies the mastermind behind Mormonism and all other occultism.

Even much of the esoteric terminology is the same. Not only the Mormon Church, but also many other neopagan organizations have long been obsessed with "restoration" doctrines, secret "revelations," and various kinds of "seer stones." Another recurring theme has involved mysterious "hieroglyphics" translated by a "Urim and Thummim," exactly as Joseph Smith claimed he had done. Myths about "Enoch," similar to Joseph Smith's, figured not only in Masonry, but among Rosicrucians and many others, who also had their "High Priesthoods" and "Melchisedec" degrees and Lodges.[16] The "laying on of hands" for passing on occult power, as well as reports of healings and other "miraculous" occurrences, are also common to most of these groups—just as among Mormons. The similarities are too close and too many to be dismissed as coincidence.

Mormonism's founding Prophet both employed the stock-in-trade occult jargon common to secret revolutionary groups of his time and shared their obsessive vision of uniting the world under a new order of government ruled by an esoteric "Priesthood." This was expanded upon by Joseph Smith's successors and is still the real goal of Mormonism. In 1878 President John Taylor declared: "God is determined to carry out his purposes, and to build up his [Independence, Missouri] Zion.... Hear it, you Latter-day Saints... it is a revelation from the Most High...."[17] Presidents Wilford Woodruff, Joseph F. Smith, and Lorenzo Snow confirmed this in no uncertain terms. Snow stated with conviction in 1898: "... You will go back to Jackson

County, many of you whom I am addressing this afternoon. I am sure of this."[18]

Having failed to establish their worldwide theocracy within the designated time limit, Mormons refuse to admit that this proves Joseph Smith and all those who followed him as "Prophet, Seer and Revelator" of the Latter-day Saints were false prophets. Though still obsessed with Smith's vision of a Missouri-based world takeover, the Mormon Church no longer flaunts that ambition but keeps it in the background. In a significant change in tactics, The Brethren have spent millions of advertising dollars and decades shedding the former image of the rebel-polygamist-heretic Mormon and building a new reputation of solid citizenship, good morals, and conservative politics. More recently the Mormon Church has begun to cultivate cooperation with "Gentiles" as part of its new strategy for fulfilling Joseph Smith's grandiose dream.

The Divine Rights of the Mormons

Mormons believe that the United States Constitution "was given by the inspiration of God"[19] and is both a divine[20] and *global* document that holds the key to a coming peace and prosperity for the whole world.[21] President Taylor said:

> When the people have torn to shreds the Constitution of the United States, the [Mormon] Elders of Israel will be found holding it up to the nations of the earth. . . .[22]

Brigham Young declared:

> . . . As Joseph Smith said, "The time will come when the destiny of the nation will hang upon a single thread. At that critical juncture, this people will step forth and save it from destruction." It will be so. . . . The "Mormon" elders . . . will step forth and do it.[23]

The prophesied Mormon takeover (to save the Constitution and the nation) was to have been administered through Joseph Smith's Council of Fifty. Today the work is expected to be administered by the Prophet reigning from his Temple in Washington D.C. and his Priesthood leaders spread across the nation. President David O. McKay declared in 1956:

Next to being one in worshipping God, there is nothing in this world upon which this Church should be more united than in upholding and defending the Constitution of the United States.[24]

Mormons know what this means. The Brethren are dedicated to reviving the "United Order." Every Temple Mormon swears absolute obedience to the Law of Consecration which means that when the time comes the Church will own and control all his assets and income.[25] President Joseph F. Smith said, "Zion can only be built up by the law that God revealed for that purpose, which is the law of consecration—not the law of tithing." (This means turning over 100 percent to the Church, not just 10 percent.)[26] President Wilford Woodruff declared:

> ... We should commence to prepare and fit ourselves for the United Order.
>
> ... The New Jerusalem [in Independence, Missouri] will be built up in our day and generation, and it will have to be done by the United Order of Zion and according to celestial law.[27]

From "Zion" The Brethren expect to rule the world, and everything they do is directed to that ultimate goal. This is the great hope of every devout Mormon.

New Age Ecumenism

Mormonism can best be understood in relation to the larger occult conspiracy of which it is a part. The pieces are now beginning to fall into place. Joseph Smith's revelations blueprinting the human path to "godhood" were right on target with the Hindu-Buddhist occultism that is sweeping the West today as the New Age movement.* It offers numerous here-and-now shortcuts to the "godhood" that Mormons can only hope to reach during eons of time into the future. For this reason, Mormons who become disillusioned with their Church are particularly susceptible to New Age delusions.

Similarity in beliefs and goals could bring about increasing cooperation between Mormons and New Age groups. Already Mormons have begun to work closely with the Unification Church, headed by Korean "Messiah" Sun

---

* For an in-depth analysis of the New Age Movement and its place in biblical prophecy, see Dave Hunt, *Occult Invasion* (Harvest House Publishers, 1997).

Myung Moon. *The New Republic* has said, "Sun Myung Moon is to cults what Henry Ford was to cars."[28]

The Mormon Church has a great deal in common with the Unification Church.

Much like Joseph Smith, Sun Myung Moon claims to have been visited by angels, Moses, Buddha, and Jesus. Jesus allegedly gave Moon at age 16 the same assignment that Joseph Smith's "god" from Kolob had already given him at the same age: to "restore" true Christianity, beginning in the United States, and eventually to take over the entire world. Although the main characters are different, the basic Unification Church scenario, including blind obedience by members, is much the same as Mormonism's. Reminiscent of Joseph Smith, Sun Myung Moon says:

> I am your brain. Every people or every organization that goes
> against the Unification Church will gradually come down and die.[29]

The Unification Church hopes to install Sun Myung Moon as world ruler; the Mormon Church holds the same ambition for its "Prophet, Seer and Revelator"; and Christians await the return of Jesus Christ to establish His kingdom. The Bible declares that the world will be united first under a great political and religious leader known as the Antichrist.[30] This gives the new ecumenism special importance and perhaps even frightening possibilities. Yet this New Age ecumenism is growing in popularity.

Unity by Lunacy

The Bible declares that the world will be united religiously under the Antichrist, who will declare himself to be God.[31] Under a "strong delusion,"[32] the entire world will accept this preposterous claim and worship him.[33] Such worldwide religious unity seems impossible. Yet in the popular motion picture *Gandhi,* that amazing hero embraces this very impossibility and makes it sound heroic and generous if not reasonable. Gandhi declares: "I am a Muslim, I am a Hindu, I am a Buddhist, I am a Christian!" He should have added, "And I am irrational!" No one can rationally be all of these, because they strongly disagree in the three most basic elements of religion: God, heaven, and salvation.

In Buddhism there is no God; in Hinduism there are millions of gods; in Islam there is one God, Allah, who is a single Person; in the Judeo-Christian

Scriptures three Persons—Father, Son, and Holy Spirit—comprise the one God. "Heaven" in Buddhism is Nirvana, a return to the void or nothingness; in Hinduism the goal is Moksha or self-realization, to realize that one *is* God; in the Judeo-Christian view the goal is to be in heaven *with* God,[34] not to *be* God; and in Islam the goal is Paradise. These concepts of God, heaven, and the way to reach it are all different. So it is indeed irrational for a person to declare that he is a Muslim, Buddhist, Hindu, and Christian. Nevertheless, moviegoers find this particular statement by Gandhi to be one of the most moving and appealing parts of the film. This unity by lunacy seems to be an idea whose time has come.

If morality is to be based upon more than changeable fads, opinions, customs, or fanaticism, it must come as a communication from God in the conscience. There must be a higher basis than culture for determining what is right and wrong if those concepts are to have any real meaning. This is exactly what the Bible claims.[35] There is no real hope for moral stability in family or society until immorality is seen as not just "hurting others," but as sin against God. Again, this is what the Bible teaches.[36] But who is God, and how can we be sure that He exists—and if He does, how can we know Him? This is very important, because our view of God determines our morality and everything else.

The atheist counters with this standard argument: "You only believe in God because science hasn't yet explained everything. One day science will have explained *everything* in terms of cause and effect governed by natural laws, and there won't be any need for God anymore." However, if *everything* is explainable in terms of natural processes, then the very theory that says so must itself be explainable as the result of natural causes and would therefore be meaningless. As C.S. Lewis says, "It would be like proving that there are no such things as proofs." This is why atheism has no basis for morality in spite of its proud and specious talk about "ethics." If everything results from natural causes, then to say "I love you!" or "That's beautiful" or "That's wrong" would be no more significant than to say, "I'm hungry" or "I have a headache."

Unless there is a transcendent Creator-God above and outside of nature, a God who made us in His image, we would not have the power to reason or choose any more than a computer could write its own program. Unlike the Mormon "gods," the God of the Judeo-Christian Bible created everything out of nothing. He established the laws that govern the universe and therefore these natural laws don't govern Him. This means that, unlike the "gods" of Mormonism and occultism, the biblical God can reach into the universe and into human hearts with forgiveness, redemption, and resurrection. It also means that salvation cannot be demanded, earned, or induced by ritual; far from flowing from natural laws, it must overcome them. This transcendent God cannot be found by our reasoning, no matter how brilliant, but must reveal Himself. This He has done when He came in the Person of Christ through the virgin birth. God demands to be known for who He is and on His terms.

Mormonism, Atheism, Humanism, and Occultism

A "God" that fits anyone's definition is clearly man's *creature* and not his *Creator*. The human arrogance that defines God in its own terms has already enthroned self in His place. Self-deification is at the heart of Hinduism, is the foundation of all occultism, and is the meeting point between atheism and false religion. As with the Yogi, self-realization has always been the goal of classical atheism and humanism, and is being expressed in psychological terminology in the West today as the Human Potential (New Age) movement.

Most Mormons are naively unaware of the fact that Mormonism is simply classical atheistic humanism deceptively packaged in pseudo-Christian terminology. Secular humanism, which most Mormons would sincerely see as their enemy, makes man the center and measure of all things. So does Mormonism. Atheist/humanist Henri de Lubec declared: "The turning point in history will be the moment man becomes aware that the only God of man is man himself."[37] Like many other New Age cult leaders, Werner Erhard is trying to bring about that very transformation through est (Erhard Seminars Training) by brainwashing his disciples (trainees) into believing that "human beings [are] God."[38] In perfect agreement with Lubec, Erhard, and countless other atheists/humanists/occultists, Joseph Smith declared that all "gods" are men and that men are the only "gods"; that the "intelligence which man possesses is co-equal with God himself"; and that men and all spirits are co-equal . . .[and] self-existent with God."[39] How odd that the current Mormon president seems unaware of this key doctrine!

If all "gods" were once men, one logically wonders who was the first god who created the first man. In Mormonism that is a meaningless question, because Joseph Smith taught that the universe of "matter and intelligence" has always existed.[40] As in all nature (witchcraft) religions, so in Mormonism there is neither creator nor creation. The Mormon "gods" don't *create* but *manufacture* suns and worlds out of available materials.[41] According to Joseph Smith, "God... never had the power to create the spirit of man" or anything else.[42]

Mormonism's Restored Gospel of Atheism

Joseph Smith was a classical humanist atheist. He rejected the one true God of the Bible, and in His place proposed an infinite and ever-increasing number of self-made "gods" who had each once been a man. No Mormon "god" even pretends to be God in the biblical-classical sense: always God,[43] the only true God,[44] and Creator of everything that is.[45] As in classical occultism and atheistic humanism, the Mormon "gods" are "Ascended Masters"— men who through initiation into ever-higher levels of secret knowledge have learned to apply universal laws and principles and have thereby become Masters over the forces of nature that have somehow always existed on their own.

Far from being omnipotent, omniscient, and omnipresent—as is the biblical God—the Mormon "God" is a highly evolved creature of the cosmos governed by these self-existent laws that are therefore greater than the "gods" themselves. To become this kind of a "god" through absolute obedience to The Brethren is the ambition of every Mormon male. This celestial existence can be achieved by recognizing that we are all gods-in-embryo and lifting ourselves up by our spiritual bootstraps. In the same terms that a thousand pagan myths have recited and modern occultists still employ, Mormon General Authority Milton R. Hunter gives this astonishing LDS definition of "the Gospel of Jesus Christ":

> Our heavenly parents have through eons of time and a multitude of experiences gradually become acquainted and applied in Their lives an untold number of these everlasting laws.

> As they learned these verities and how to operate them, these laws thereby became subject unto Elohim and henceforth were His laws—or, in other words, the Gospel of Jesus Christ.[46]

Many sincere Mormons are not aware that: 1) the "godhood" they pursue in obedience to The Brethren will take "eons of time" to achieve at great effort and danger; and 2) once gained, it can be lost in a moment if they fail to perfectly obey the thousands of laws that govern Mormon "gods." Milton R. Hunter writes, "He became God by absolute obedience to all the eternal laws of the Gospel...."[47] The Mormon "god" is an ambitious man who has become a "white magician" through acquisition of occult powers and can as readily lose them.

The "god" of Mormonism is unquestionably not the God of Christianity and the Bible. Therefore, even if every prophecy Joseph Smith uttered came true (in fact, almost none did), the people of God would still be required to reject him. The very first mark of a false prophet in the Bible is that he entices people to follow "other gods" than the God of Israel.[48] Joseph Smith fits that description.

Escape at Last

Today's world trembles under the threat of nuclear devastation and teeters on the brink of ecological, financial, and social collapse. We have been on a selfish binge that is destroying ourselves as God's creatures and the creation in which He has placed us. The theory of man's inherent goodness and infinite potential for good as a "god-in-embryo" hardly fits the rampant lust, jealousy, hatred, murder, rape, disease, hunger, war, and other sorrows and crimes that are a blight on planet Earth. A much better explanation would be that all of this horror and shame can be traced to the fact that we have almost six billion little counterfeit gods in the world. The only hope is to give up our rebellion and surrender to the one true God on His own terms.

Thousands of Mormons are doing exactly that, but not without a struggle. It is not an easy step to take. The Mormon Church offers a great deal of comfort and security, and to step away from all that and in the process see family and friends become enemies is more than anyone can bear without the comfort of the real Jesus Christ. Jolene became a Christian, and her Church-destroyed marriage to Greg has been restored. The family that encouraged her to leave Greg has now rejected her. Sadly, Jolene told us:

> When I was growing up, my sisters and I were the best of friends and had a beautiful relationship. Since I've come out of the Mormon Church, however, my sisters and I have no relationship at all.

It's primarily because they're Temple Mormons, and one of the rules is that Temple Mormons can't associate with "apostates," which is what the Mormon Church calls me.

Although she knew that much was wrong with Mormonism, Janet went back "just one more time" to a Relief Society meeting. There she was reminded that she could become a "goddess." Hooked on that vain hope, she lingered for another three years of frustration. Finally she could keep up the pretense no longer. However, it seemed as though there was nowhere else to turn. "I believed," Janet told us, "that if the Mormon Church wasn't true, there was no true Church. I had one of those burning testimonies of the Mormon Church."

Doug and Janet were an ideal Mormon couple. Janet had been raised in the Church, and Doug had become a Mormon when he was 24 years old. "We were married in the Temple," Doug said, "and raised seven beautiful children as Mormons. I had served a stake mission and we were very happy in the Mormon Church." Then he learned of Janet's disillusionment and unhappiness, and of the person she had met who was telling her of the Jesus in the Bible—the Jesus that she realized for the first time was not the Jesus of Mormonism.

"This man told me how wonderful Jesus was and how He had changed his life," Janet related. "That really threw me. I had never heard a Mormon talk that way. We would talk about the Church, the organizations, and the Prophet, but this man talked about Jesus with such love as if he knew Him personally." Janet's story was like that of many others:

> Reading the Bible, I began to understand it for the first time. I realized that the Bible was teaching something different from the Mormon Church.
>
> That sent me into great despair. If the Mormon Church wasn't true, then we have been teaching a lie to our children all of their lives, and we were all doomed. I was beside myself with grief.
>
> I remembered then that my Christian friend had encouraged me to ask Jesus into my heart. So I got down on my knees when I was all alone and did just that. I didn't know what I was doing, but something wonderful happened. I knew that I had been born again, and that salvation and eternal life are in Jesus Christ, not in an organization.

> The joy I felt to know that Jesus had really come to live in my heart was inexpressible. I fell in love with the Bible also, and couldn't read it enough.
>
> I sat down and wrote a letter to all of my Mormon friends, relatives, and everyone in the ward, telling them about Jesus. I immediately got a visit from the Bishop, who told me that if I didn't stop writing letters I would be excommunicated.

Her husband Doug's life was shattered when Janet became a Christian, even though until that time he would have argued that Mormons were Christians. Now he realized that Mormonism and Joseph Smith, not the Christ that Janet knew, were everything to him. Bewildered and angry at first, her family began to notice a tremendous change in Janet that intrigued and finally convinced them that they needed what she had found. It wasn't long until she had won them all to Christ. Her eldest son told us:

> I had been looking all my life for something in the Mormon Church. And I couldn't put my finger on what I was looking for. Now when my mom accepted Christ into her life, she shared it with me.
>
> I saw a joy in her life that I had never seen before in all her activity in the Mormon Church. And this was what I needed.

* * *

The lawyers refused to file that class-action suit. They told Ed Decker and Dick Baer, "You've taken us to Kolob and back, but we don't think we could get a jury to accompany us. The Mormon Church has *billions* of dollars. You don't have the money to fight them through the courts."

At first, Ed and Dick were bitterly disappointed. However, it was out of that disappointment that the inspiration for the movie and for this book came. It was one way to tell the story, to explain the truth. At least now many thousands of people who might otherwise have been deceived will know what lies behind those sincere words and innocent smiles the next time two well-groomed and wholesome-appearing young men ride up on their bicycles, knock at the door, and pleasantly say:

> Hello! We'd like to talk to you about the Church of Jesus Christ of Latter-day Saints. . . .

NOTES

Chapter 1—The Mormon Challenge

1. *Denver Post*, Special Reprint, Sunday Supplement, "Utah: Inside the Church State," Nov. 21-28, 1982, from introductory comments by Will Jarret, Executive Editor.
2. A takeoff from the fact that Mormons consider themselves to be the real Jews and believe that Zion in the Bible isn't Jerusalem, Israel, but Independence, Missouri, where Joseph Smith and Jesus Christ will one day have their headquarters for ruling the world.
3. *Los Angeles Times*, June 26, 1983, p. 1.
4. *Denver Post*, op. cit.
5. Ibid.
6. Ibid.
7. *Los Angeles Times*, op. cit.
8. *Denver Post*, op. cit., p. 8.
9. Ibid., p. 2
10. *Time* magazine, August 4, 1997, p. 55.
11. *The Detroit News Magazine*, May 18, 1980, pp. 15, 31.
12. *Los Angeles Times*, op. cit., p. 26.
13. Cited from *Dialogue* on p. 13 of *Denver Post* article, op. cit.
14. *Denver Post*, op. cit., p. 2.
15. *Orson Pratt's Works*, "Divine Authenticity of the *Book of Mormon*" (Liverpool, 1850), pp. 1-2.

Chapter 2—A Fascinating Question

1. *Denver Post*, op. cit., p. 10.
2. Ibid.
3. Journal of Discourses, vol. 7, p. 289.

Chapter 3—The Pagan Connection

1. *Doctrine and Covenants* 29:36-41.
2. Bruce R. McConkie, *Mormon Doctrine* (Salt Lake City, 1966), p. 527.
3. *Journal of Discourses*, vol. 10, p. 110.
4. Ibid., vol. 7, pp. 290-91.
5. Ibid., vol. 2, p. 143.
6. Ibid., vol. 11, p. 272.
7. *Book of Mormon*, 2 Nephi 30:6.
8. Bruce R. McConkie, op. cit., pp. 516-17.
9. *History of the Church*, vol. 6, p. 306.
10. Joseph Fielding Smith, *Doctrines of Salvation*, vol. 2, 1960 ed., p. 86.
11. Ibid., pp. 87-89.
12. The Osmonds, *A Testimonial of The Church of Jesus Christ of Latter-day Saints* (Salt Lake City), pp. 3-5.

13. *The Ensign*, "Jesus of Nazareth" by President Spencer W. Kimball, Dec. 1980, p. 3.
14. *The Seer*, edited by Orson Pratt, Jan. 1853–July 1854, pp. 37-38.
15. James E. Talmage, *Jesus the Christ*, pp. 6-8, 15-16; *The Seer*, pp. 50-54.
16. *Journal of Discourses*, vol. 16, p. 334; *The Seer*, p. 21.
17. Milton R. Hunter, *The Gospel Through the Ages* (Salt Lake City, 1958), p. 110.
18. *Doctrine and Covenants* 9:8.
19. Isaiah 14:14.
20. Bruce R. McConkie, op. cit., pp. 210-11, 251.
21. John 8:44.
22. 1 Timothy 2:14.
23. Romans 5:12-21.
24. Romans 6:23.
25. 2 Nephi 2:25.
26. *Deseret News*, Church Section, July 31, 1965, p. 7.
27. Ibid., June 18, 1873, p. 308.
28. *Doctrines of Salvation*, vol. 1, 1960 ed., pp. 113-15.
29. *The Seer*, pp. 102-03.
30. Manley P. Hall, *The Secret Teaching of All Ages* (Los Angeles, 1969, Sixteenth Edition), p. LVI.
31. Bruce R. McConkie, op. cit. pp. 322-33; *Journal of Discourses*, vol. 2, p. 345.
32. *Salt Lake City Tribune*, Oct. 7, 1974 and Sept. 18, 1974.

Chapter 4—Up to Godhood

1. *Life of Heber C. Kimball*, pp. 335-36; *Journal of Discourses*, vol. 11, p. 269.
2. *Deseret News*, Church Section, Nov. 12, 1977.
3. Matthew 22:23-33.
4. Matthew 16:24; Mark 8:34; Luke 9:23.
5. *Doctrines of Salvation*, vol. 1, pp. 189-90.
6. *Journal of Discourses*, vol. 7, p. 289.
7. Ibid.
8. LDS Hymnal, no. 147.
9. *The Ensign*, Apr. 8, 1973, p. 74.
10. Joseph Fielding Smith, *Answers to Gospel Questions*, vol. 2, p. 205; *Doctrines of Salvation*, vol. 1, p. 186.
11. Bruce R. McConkie, op. cit., pp. 155-56, 416.
12. *Journal of Discourses*, vol. 6, p. 32.
13. Fourteen Fundamentals in Following the Prophets, President Ezra Taft Benson, BYU Devotional Assembly, Feb. 26, 1980.
14. Isaiah 8:20.
15. S. Dilworth Young, BYU Stake Fireside, May 5, 1974, from Saints Alive in Jesus, Mormon Plan for America, assorted notes.
16. *Journal of Discourses*, vol. 99, p. 324.
17. *The Ensign*, op. cit., p. 69.
18. *Doctrine and Covenants* 9:8.
19. *History of the Church*, vol. 6, pp. 408-09.
20. *Journal of Discourses*, vol. 13, p. 95.
21. *The Improvement Era*, Ward Teachers' Message, "Sustaining the General Authorities of the Church," June 1945, p. 1.

Chapter 5—The Mormon Dilemma

1. *Time* magazine, August 4, 1997, p. 54.
2. *Sunstone Review*, vol. 2, no. 10, Oct. 1983, p. 5.
3. *Birth Control, General Handbook of Instructions*, no. 21/1976, The Church of Jesus Christ of Latter-day Saints, p. 105.
4. *Los Angeles Times*, June 26, 1983, Part 1, p. 25.
5. *Church News*, Apr. 17, 1983, pp. 8-9; U.S. News and World Report, Nov. 21, 1983, p. 62.
6. *Church News*, Jan. 16, 1982, pp. 4-6; *Eastern Standard Times*, June 1983, p. 10.

7. Bruce R. McConkie, op. cit., p. 670.
8. *Los Angeles Times*, op. cit.
9. *National NOW Times*, "The Wage Gap," Aug. 1980, pp. 8-9.
10. *Denver Post* Special Reprint, "Utah: Inside The Church State," Nov. 21-28, 1982, p. 22.
11. *Utah Holiday*, "Loving in Violence—The Betrayal of Battered Wives" by Margaret Crapo, July 1980, pp. 32-44.
12. *Sunstone*, "Mormon Women and Depression," Mar./Apr. 1979, pp. 16-26 (transcript of KSL-TV news special).
13. *Time* magazine, August 4, 1997, p. 52.
14. *Church News*, July 1, 1978, p. 3; *Latter Day Sentinel*, Apr. 22, 1983, p. 20.
15. The Mormon Church is organized by "Wards" (local churches or chapels) and "Stakes" (a group of local chapels).
16. *Latter-day Sentinel*, op. cit., p. 1.
17. From a speech delivered by Paul H. Dunn, General Authority, to a missions conference at Rose Park, Salt Lake City, February 1982.
18. *The Ensign*, Oct. 1977, p. 10.
19. For an explanation of the relationship of cults and the occult to Hinduism and Christianity, see Dave Hunt, *The Cult Explosion* (Harvest House Publishers: 1980).
20. Bhagavad Gita 4:6-8.
21. 1 Timothy 1:15.
22. Bruce R. McConkie, op. cit., pp. 654-55, 669.
23. Luke 5:32.
24. Ecclesiastes 7:20.
25. Luke 18:19.

Chapter 6—An Astonishing Legacy

1. Hebrews 9:27.
2. John 8:21-24.
3. *Doctrine and Covenants* 128:15.
4. 1 Timothy 1:4; Titus 3:9.
5. *Doctrines of Salvation*, vol. 2, p. 149.
6. Matthew 22:35-38.
7. *Doctrines of Salvation*, vol. 2, p. 146.
8. *Temple Mormonism* (New York, 1931), p. 10.
9. *Deseret News*, Church Section, Apr. 23, 1966, p. 14.
10. *Journal of Discourses*, vol. 6, p. 163.
11. *The Ensign*, May 1976, p. 102.
12. Ibid., May 1982, pp. 71-72.
13. *Journal of Discourses*, vol. 19, p. 229.
14. *Doctrines of Salvation*, vol. 3, p. 60.
15. *Journal of Discourses*, vol. 4, p. 223.
16. Ibid., vol. 3, p. 109.
17. 1 Samuel 28:7-19; Matthew 17:1-9.
18. 1 Nephi 15:35; Alma 5:24,25.
19. For a full discussion, see Dave Hunt, *The Cult Explosion* (Harvest House Publishers: 1980), pp. 143-82.
20. Deuteronomy 18:9-12; Leviticus 19:31; 20:6.
21. *The Ensign*, May 1982, p. 65.
22. *The Instructor*, Nov. 1964, p. 456.
23. *Journal of Discourses*, vol. 19, p. 229.
24. Dave Hunt, op. cit., pp. 143-44.
25. 2 Corinthians 11:14.
26. *Doctrine and Covenants*, Introduction, p. iii.
27. Joseph Heinerman, *Temple Manifestations* (Mountain Valley Publishers: Manti, UT), pp. 94-97.
28. Ibid., pp. 134-37.
29. 2 Corinthians 4:4.
30. Chuck Sackett, *What's Going On in There?* p. 27.
31. *The Nauvoo Expositor*, June 7, 1944.
32. *Doctrine and Covenants* 137:293; *Teachings of Prophet Joseph Smith*, p. 367.
33. *Joseph Smith—Seeker After Truth* (Salt Lake City, 1951), pp. 177-78.
34. 2 Nephi 23:21-22.
35. Alma 34:32-35.
36. *Mormon Doctrine*, p. 421.
37. *Journal of Discourses*, vol. 6, p. 4.

Chapter 7—*Myths, Zion, Mecca, and Magic*

1. *Journal of Discourses*, vol. 1, p. 275.
2. *The Seer*, pp. 33-38.
3. Ibid., pp. 102-03.
4. *History of the Church*, vol. 3, p. 380.
5. *The Young Woman's Journal*, by Oliver B. Huntington, 1892, vol. 3, p. 263.
6. *Journal of Discourses*, vol. 13, p. 271.
7. Ibid., vol. 6, p. 176; vol. 4, p. 269; *Doctrines of Salvation*, vol. 1, p. 236; *Journal of Discourses*, vol. 6, p. 229; *History of the Church*, vol. 7, p. 287.
8. George Laub's journal as cited in *Brigham Young University Studies*, Winter 1978, vol. 18, no. 2, p. 177.
9. *Young Woman's Journal*, op. cit., pp. 267-64.
10. Cited from a Michael Marquardt typed extract in Jerald and Sandra Tanner, *Mormonism—Shadow or Reality?* (Salt Lake City), p. 4A
11. *The Story of the Mormons* (New York, 1902), p. 35.
12. From last page in introduction to *The Book of Mormon*, "The Testimony of Three Witnesses," and also "The Testimony of Eight Witnesses."
13. *Journal of Discourses*, vol. 7, p. 164.
14. *Story of the Mormons*, op. cit., p. 35.
15. Genesis 2:10-14.
16. *Doctrine and Covenants*, Section 116.
17. Zechariah 14:4; Acts 1:9-14.
18. *Journal of Discourses*, vol. 18, pp. 160, 241; *Reed Smoot Case*, vol. 2, p. 159; Andrew Jensen, *Church Chronology*, p. 55; *Temple Lot Case*, p. 341; Joseph Smith, *Blessings of Joseph Smith*, vol. 3.
19. Elder Mark E. Petersen, *Which Church is Right?* (LDS pamphlet, 1974), p. 19.
20. *Denver Post*, op. cit., p. 14.
21. *Time* magazine, August 4, 1997, p. 57.
22. Ibid.
23. Ibid.
24. *Dialogue: A Journal of Mormon Thought*, "Mormons and Archaeology: An Outside View," Summer 1973, pp. 41-42, 46.
25. Ibid., p. 45.
26. Letter to Jack Sande dated Oct. 5, 1981.
27. John L. Sorenson, "Instant Expertise on Book of Mormon Archaeology," in *BYU Studies*, Spring 1976, pp. 429-32.
28. J.N. Washburn, *Contents, Structure and Authorship of the Book of Mormon*, p. 203.
29. *Fourteenth Annual Symposium on the Archaeology of the Scriptures* (BYU, Apr. 13, 1963), p. 61.
30. *Dialogue*, op. cit., Summer 1969, pp. 77-78.
31. Ibid., p. 76.
32. Jerald and Sandra Tanner, *Mormonism—Shadow or Reality?* p. 103.
33. Thomas Stuart Ferguson, personal letter dated Oct. 23, 1980.
34. Jerald and Sandra Tanner, op. cit., p. 125-J.
35. Fletcher B. Hammond, *Geography of the Book of Mormon* (Salt Lake City, 1959), "Where Is the Hill Cumorah?" p. 7.
36. The 109th Annual Conference Report, pp. 128-29, cited in Fletcher B. Hammond, op. cit., pp. 122-26.
37. *Church News*, July 29, 1978, vol. 48, no. 30, p. 16.
38. *History of Joseph Smith*, by his mother, Lucy Mark Smith (Salt Lake City, 1945), pp. 91-92.
39. Ibid.
40. Hyrum L. Andrus, *God, Man and the Universe* (Salt Lake City, 1968), pp. 70-75.
41. B.H. Roberts, *A Comprehensive History of the Church*, vol. 1, pp. 81-82.
42. *The Chenango Union*, Norwich, NY, May 3, 1877.
43. Dr. Hugh Nibley, *The Myth Makers*, p. 142.
44. Sworn Affidavit by Wesley P. Walters,

Oct. 28, 1971: Leonard J. Arrington and Davis Britton, *The Mormon Experience,* pp. 10-11.

45. *Palmyra Herald,* July 24, 1822.

46. *Wayne Sentinel,* Feb. 16, 1825.

47. Ibid., Dec. 27, 1825, p. 2.

48. Reed C. Durham, Jr., typed syllabus published by the Church Educational System.

49. Deuteronomy 18:9-14.

50. Reed C. Durham, Jr., *No Help for the Widow's Son* (Martin Publishing Co.: Nauvoo, IL, 1980), pp. 22-25.

51. *The Palmyra Reflector,* Feb. 28, 1931; B.H. Roberts, op. cit., pp. 26-27; Jerald and Sandra Tanner, *Mormonism and Magic,* Dec. 1982, pp. 1-7.

Chapter 8—The World's Most Perfect Book?

1. *Overland Monthly,* Dec. 1890, p. 630.

2. *Warsaw Signal,* May 22, 1844.

3. *Times and Seasons,* vol. 5, p. 405.

4. Joseph Smith, *History of the Church of Jesus Christ of Latter-day Saints* (Salt lake City, 1967), vol. 5, p. 372.

5. James D. Bales, *The Book of Mormon?* (1958), pp. 95, 97-99.

6. *Doctrine and Covenants* 5:10-15.

7. *The Prophet Joseph Smith's Testimony,* pp. 19-20, a proselytizing booklet published by The Church of Jesus Christ of Latter-day Saints.

8. Ibid.

9. Introduction, *Book of Mormon,* "Testimony of Eight Witnesses."

10. David Whitmer, *An Address to All Believers,* 1887, p. 27.

11. *Joseph Smith—Seeker After Truth,* p. 58; *Journal of Discourses,* vol. 24, p. 364.

12. Max H. Parkin, *Conflict at Kirtland,* pp. 82-83, quoting "Mary Elizabeth Rollins Lightner Journal."

13. *Latter-day Saints Millennial Star,* vol. 8, Nov. 15, 1846, pp. 124-28.

14. Letter quoted in *Senate Document 189,* Feb. 15, 1841, pp. 6-9.

15. *Pearl of Great Price,* JS 2:72-76.

16. Private letter to brother Warren Cowdery, by Oliver Cowdery, Jan. 21, 1838.

17. *History of the Church,* vol. 3, pp. 16-18; Joseph Smith, *Elder's Journal,* July 1838.

18. *Historical Record,* 1886, vol. 5, p. 233.

19. *History of the Church,* vol. 3, pp. 16-18.

20. *Times and Seasons,* vol. 2, p. 482; *Improvement Era,* Jan. 1969, p. 56; Joseph Greehalgh, "Oliver Cowdery—The Man Outstanding," 1965, p. 28.

21. Charles Shook, *The True Origin of The Book of Mormon,* 1914, pp. 58-59.

22. *Historical Record,* 1886, vol. 5, p. 201.

23. *The Mormon Frontier, Diary of Hosea Stout,* vol. 2, p. 336.

24. *Senate Document 189,* Feb. 15, 1841, pp. 6-9; Roberts, *Comprehensive History of the Church,* vol. 1, pp. 438-39.

25. E.D. Howe, *Mormonism Unveiled,* 1834, pp. 260-61.

26. *Improvement Era,* March 1969, p. 63; Brigham Young, *Journal of Discourses,* vol. 7, p. 164.

27. Andrew Jensen, *Church Chronology,* 1899, p. 31; *Millennial Star,* vol. 8, Nov. 15, 1846, pp. 124-28.

28. Tanner, *The Case Against Mormonism,* vol. 2, pp. 50-58; Wayne C. Gunnell, *Martin Harris—Witness and Benefactor* (BYU 1955 thesis), p. 52; *The Braden and Kelly Debate,* p. 173.

29. J.A. Clark, *Gleanings by the Way,* pp. 256-57.

30. *Times and Seasons,* vol. 2, p. 482.

31. *Palmyra Reflector,* Mar. 19, 1831.

32. *Millennial Star,* vol. XL, pp. 771-72.

33. Lucy Smith, *Biographical Sketches,* pp. 211-13.

34. Letter to Oliver Cowdery, by David Whitmer, Sept. 8, 1847, printed in the *Ensign*

of Liberty, May 1848, p. 93; also see *Ensign of Liberty,* Aug. 1849, pp. 101-04.

35. *John Whitmer's History of the Church,* Modern Microfilm, SLC, p. 22.

36. Ibid., vol. 3, p. 228.

37. Jerald and Sandra Tanner, op. cit. p. 55.

38. *John Whitmer's History,* p. 23.

39. *The Gospel Herald,* May 4, 1848, p. 27.

40. *A Holy, Sacred and Divine Roll and Book,* 1843, p. 358.

41. *The Braden and Kelly Debate,* p. 173; Wayne Gunnell, *Martin Harris—Witness and Benefactor to the Book of Mormon,* (BYU thesis, 1955), p. 52.

42. *Holy, Sacred and Divine Roll and Book,* op. cit., p. 304.

43. Jerald and Sandra Tanner, op. cit. p. 63.

44. *Psychic Magazine,* "The Making of a Ghost" by I.M. Owen, July/Aug. 1975; *New Horizons,* "Generation of Paranormal Physical Phenomena with an Imaginary Communicator" and "Philip's Story Continued," vol. 1, nos. 3,4; *Conjuring Up Philip* (New York: Harper and Row, 1976).

45. For a full explanation of these four lies, see Dave Hunt, *The Cult Explosion* (Harvest House Publishers: 1980), pp. 109-17.

46. For a broader consideration of this subject, see Dave Hunt, op. cit., chapters 1, 2, 3, 12, 14, 15.

47. *John Whitmer's History,* chapter 6.

48. *Times and Seasons,* edited by Joseph Smith, Apr. 1, 1842, vol. 3, p. 747.

49. Max H. Parkin, op. cit., p. 331.

50. *Journal of Discourses,* vol. 11, p. 10.

51. *The Des Moines Daily News,* Oct. 16, 1886.

52. *Journal of Discourses,* vol. 11, p. 4.

53. Max H. Parkin, op. cit., pp. 79-80.

54. Ibid.

55. *Doctrine and Covenants,* Section 129.

56. *Teachings of the Prophet Joseph Smith,* pp. 214-15.

57. *Journal of Discourses,* vol. 5, p. 164.

58. Ibid., vol. 1, p. 244.

59. *The Seer,* op. cit., p. 215.

60. *Teachings of the Prophet Joseph Smith,* p. 71.

61. Ibid., p. 194.

62. Ibid., p. 370.

63. 1 Nephi 11:18,21,32; etc.

64. Published several years before the *Book of Mormon* and undoubtedly known to Joseph Smith, *View of the Hebrews* has far too many close parallels to the *Book of Mormon* to be coincidence.

65. B.H. Roberts, *Book of Mormon Difficulties,* a typewritten, unpublished manuscript reproduced in Jerald and Sandra Tanner, *Roberts' Manuscripts Revealed.*

66. *Doctrine and Covenants* 20:9; 42:12; see also 135:3.

Chapter 9—The Masonic Connection

1. From an "underground" typewritten copy of Dr. Durham's talk carefully compared with a tape recording thereof and certified to be accurate by Mervin B. Hogan, Secretary of the Masonic Research Lodge of Utah in Salt Lake City; Reed C. Durham, Jr., *No Help for the Widow's Son,* op. cit., p. 25.

2. Ibid.

3. Ibid., p. 27.

4. *Doctrine and Covenants* 78, 104, etc.

5. Reed C. Durham, op. cit. pp. 27-28.

6. Ibid., pp. 15-16, 19.

7. Ibid., pp. 15-17.

8. *Doctrine and Covenants* 78, 104.

9. *Times and Seasons,* vol. 1, p. 133; *Teachings of Prophet Joseph Smith,* p. 146.

10. Albert Pike, *Morals and Dogma of the Ancient and Accepted Scottish Rite of Freemasonry* (Washington, D.C., 1958), p. 210.

11. Ibid., pp. 213, 219.
12. Albert G. Mackey, *An Encyclopedia of Freemasonry* (1921), pp. 618-19.
13. Albert Pike, op. cit., pp. 277, 525.
14. Ibid., p. 744.
15. Reed C. Durham, op. cit., p. 21.
16. Ibid., pp. 20-21.
17. Apostle John A. Widtsoe, Evidences and Reconciliations (first edition), vol. 3, p. 358.
18. *History of Freemasonry in Illinois*, p. 184, as quoted in S.H. Goodwin, *Mormonism and Masonry*, p. 34.
19. B.H. Roberts, *Comprehensive History of the Church*, op. cit., vol. 2, pp. 135-36.
20. Reed C. Durham, op. cit., p. 21.
21. Ibid.
22. Ibid.
23. Ibid., p. 22.

24. Ibid., p. 23.
25. Albert Pike, op. cit., pp. 104-05.
26. Ibid., p. 819.
27. For a broader analysis of the Luciferian foundation of Freemasonry, see Ed Decker, *The Question of Freemasonry.*
28. Manly P. Hall, *Locked Keys of Freemasonry,* p. 48.
29. Albert Pike, op. cit. p. 321.
30. Instructions to the 23 Supreme Councils of the World, by Albert Pike, Grand Commander, Sovereign Pontiff of Universal Freemasonry, July 14, 1889, recorded by A.C. De La Rive and reported in *La Femme et l'Enfant dans la Franc-Maconnerie Universelle*, p. 588, as found in Edith S. Miller, *Occult Theocracy*, vol. 1, pp. 220-21.

Chapter 10—Sacred or Secret?

1. "Historic Temple Square," an official brochure published by The Church of Jesus Christ of Latter-day Saints.
2. Ibid.
3. Genesis 3:15.
4. Genesis 3:24.
5. Revelation 22:14.
6. John 1:29.
7. Hebrews 11:4.
8. Romans 10:17.
9. The Hebrew words for sin and sin offering are the same. The better rendering is obvious. Sin requires an offering and would therefore hardly be a hindrance to an offering. The problem wasn't that Cain had sinned, for this is true of all, but that he refused the sin offering that God had commanded and that was available.
10. John 3:16; Romans 3:19-26; Ephesians 2:8-10; 1 John 5:9-13; etc.
11. *Plan of Salvation* (Salt Lake City 1978), p. 8.

12. Ecclesiastes 7:20; Romans 3:23.
13. Romans 3:28.
14. Acts 13:39.
15. *Plan of Salvation*, op. cit.
16. John 3:36.
17. *Plan of Salvation*, op. cit., p. 20.
18. John 1:17.
19. Romans 3:20.
20. Romans 3:24.
21. Manly P. Hall, op. cit., p. XXI.
22. *Deseret News*, Church Section July 18, 1873, p. 308.
23. Ibid., July 31, 1965, p. 7.
24. 1 Corinthians 15:3; John 3:16.
25. *What Mormons Think of Christ* (Salt Lake City, 1976), p. 21.
26. Manly P. Hall, op. cit.
27. Hebrews 10:1-10.
28. John 18:20.
29. Luke 8:17; 12:1-3; Romans 2:16.
30. Ephesians 5:11-13.
31. Ecclesiastes 12:14; Romans 2:16.
32. 2 Timothy 3:16,17.

33. 2 Peter 1:3.
34. Revelation 22:18.
35. James H. Billington, *Fire in the Minds of*

Men: Origins of the Revolutionary Faith (Basic Books: New York, 1980), pp. 8-93.
36. Ibid., p. 85.

Chapter 11—Lying Prophets and Apostles

1. *Church*, week ending March 28, 1981.
2. Ibid.
3. *Los Angeles Times*, op. cit., p. 24.
4. *The Gospel Through the Ages* (1968), pp. 118-19.
5. Ibid., p. 9; *Mormon Doctrine*, 1966, p. 238.
6. *Doctrines of Salvation*, vol. 2, p. 44.
7. Ibid., pp. 61-63.
8. Ibid.
9. *Journal of Discourses*, vol. 1, p. 361.
10. *Latter-day Saints' Millennial Star*, vol. 40. pp. 226-27.
11. Joseph Smith, *History of the Church*, introduction to vol. 5.
12. From a typed copy of the letter, cited in Jerald and Sandra Tanner, op. cit., p. 230-A.
13. *Journal of Discourses*, vol. 11, p. 128.
14. *Deseret News*, Aug. 6, 1862.
15. Ibid.
16. Ibid.
17. *Journal of Discourses*, vol. 1, p. 361.

18. Exodus 20:16.
19. Hyrum L. Andrus, *Doctrines of the Kingdom* (Salt Lake City, 1973), p. 450.
20. *History of the Church*, vol. 6, p. 411.
21. *Historical Record*, p. 220.
22. *Evidences and Reconciliations*, p. 282.
23. *The Restored Church*, pp. 181-85.
24. *History of the Church*, vol. 5, pp. 60-61.
25. Thomas Edgar Lyon, "Orson Pratt—Early Mormon Leader," M.A. Thesis, University of Chicago, 1932, pp. 26, 28 of typed copy. Lyon was a devout Mormon.
26. Ibid., p. 29.
27. Ibid.
28. John J. Stewart, *Joseph Smith the Mormon Prophet*, p. 180.
29. *Journal of Discourses*, vol. 17, pp. 224-25.
30. Andrew Jensen, *Historical Record*, pp. 225-26.
31. *Journal of Discourses*, vol. 20, p. 29.
32. Ibid., vol. 2, pp. 216-17.
33. *Temple Lot Case*, pp. 309, 320-22.
34. Andrew Jensen, op. cit., p. 226.

Chapter 12—Another Angel Story

1. Joseph F. Smith, *Teachings of the Prophet Joseph Smith*, p. 194.
2. Ibid., p. 71.
3. *Orson Pratt's Works*, "Divine Authenticity of the *Book of Mormon*," op. cit.
4. *Journal of Discourses*, vol. 11, p. 211.
5. *Millennial Star*, vol. 40, pp. 226-27.
6. *Journal of Discourses*, vol. 20, pp. 28-31.
7. Ibid., vol. 25, p. 21.
8. Ibid, vol. 20, pp. 28-31.
9. Ibid., vol. 25, p. 21.
10. Ibid., vol. 17, pp. 224-25.
11. *The Contributor*, vol. 6, no. 4, Jan. 1885,

p. 131.
12. Cited from "The History of Joseph C. Kingsbury," a document in the University of Utah Library, Western Americana section, by Michael Marquardt in his pamphlet, *The Strange marriages of Sarah Ann Whitney*.
13. *Journal of Discourses*, vol. 2, pp. 13-14.
14. Max. H. Parkin, op. cit., p. 166; John J. Stewart, op. cit., pp. 103-04.
15. *Historical Record*, p. 233.
16. John J. Stewart, *Brigham Young and His Wives*, p. 31.

17. Dr. Wyl, *Mormon Portraits*, 1886, pp. 70-72; Orson F. Whitney, *Life of Heber C. Kimball*, pp. 333-35, 339.

18. Dr. Wyl, op. cit.

19. *Confessions of John D. Lee*, 1880 p. 132; Juanita Brooks, *On the Mormon Frontier*, vol. 1, p. 141, footnote 18; Andrew Jensen, *Historical Record*, p. 233; Stanley Ivin, *Joseph Smith and Polygamy*, p. 42.

20. Fawn M. Brodie, *No Man Knows My History*, p. 466.

21. Ibid.

22. Ann-Eliza Young, *Wife No. 19*, 1876, pp. 70-71.

23. *Evidences and Reconciliations*, 1960, p. 343.

24. Matthew 22:23-30.

25. Speech by Mary E. Lightner, Brigham Young University, Apr. 14, 1905. Cited in Jerald and Sandra Tanner, *Mormonism—Shadow or Reality?* (Modern Microfilm Company, P.O. Box 1884, Salt Lake City, Utah 84110, Fourth Edition, Enlarged and Revised), p. 215.

26. Fawn M. Brodie, op. cit., pp. 466-67, citing affidavit of Mary E.R. Lightner.

27. *Journal of Discourses*, vol. 11, p. 269.

28. Ibid., vol. 4, p. 209.

29. John J. Stewart, op. cit., p. 22.

30. *Journal of Discourses*, vol. 13, p. 166.

31. *Mormon Portraits*, pp. 61-62.

32. *Journal of Discourses*, vol. 1, pp. 50, 345-46; vol. 2, p. 210; vol. 4, pp. 259-60; vol. 13, p. 309; vol. 26, p. 115; *Millennial Star*, vol. 15, p. 285; *The Seer*, op. cit., pp. 158, 172.

33. *Journal of Discourses*, vol. 17, pp. 224-25; *Millennial Star*, Oct. 28, 1865.

34. *The Seer*, op. cit., pp. 124-25; *Journal of Discourses*, vol. 13, pp. 195-208.

35. *Journal of Discourses*, vol. 25, p. 21.

36. Ibid., vol. 17, pp. 224-25.

37. *Under the Prophet in Utah*, pp. 268-70; *Reed Smoot Case*, vol. 1, pp. 197, 312, 334-35, 408-09, 430, 718, etc.

38. *Nauvoo Expositor*, June 7, 1844, p. 2.

39. *History of the Church*, vol. 6, pp. 432, 441, 445; John J. Stewart, op. cit., p. 34.

40. *Journal of Discourses*, vol. 17, pp. 224-25.

Chapter 13—Secrets, Surprises, and Perils of God-Making

1. *Journal of Discourses*, vol. 21, p. 10.

2. Ibid., vol. 6, p. 4.

3. Spencer W. Kimball, *The Miracle of Forgiveness* (Bookcraft: 1981), p. 6.

4. John 5:24.

5. Revelation 3:20.

6. 1 John 5:13.

7. Spencer W. Kimball, op. cit., p.16.

8. Ibid., p. 5.

9. *Messages of the First Presidency*, edited by James R. Clark (Bookcraft), vol. 4, pp. 203-06, as cited in *Temple Preparation Seminars Instructor's Discussion Guide*, p. 10.

10. Cited in C. Penney Hunt, *The Menace of Freemasonry to the Christian Faith*, pp. 47-48.

11. *The Freemason's Pocket Companion*, p. 154.

12. W. Cleon Skousen, *The First 2000 Years* (1980), pp. 354-55; *Journal of Discourses*, vol. 1, p. 117.

13. Milton R. Hunter, *The Gospel Through the Ages* (1968), pp. 104, 114-15.

14. Ibid. p. 4.

15. Personal interview for the movie, *The God Makers*.

16. 2 Corinthians 5:8.

17. 1 Corinthians 15:52; 1 Thessalonians 4:17.

18. *Temple Preparation Seminar Discussions*, 1978 Edition (LDS Church publication), pp. 78, 83.

19. Bernard P. Brockbank, *Commandments and Promises of God* (Deseret Book Co.:

1982); Spencer W. Kimball, op. cit., p. 208.

20. James E. Talmage, *Articles of Faith*, pp. 477-78; *Doctrines of Salvation*, vol. II, pp. 10-11.
21. *Journal of Discourses*, vol. 13, p. 143.
22. Ibid., vol. 1, pp. 97, 134-35; vol. 3, p. 247; vol. 4, pp. 49-54, 219-20; Bruce R. McConkie, *Mormon Doctrine*, p. 92.
23. *Doctrines of Salvation*, vol. 1, 1954, p. 303; *Doctrine and Covenants*, sec. 131, vv. 5-6.
24. *The Improvement Era*, June 1954, p. 354.
25. 1 John 1:8-10.

26. Chuck Sackett, op. cit., p. 20.
27. J.R. Clark, *Messages of the First Presidency* (1971), vol. 5, p. 110.
28. *Journal of Discourses*, vol. 9, p. 376.
29. *The Improvement Era*, vol. 9, p. 813.
30. Chuck Sackett, op. cit., pp. 31-32.
31. Ibid., pp. 33-46.
32. John 19:30; Matthew 27:51; Mark 15:37-38.
33. Chuck Sackett, op. cit., p. 52.
34. Ibid., p. 38.
35. John 10:11, 27-30.
36. *Journal of Discourses*, vol. 3, pp. 50, 369.
37. *Time* magazine, August 4, 1997, p. 56.

Chapter 14—The Great Temple/Priesthood Scam

1. *Journal of Discourses*, vol. 1, p. 219.
2. *The Improvement Era*, June 1945, p. 354; *The Ensign*, "The Debate Is Over" by President N. Eldon Tanner, Aug. 1979, p. 3.
3. *BYU Today*, "Fourteen Fundamentals of Following the Prophet" by President Ezra Taft Benson, BYU Devotional Assembly, Feb. 26, 1980, pp. 190-93.
4. LeGrand Richards, *A Marvelous Work and a Wonder*, p. 190.
5. 1 Corinthians 3:16,17; 6:19; 2 Corinthians 6:16.
6. Ephesians 2:21,22.
7. 1 Peter 2:5.
8. *Doctrines of Salvation*, vol. 2, p. 169.
9. Hebrews 9:24–10:18.
10. Matthew 24:1,2.
11. Hebrews 9:9; 10:1.
12. Hebrews 9:14.
13. Hebrews 9:25-28; 10:12-14.
14. Milton R. Hunter, *Christ in Ancient America*, vol. II, pp. 51-53.
15. Ibid., p. 121.
16. J.S.M. Ward, *The Entered Apprentice's Handbook*, p. 40.
17. *Doctrines of Salvation*, vol. 2, p. 45.
18. *Journal of Discourses*, vol. 1, p. 51; *Dialogue: A Journal of Mormon Thought*, Autumn 1967, pp. 100-01; *Doctrines of Salvation*, vol. 1, p. 19.
19. *History of the Church*, vol. 6, p. 474; Bruce R. McConkie, *Mormon Doctrine*, pp. 317, 576-77.
20. Nehemiah 9:6; Psalm 90:2; Isaiah 43:10-12; 44:24; 45:5,6,12,18,21-22.
21. *Doctrines of Salvation*, vol. 1, pp. 16, 65; *Journal of Discourses*, vol. 5, p. 331.
22. *Doctrine and Covenants*, 1835 Edition, pp. 52-53, 55, 57-58 removed from subsequent editions beginning in 1921.
23. *Journal of Discourses*, vol. 2, p. 338; *Millennial Star*, vol. 12, p. 308.
24. "The Holy Spirit," a pamphlet by Orson Pratt, p. 50.
25. *Doctrines of Salvation*, vol. 1, p. 39.
26. Genesis 14:18.
27. *Articles of Faith*, James E. Talmage, p. 189.
28. Jerald and Sandra Tanner, op. cit., p. 180, letter on file.
29. *History of the Church*, vol. 1, p. 40 footnote.
30. David Whitmer, *An Address to All Believers in Christ* (1887), pp. 35, 49.

31. LaMar Petersen, *Problems in Mormon Text*, pp. 7-8.
32. *William Smith on Mormonism* (Lamoni, Iowa, 1883), pp. 19-20.
33. *Doctrine and Covenants* 107:12-14.
34. *Defense in a Rehearsal of My Grounds for Separating Myself from the Latter-day Saints* (Norton, Ohio, 1839).
35. *Deseret News*, Apr. 13, 1859, vol. IX, p. 48.
36. *History of the Church*, vol. 3, p. 232.
37. Letter quoted in *Senate Document 189*, Feb. 15, 1841, pp. 6-9.
38. Jerald and Sandra Tanner, op. cit., pp. 52-59.
39. John A. Widtsoe, op. cit., pp. 338-39.
40. *Doctrine and Covenants* 3:12; 10:6-7.

41. *Millennial Star*, Nov. 15, 1846, vol. 8, pp. 124-28.
42. Jerald and Sandra Tanner, op. cit., p. 31-B.
43. Revelation 20:7-9.
44. Revelation 21:22.
45. Parley P. Pratt, *Key to the Science of Theology* (1863), p. 66.
46. *History of the Church*, vol. 6, p. 365.
47. *Journal of Discourses*, vol. 7, p. 53.
48. Ibid., vol. 11, p. 53.
49. Affidavit of Thomas B. Marsh, cited in Leland Gentry, *A History of Latter-day Saints in Northern Missouri from 1836–1839* (Brigham Young University, 1965), p. 414.
50. *Journal of Discourses*, vol. 10, p. 320.

Chapter 15—A Non-Prophet Organization

1. *Journal of Discourses*, vol. 9, p. 267; vol. 11, p. 298; vol. 12, p. 59; vol. 14, p. 205.
2. *History of the Church*, vol. 6, pp. 319-20.
3. Jerald and Sandra Tanner, op. cit., pp. 186-95; Walter Martin, *The Maze of Mormonism* (Vision House: 1978), pp. 352-59.
4. *Orson Pratt's Works*, "The Bible Alone an Insufficient Guide," p. 187.
5. Bruce R. McConkie, *Mormon Doctrine*, op. cit., p. 650.
6. Jerald and Sandra Tanner, op. cit., p. 18-A.
7. *Reed Smoot Case*, vol. 1, p. 483-84, 499.
8. Walter Martin, op. cit.
9. *The Prophet Joseph Smith's Testimony*, official booklet published by The Church of Jesus Christ of Latter-day Saints, p. 3.
10. Ibid., p. 4.
11. *Dialogue: A Journal of Mormon Thought*, Autumn 1966, pp. 30-34.
12. Ibid.
13. *Doctrine and Covenants* 84:21,22.
14. *Doctrine and Covenants*, sec. 5, 1835 edition.

15. *BYU Studies*, Spring 1969, p. 384.
16. *Amboy Journal*, June 11, 1879, p. 1.
17. Letter of Hill and Joseph Lewis, dated Apr. 23, 1874, cited in Walter Martin, op. cit., p. 336.
18. From a copy of the letter, carefully compared to the original, quoted in *The Zarahemla Record*, Summer and Fall 1982, pp.14-15.
19. *Journal of Discourses*, vol. 14, pp. 261-62.
20. *Journal of Discourses*, vol. 6, p. 335.
21. Ibid., vol. 2, p. 171; vol. 18, p. 239.
22. Ibid., pp. 196-97.
23. Ibid., vol. 20, p. 167.
24. Ibid., vol. 12, pp. 333-34; vol. 6, p. 29.
25. Jerald and Sandra Tanner, *The Changing World of Mormonism* (Moody Press: 1980), pp. 29-66.
26. Letter dated July 22, 1844, from Sarah Scott, as cited in *Among the Mormons*, pp. 152-53.
27. *History of the Church*, vol. 67, p. 408.
28. Ibid., vol. 5, p. 289.
29. Ibid., vol. 5, p. 467.
30. Ibid., vol. 6, p. 78.

31. Hyrum L. Andrus, *Joseph Smith and World Government*, p. 33.
32. Cited in Jerald and Sandra Tanner, *Mormonism—Shadow or Reality?* pp. 415-16.
33. *Doctrine and Covenants* 42:30-35.
34. Leland Gentry, op. cit., p. 322.
35. *Senate Document 189*, pp. 21-25.
36. *History of the Church*, vol. 1, p. 441.
37. *A Brief History of the Church of Jesus Christ of Latter-day Saints* (1839), p. 41.
38. *History of the Church*, vol. 1, pp. 498-99.
39. The 26th Congress, Second Session, pp. 1-6, 9.
40. *Doctrine and Covenants* 87:1-3.
41. William E. Berrett, *The Restored Church* (Salt Lake City, 1956), pp. 197-98.
42. Leland Gentry, op. cit., p. 339.
43. Governor Thomas Ford, *History of Illinois*, as quoted in Klaus J. Hansen, op. cit., p. 155.
44. Ibid., pp. 116-17.
45. *History of the Church*, vol. 5, p. 394.
46. Ibid., vol. 1, pp. 315-16.
47. *Journal of Oliver Boardman Huntington*, vol. 2, pp. 128-99.
48. *History of the Church*, vol. 2, p. 182.
49. *Millennial Star*, vol. XV, p. 205.
50. *Dialogue: A Journal of Mormon Thought*, Autumn 1966, p. 76.
51. *Times and Seasons*, vol. 6, p. 956.
52. *Journal of Discourses*, vol. 5, p.134; vol. 6, p. 190.
53. Ibid., vol. 9, p. 71.
54. *Dialogue: A Journal of Mormon Thought*, Autumn 1966, p. 74.
55. *Journal of Discourses*, vol. 13, p. 362.
56. Deuteronomy 18:22.
57. A copy of this letter may be obtained by request from Dick Baer, P.O. Box 530, Orangevale, CA 95662.
58. The False Prophet, Joseph Smith "...AND IT DIDN'T COME TO PASS..." 1997, Saints Alive Ministries, Internet edition, www.Saintsalive.com.

Chapter 16—The Secret Kingdom

1. Jeffrey Kaye, "An Invisible Empire: Mormon Money in California," in *New West*, May 8, 1978, pp. 36-41.
2. Michael Parrish, "The Saints Among Us," in *Rocky Mountain Magazine*, Jan./Feb. 1980, pp. 17-32.
3. *The Wall Street Journal*, Nov. 9, 1983, Front Page.
4. Claudia Capos, "The Mormon Kingdom: The Power and the Prophet," second of two parts, in *The Detroit News Magazine*, May 25, 1980, p. 26.
5. Bruce R. McConkie, *Mormon Doctrine*, op. cit., pp. 338, 813.
6. *Doctrine and Covenants* 104:16. See all of *Doctrine and Covenants*, Sections 42 and 104.
7. Bruce R. McConkie, *Mormon Doctrine*, op. cit., pp. 92-93.
8. *Journal of Discourses*, vol. 3, p. 247.
9. Ibid., vol. 4, pp. 49-50.
10. *Times and Seasons*, vol. 4, pp. 183-84; *History of the Church*, vol. 7, p. 597; *Journal of Discourses*, vol. 1, pp. 73, 108-09.
11. *Journal of Hosea Stout*, vol. 2, p. 71.
12. *Journal of Discourses*, vol. 10, p. 110.
13. "Manuscript History of Brigham Young," Feb. 24, 1847, cited in Jerald and Sandra Tanner, op. cit., p. 402.
14. Klaus J. Hansen, *Quest for Empire, The Political Kingdom of God and the Council of Fifty in Mormon History*, p. 127.
15. *Journal of Discourses*, vol. 1, p. 83.
16. *Doctrines of Salvation*, vol. 1, p. 135.
17. *Journal of Discourses*, vol. 4, pp. 219-20.
18. McConkie, *Doctrine*, p. 93.
19. *Journal of Discourses*, vol. 7, p. 170.
20. Klaus J. Hansen, op. cit., pp. 55-56.

21. John J. Stewart, op. cit., p. 204.
22. Klaus J. Hansen, op. cit., pp. 55-56.
23. *American Universal Encyclopedia*, 1884, p. 219.
24. Klaus J. Hansen, op. cit., p. 161.
25. *History of the Church*, vol. 6, pp. 568-69; Hansen, op. cit., pp. 66-67; *Dialogue: A Journal of Mormon Thought*, Summer 1966, p. 104; *Zion's Harbinger and Baneemy's Organ*, St. Louis, July 1853, p. 53.
26. Klaus J. Hansen, op. cit., p. 66, and footnote 74, p. 200.
27. From a typed copy of Franklin D. Richards's journal, entry Feb. 4, 1885, original in Church Historian's office. Cited in Jerald and Sandra Tanner, op. cit., p. 418.
28. Bruce R. McConkie, *Mormon Doctrine*, op. cit., pp. 415-16.
29. Chuck Sackett, op. cit., p. 44.
30. Ibid., p. 30.
31. *Dialogue: A Journal of Mormon Thought*, Summer 1966, pp. 46-47.
32. Klaus J. Hansen, op. cit., pp. 4-5.
33. John 18:20.
34. Jeremiah 17:9.
35. *Los Angeles Times*, Apr. 5, 1980, Part 1-A, p. 1.
36. Kostman et al., op. cit.
37. *Salt Lake Tribune*, Oct. 1, 1981.
38. Ibid.
39. Kostman et al., op. cit.
40. *Wall Street Journal*, Nov. 9, 1983, p. 16.
41. *Journal of Discourses*, vol. 7, p. 15.
42. Hyrum L. Andrus, *Joseph Smith, the Man and Seer*, p. 5.
43. John J. Stewart, op. cit., p. 209; Hyrum L. Andrus, *Joseph Smith and World Government*, op. cit., p. 54.
44. *The Ensign*, Jan. 1979, "To Prepare a People," p. 18.
45. *Journal of Discourses*, vol. 1, p. 230.

Chapter 17—A Time to Choose

1. From an October 8, 1854 Conference discourse in which he clearly stated that Adam is God. The Brethren have suppressed this, and it is presently located in the LDS Archives in order to persist in denying that Brigham Young taught the "Adam-God Doctrine." Although the Mormon Church has never published this sermon, others have. This quote was taken from *Brigham Young 1854* (States West Publishing Co.: Scottsdale, AZ).
2. *Journal of Discourses*, vol. 12, p. 66.
3. Ibid., vol. 5, p. 73.
4. Ibid., p. 331.
5. Ibid., vol. 6, p. 176.
6. Ibid., p. 167.
7. Chuck Sackett, *What's Going On in There?—The Verbatim Text of the Mormon Temple Rituals Annotated and Explained by a Former Temple Worker* (Ex-Mormons for Jesus, P.O. Box 5044-154, Thousand Oaks, CA 91359: 1983), pp. 34-38.
8. *Seventh East Press*, Nov. 18, 1981. From a speech at the "Fourteenth Brigham Young University Stake Conference," Oct. 31, 1981.
9. Ibid.
10. Ibid.
11. John 3:16; 10:27-30; 1 John 5:9-13.
12. Matthew 24:24.
13. 2 Thessalonians 2:3-9.
14. 2 Thessalonians 2:10-12.
15. Revelation 13:13-18.
16. Nesta H. Webster, *Secret Societies and Subversive Movements* (Christian Book Club of America: 1924), pp. 152-76; Manly P. Hall, *The Secret Teachings of All Ages: Masonic, Hermetic, Cabalistic and Rosicrucian Symbolical Philosophy* (The Philosophical Research Society, Inc.: 1969), pp. CLXXIII, CLXXVIII, CXXX,

CXXXVI.

17. *Journal of Discourses*, vol. 20, p. 43.

18. *Conference Report*, April 1898, p. 14.

19. Joseph Smith as quoted by John Taylor, *Journal of Discourses*, vol. 21, p. 31.

20. Hyrum L. Andrus, *Doctrines of the Kingdom* (Bookcraft, Inc.: Salt Lake City, Utah, 1973), pp. 101-05.

21. Michael Loyd Chadwick, "Republican Government: A Model for the Western Hemisphere," in *Freemen Digest*, no. 6, 1980, pp. 1-3.

22. *Journal of Discourses*, vol. 21, p. 8.

23. Ibid., vol. 7, p. 15; vol. 2, p. 182.

24. From an editorial in *The Instructor*, cited in Lund, op. cit., p. 59.

25. Chuck Sackett, op. cit., p. 44; *Doctrine and Covenants* 42:30-37; 58:35-36; 85:1-3.

26. *Millennial Star*, vol. 56, June 18, 1894, pp. 385-87.

27. *Journal of Discourses*, vol. 17, p. 250.

28. Laurence Grafstein, "Messianic Capitalism," in *The New Republic*, Feb. 20, 1984, p. 16

29. Ibid.

30. 2 Thessalonians 2:3-10; 1 John 2:22; 4:1-3; Revelation 13:1-17.

31. 2 Thessalonians 2:4.

32. 2 Thessalonians 2:11,12.

33. Revelation 13:4-8.

34. John 14:1-3; 2 Corinthians 5:1-8; 1 Thessalonians 4:16,17.

35. Romans 2:12-15.

36. Psalm 51.

37. Henri de Lubec, *Atheistic Humanist*, p. 10.

38. Luke Rinehart, *The Book of est* (New York, 1976), pp. 216-17.

39. *Journal of Discourses*, vol. 6, pp. 4-7.

40. Ibid.

41. Ibid.

42. Ibid.

43. Psalm 90:2.

44. Isaiah chapters 43–46; John 17:3.

45. Genesis 1:1; John 1:3; Jeremiah 10:10.

46. Milton R. Hunter, *The Gospel Through the Ages*, op. cit., p. 4.

47. Ibid., p. 115.

48. Deuteronomy 13:1-3.

Other Books by Ed Decker:

Deckers Complete Book of Mormonism — The ultimate A-to-Z reference on the beliefs, teachings, and traditions of the Church of Jesus Christ of Latter-day Saints. This book presents the official Mormon position and the corresponding biblical response on more than 150 topics.

Fast Facts on False Teachings — An all-in-one volume designed to give the facts *instantly.* A great time-saver with short, informative chapters that highlight exactly what you need to know about today's major cults and false teachings.

The Godmakers II — Though the new face of Mormonism is dramatically different, the changes are only cosmetic. Lays bare the secrets and frightening new dangers this sophisticated cult poses to the unwary.

Ed Decker's newsletter may be received by request.
Write to:

Saints Alive, P.O. Box 1347,
Issaquah, WA 98027

E-mail: edecker@nwlink.com
Website: http://www.Saintsalive.com

Other Books by Dave Hunt

A Woman Rides the Beast — An eye-opening book about prophecy, Catholicism, and the last days. Has the view of the Church of Rome as the woman who rides the beast in Revelation 17 become outdated? Hunt carefully sifts through history and prophecy to provide an answer.

In Defense of the Faith — Drawing from the most-asked questions of his years in ministry, noted cult and prophecy expert Dave Hunt addresses the toughest questions that Christians and non-Christians alike ask.

A Cup of Trembling — Through careful study of biblical prophecy, this definitive examination shows why Jerusalem, a small city with no strategic or industrial importance, is the key to peace in the world. Hunt explores Jerusalem's past and future roles in God's plan.

Dave Hunt's newsletter may be received by request.
Write to:

Dave Hunt
P.O. Box 7019
Bend, OR 97708